ORDINARY PEOPLE

In and out of Poverty in the Gilded Age

David Wagner

Paradigm Publishers

Boulder • London

Paradigm Publishers is committed to preserving ancient forests and natural resources. We elected to print *Ordinary People* on 30% post consumer recycled paper, processed chlorine free. As a result, for this printing, we have saved:

4 Trees (40' tall and 6-8" diameter)
1,753 Gallons of Wastewater
705 Kilowatt Hours of Electricity
193 Pounds of Solid Waste
380 Pounds of Greenhouse Gases

Paradigm Publishers made this paper choice because our printer, Thomson-Shore, Inc., is a member of Green Press Initiative, a nonprofit program dedicated to supporting authors, publishers, and suppliers in their efforts to reduce their use of fiber obtained from endangered forests.

For more information, visit www.greenpressinitiative.org

Copyright © 2008 Paradigm Publishers

Published in the United States by Paradigm Publishers, 3360 Mitchell Lane Suite, E, Boulder, CO 80301, USA.

Paradigm Publishers is the trade name of Birkenkamp & Company, LLC, Dean Birkenkamp, President and Publisher.

Library of Congress Cataloging-in-Publication Data

Wagner, David.
    Ordinary people : in and out of poverty in the gilded age / David Wagner.
        p. cm.
    Includes bibliographical references and index.
    ISBN 978-1-59451-460-9 (hardcover : alk. paper)   1. Almshouses—United States—History—19th century.   2. Poor—United States—History—19th century.   3. Public welfare—United States—History—19th century.   I. Title.
    HV61.W33 2008
    362.5'85097309034—dc22

                                                                    2007043348

Printed and bound in the United States of America on acid-free paper that meets the standards of the American National Standard for Permanence of Paper for Printed Library Materials.

Designed and typeset by Straight Creek Bookmakers.

12 11 10 09 08   1 2 3 4 5

Contents

Boxes and Tables

Acknowledgments

Some books have so many sources of assistance and inspiration that a long set of pages is required. Although the intellectual origins of this book are many, laid out in some detail in my earlier work *The Poorhouse: America's Forgotten Institution,* I feel two people were particularly inspirational in this book. One was Chet Kennedy. Chet is a spry octogenarian with an interesting career as an artist and then, for decades, the Massachusetts Public Health Department's publicity campaign manager. In a parallel volunteer life that has lasted for decades, he founded the Massachusetts Public Health Museum, on the grounds of one of the few remaining buildings from the nineteenth century at the Tewksbury Hospital (formerly the Massachusetts State Almshouse at Tewksbury). Beyond providing the serendipitous find of the many old binders of inmate biographies at the Museum, Chet's (and later his daughter Karen's, who was a volunteer at the Museum as well) enthusiasm for history, and his kindness and openness to assistance in what was clearly his labor of love is so much appreciated. Secondly, once I was deeply involved in the archives of Tewksbury, I was accepted into a National Endowment of the Humanities history seminar at the University of Connecticut, where I met Professor Richard Brown. Richard was of enormous assistance despite the fact that our work is quite different in many ways. While I was not a student of Richard's nor had any claim on his time, he contributed greatly to my learning about genealogical and other official records for use in this book and further aided in me in his reading and criticism of the book.

Others, of course, were important. The College of Arts and Sciences at the University of Southern Maine provided me with a Faculty Creativity grant in the late Spring of 2004, which enabled me to begin preliminary research, and I was aided all too briefly by a student assistant, Joy Golding (now Powell). Later I was aided by two other University of Southern Maine students, Jennifer L. Brown and Erin Wilford. The Center for Lowell History at the University of Massachusetts at Lowell provided a very comfortable and hospitable place to read and copy the state-archived *Inmate Biographies,* and its director, Martha Mayo, was helpful with questions and with securing illustrations for the book. William Barry of the Maine Historical Society was as usual helpful, as he aided me in the initial stages of approaching the genealogical work, as well as reading some chapters. Other readers included Joseph Conforti of USM's American and New England Studies Department, Lawrence Goodheart at the University of Connecticut's Department of History, and Stephen Murphy of USM's School of Education.

There are some "usual suspects" to thank as well. Marcia B. Cohen, my wife and colleague at the University of New England, read each chapter as they came off the press, and even read some of the *Inmate Biographies.* Frances Fox Piven of the City University Graduate Center has served in her steady mentor role, and my friend and long-term editor, now publisher, Dean Birkenkamp, has provided me a forum for ideas and publishing.

Annie Sullivan, "The Miracle Worker." Tewksbury's most famous inmate pictured in 1881 at age eleven, see Chapter 1 (courtesy, Perkins Institution for the Blind).

GEN! BENJ. F. BUTLER.
Published & Lith⁴ by L. Prang & C⁰ Boston.
Sole Agent J. Haven, 31 Exchange St

Benjamin Butler, the populist governor of Massachusetts, led an 1883 investigation of Tewksbury (courtesy, Center for Lowell History).

Discharged .... Jan 28 1875

Removed .... Boston 1875

By whom Hanson

For Nos ....

326 Finland Lane Boston
Feb or March 1870 as a Seaman
on Ship Antrim - Has followed
the seas since - Single Seaman
N. N. No Prop. No Exps - Pa
Adolph in Finland Mo
Johanna d° No Rels or fds
in A. No other Inst Had
Syph 3 yrs ago in Eng
Now has sore Legs. See Syph
Recently came to Boston from
Coast of Africa on Barque
"Jennie Goosman" In Marine
Hospital past 6½ mos - writ
... an nearly

Tewksbury inmate biography, a sample of an archived biography found at the
Massachusetts Public Health Museum (photo, David Wagner).

The Departure of the Emigrants' Ship.

Departure of an immigrant ship with Irish immigrants (courtesy, Center for Lowell History).

Railroad workers, 1886. Many Tewksbury inmates were rail workers (courtesy, Center for Lowell History).

Laborers, 1880s. This was the most common male job of Tewksbury inmates (courtesy, Center for Lowell History).

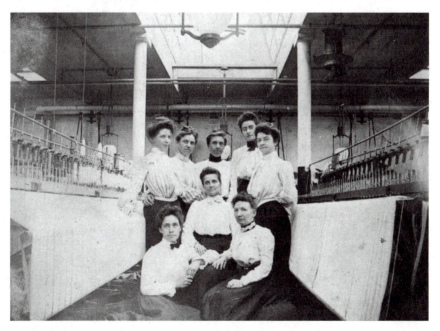

Workers at Arlington Mills, also a common occupation of inmates (courtesy, Center for Lowell History).

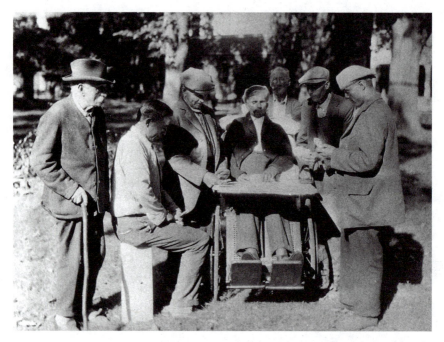

Card players, Tewksbury Infirmary, 1930s. Despite the renaming of the institution as an "Infirmary," Tewksbury remained a home for poor people, ill or not, for most of its history, housing many hundred indigent people at a time during the Great Depression (courtesy, Massachusetts Public Health Museum).

ONE

Ordinary People

"Let it be remembered that a large proportion of these poor people, called 'paupers' by the newspapers and officials, are honest working men and women, the profit of whose toil goes to make up the fortunes—the millions—of the few whose costly equipage jostle the starving mechanic in the same street."
—William Sylvis, nineteenth-century labor leader

In every era, those who are labeled "poor" tend to be viewed as frozen in time and space as a permanent class. In the nineteenth century, those at the bottom of the social order were variously known as: paupers; the indolent, vicious, and intemperate; the dangerous classes; the rabble; or, as the 1880 census labeled them, "the defective, dependent and delinquent classes." One of the important opportunities of historical research is the ability to explore the lives of ordinary people who were classified as "poor" at one point in time and gain some measure of a longer look at their lives. The following seven people—a native-born American orphan who was placed out of his family, an African American born in the South arriving in Massachusetts, an Irish immigrant to America with family problems, an Irish-Canadian immigrant who had a child out of wedlock, a French immigrant and her children fleeing domestic violence, another Irish immigrant who lost his leg working on the railroad, and an elderly native New Englander who lost his money—all hit "rock bottom" and were admitted to a poorhouse between the end of the Civil War and the mid-1890s. As different as each person was, they shared the characteristic of being *ordinary people*.

FRANK CROSS

Frank Cross was a ten-year-old boy made homeless in 1880 when his father, Solomon, was imprisoned for nine months in the House of Correction in South Boston "for obtaining goods under false pretenses." Frank was born in a small town in rural Maine but grew up in the growing industrial center of Lewiston where his father was a blacksmith. When Frank was a little boy, his mother Etta deserted the family. His father migrated to the Boston area where he became a grocer. As in most cases of orphans or young children of prisoners, Frank was moved from the poorhouse and was "placed out" or "bound over" to a farm family where he would labor in return for board. These placements were sometimes exploitative. We know that by age 17, Frank was a laborer in the Boston area. He then married Mary Haney, who was from a family affluent enough that she did not have to work. Frank and Mary had two children and lived in the Boston area throughout the rest of their lives. Frank tried his hand at a clothing business in the first decade of the twentieth century, but later worked as a mechanic and owned a home in Wakefield, Massachusetts, about twenty miles outside of Boston. His son followed him in becoming a mechanic.

ROBERT H. DELANEY

Robert H Delaney was an African American boy who was born in Washington, D.C. His father, Thomas, was a hotel waiter who owned some property, and his mother was Josephine. The youngest of five children, several years after his father's death, Robert headed north to Massachusetts. As a young teenager he got a job at the Harvard (University) Dining Saloon, which employed many African Americans. After Robert was admitted to the almshouse in 1875, the agents noted "he had friends William H. Jones, C. W. Turner, and George Simmons all of Washington [who are] now employed in the Harvard Dining Saloon." After a short stay at the almshouse, Robert would later return to Washington, where he continued to work as a waiter and live with his family. He married Laura Moran, a native of Georgia, in 1885. When found in records later, he seemed to have separated or divorced from Laura and had moved to New Jersey where he worked in Atlantic City as a waiter and lived with his mother, now in her seventies and listed as a nurse. Robert remarried in the early 1900s and was last found as a hotel waiter in Paterson, New Jersey.

BRIDGET HENNESSEY FERGUSON

Bridget Hennessey was born in County Cork, Ireland, in 1840. Like millions of her fellow countrymen who fled the abject poverty of Ireland, she came to America, landing in Boston in September 1858 aboard the ship *Wilbur Fiske*. As was also typical of many immigrants, her family was divided, with her father, William, staying in Ireland and dying there, while her mother, Margaret, came to America. Her siblings' history is not known, but may too have been divided by the Atlantic. In 1864, she married James Ferguson, a German immigrant, in a Roman Catholic ceremony in Boston.

In 1873, Bridget, now the mother of four children, entered the poorhouse complaining of her husband abusing her. According to her interview the troubles began the year before, and "she has had more or less trouble with her husband since. She claims that he sold her furniture and he still treats her badly. He pinches her out the doors occasionally." Bridget stated that neither she nor her husband were heavy drinkers. Interestingly, the children were left at the home in Boston with James. The examining agents described Bridget obliquely as "a trifle flighty now but one should not call her insane."

Bridget (nee Hennessey) Ferguson returned to her husband and they had five more children together. James, earlier described as having a job at the Customs House, was by 1880 a porter in a leather shop, which must have certainly made it challenging to support the family. James died in 1896 in Boston, at the age of 58, and Bridget died the following year at 57 in Taunton, Massachusetts, an industrial center in southeastern Massachusetts.

AUGUSTINE JACQUOIT

Augustine Jacquoit (maiden name not known) was a French immigrant to America, arriving in New York in October 1888 at the age of fifteen. The next year she married Julius Jacquoit, also a native of France. They gave birth to their first child, Pauline, in the Western Massachusetts Berkshires town of Great Barrington, and later had two other children, Louis and Julius Junior. Some time after they met, Julius evidently began to batter Augustine, and in 1893, Julius was sentenced to four months in the Pittsfield, Massachusetts, jail for assaulting his wife. Augustine entered the poorhouse with her three children, though we do not know whether this was for reasons of physical shelter or for other assistance, such as medical care for her children. At some point in the 1890s, both Louis and Julius Junior died. Augustine would live with her one remaining child, Pauline, the rest of her life. She would work as a cook, first in Great Barrington and later in Albany, New York, where she was also the keeper of a lodging house. Pauline found work as a typist and stenographer. We do not know for sure what became of Julius Senior. The most likely person found in censuses was a man with a similar name in the small industrial city of Torrington, Connecticut. If this is he, he remarried and started a new family, and worked throughout his life as a machinist.

KATE JOY

Kate Joy is typical of many women who were punished in the nineteenth century for having an out-of-wedlock child. Born on the barren Canadian island of Newfoundland, her family was of Irish descent. She came to the northern Massachusetts town of Newburyport in the late 1840s. Kate was the sixth of nine children. Her father, John Joy, was a seaman and fisherman, and her mother, Mary, kept house. Her father was born in Ireland, while Mary was born in Canada. As was common in the nineteenth century, the entire family worked from an early age, and in 1860, for example, all the girls were working in mills, while the older sons were fisherman sailing out of Newburyport. The Joys must have done relatively well as they owned their own home for awhile. However, upon the death of John Joy, the family had to sell the house. In 1867, Kate was admitted to a poorhouse after discovering she was pregnant. She reported that the father of her child was one Tim Sullivan, a 23-year-old sailor from the nearby northeastern Massachusetts town of Amesbury. As did many unmarried mothers, Kate reported that the father was "now off" (the father would have faced arrest and prosecution under the law at this time and made to pay support for the woman and child; whether the father had indeed "skipped town" or whether his location was actually known to the mother we cannot know). On July 1, 1867, Kate was sentenced to the Massachusetts workhouse, which more closely resembled a penal institution than an almshouse. This entailed harsh work and discipline and was meant explicitly to punish miscreants guilty of drunkenness, adultery, fornication, petty theft, and even idleness. We know that, as of 1870, Kate was still an inmate at the workhouse. This is quite an unusual length of time to be there, indicative either of another conviction which sent

Kate there after her first sentence or perhaps an assessment of her mental status as incompetent. The agents referred to her as "foolish almost," a presumed judgment of mental retardation.

DAVID RING

David Ring was an Irish immigrant who landed in New York City in 1850 on the ship *Clara Wheeler*. He married his wife, Johanna, in 1854 and settled down in Salem, Massachusetts, the old seaport city about thirty miles north of Boston. Like most Irish males of this period, he had few opportunities but to be a "laborer," which served as an all purpose catchall term to describe unskilled workers who were forced to do almost anything manual. As with many Irish laborers he worked on the vast network of railroads beginning to cross the nation. Unfortunately, the growth of the railroads, as with much of the American economy, left behind thousands of injured, maimed, and even dead workers. Railroad employment additionally relied on housing thousands of workers in railroad camps with poor health and sanitary conditions, and many workers were misled into coming for work that did not exist. In 1860, David was one the railroad's victims, losing a leg while he was loading stone onto a rail car on the Eastern Railroad. Unable to work anymore, he was lucky enough to be supported by his wife, who ran a small store. In 1873, however, his wife fell ill and broke her leg and was unable to care for him. She also was reported "to have used up all her means." David Ring entered the poorhouse that year. He did find sympathy from a member of the Overseers of the Poor in his native Salem (those officials responsible for administering local relief for three hundred years of American history) who described him as "a clever, old unfortunate man. Give him all the liberty you can." Ring was 68 years old at the time.

JOHN F. WYMAN

John F. Wyman was the tenth of eleven children of William and Mary Gibson Wyman, members of an old New England family. According to his interview on entering the poorhouse, John carried "a complete Family Record back to 1752, [with a] settlement in old Lunenberg, now a part of the city of Fitchburg." Born in 1805 in Walpole, New Hampshire, an old rural settlement, John, like many nineteenth-century Americans, was mobile and by eighteen had traveled to Massachusetts, by twenty-five out west to the Erie Canal area, and by thirty-five further west to Michigan. John married Caroline Elizabeth Metcalf in 1833, and by 1850 they had a family of five daughters. John became a merchant in Grand Rapids, Michigan, with a respectable $1,500 worth of property. At some point John caught the revivalist fever of the times and "traveled in various places [in the] West lecturing on Temperance and Phrenology." (Temperance was the budding anti-liquor movement of the time, while the study of phrenology relied on the analysis of skull characteristics to determine mental or moral characteristics). John evidently left his family, presumably to lecture or proselytize, and worked on farms in Michigan and Massachusetts. When John was sixty-eight, he reported that he was robbed of $4,300 while traveling from Lowell, Massachusetts, to Boston. According to his interview in 1874, he "was once worth $40,000, but lost his property by endorsing the paper of a friend and selling his stock in a variety store on credit." At seventy years old, John entered the almshouse and apparently remained there until he died at 78 on October 11, 1882. His wife, Caroline, died in 1861, and his daughters were in Grand Rapids, Michigan, in the late nineteenth century.

The Fluidity of Poverty

With the possible exception of Wyman (and whether he accumulated the amount of funds he claims may be dubious), what is most striking is the ordinariness of the "inmates" (as they were then called) of one of America's largest almshouses. Sadly, John Wyman and (perhaps) David Ring ended their days there. It is also possible that Kate Joy died in the workhouse, given the early life expectancy of the time and the high death rate at these institutions. Yet for Frank Cross, Thomas Delaney, Bridget Ferguson, and Augustine Jacquoit the harsh stigma of poverty and the poorhouse did not prevent them from leading what appears to be ordinary lives after leaving the poorhouse, at least as far as occupations and family constellations are concerned. Nor had the Joy, Wyman, and Ring families by any means always been "poor"; the Wyman and Joy families had been homeowners, while the Rings had run a store.

To say these and other poor people are "ordinary" people is not to deny the tragedy that is poverty nor that the poor were (and are) victims of economic events such as unemployment, as well as poor working conditions and poor living conditions which follow from poverty, from inferior housing and inadequate diet to street violence to more reported family violence. They are also the victims of how the political and social system distributes its surplus. However, a focus on poverty as victimhood not only—as so many have now argued—defeats any sense of people's own control or "agency," as academics like to say. It also, as importantly, can obscure the fact that most poor people, if never affluent, are part of a broader class of working people, who either do not make enough money or suffer losses of jobs or other reversals that prevent them from being judged as "average" working people for a period of time. This is to suggest that, economic depressions aside, few people go for years without work and without participation in both the wage and consumer culture of capitalism. While clearly some groups of people are far more vulnerable to poverty than others, predicting poverty in the cases above would not have been easy and was dependent on a complex mix of social, economic, and individual circumstances.

Specifically, there would be almost no way to predict from their earlier lives that Kate Joy, David Ring, or John Wyman would end up in an almshouse or workhouse. Kate Joy's father was a property holder and taxpayer. His daughter's apparent fate may have been a result of the simple act of an out-of-wedlock pregnancy or perhaps involved other factors (her being "foolish almost"). While we know many elderly people ended up destitute at this time, there would be no reason to predict that Wyman or Ring in particular would. Wyman was a property holder and Ring a storekeeper at one point. The deep depression that began in 1873 may well have been a breaking point for both of them and their ability to support themselves (or their family's ability to support them). In a similar vein, we could not predict that Frank Cross, an orphan who was bound out, or Augustine Jacquoit, an immigrant woman with a family who was assaulted by her husband and entered an almshouse, would each later own a home, not a common thing for most workers in the U.S. until after World War II. Since Cross and Jacquoit were both relatively young when they entered the almshouse (ten for Cross in 1880 and twenty-two for Jacquoit in 1893), they grew to later adulthood in a relatively more prosperous period in New England of the early twentieth century, in which there was more social mobility. Perhaps this in part provides an answer.

Moreover, "poverty" turns out to be a complex thing to define, consisting of at least three valid definitions. Most people think of poverty as an *absolute* monetary amount necessary to support oneself and/or one's family. Determining such levels is highly contested, and most social scientists believe the current U.S. "poverty line" is set at an inadequately low rate. Still, one can develop a measure of necessities and decide on a more liberal poverty line. Depending, of course, on what exact level of income or assets our seven people above had at any time, they may have gone in and out of being in poverty. Another definition of poverty is a *relative* one. This definition would suggest poverty exists on a comparative basis in which individuals and families, and, in fact, the whole society thinks of deprivation based on the average consumption and living standards of their area and their time. This too is an important measure of social life. You may make $20,000 as an individual in 2007, which would place you far above today's poverty level, and that would be the case even with the more liberal poverty lines some advocate. Yet you may feel absolutely poor, being unable to buy an automobile, afford much of a vacation, or perhaps purchase the latest computer, television, and high tech equipment. While once seen as luxuries, most of these items are now thought of as necessities. By relative measures, certainly some of our seven people above appear to have been above the relative level of the times, particularly when including the home ownership information.

Another definition of poverty that is underexplored is the *legally ascribed status* that poverty had until relatively recently, and which arguably has some carry-overs in our current time. From the first Colonial settlements in America until the Warren Court's striking down of certain regulations in the 1960s, poverty had a legal meaning. To be a "pauper," one who was destitute and receiving public aid, was to *lose all rights,* including usually the right to vote in elections. This is to remind the reader that all seven of our ordinary people lost whatever rights they had not only while on relief but, although not always enforced, potentially for years afterward. Also, from the seventeenth century to the mid-twentieth century, legal poverty entailed the laws of settlement, which privileged those who had lived in one place steadily and paid taxes such as property and poll taxes. For women, who of course could not vote during most of this time period, their settlement was usually established through their husbands or fathers. To have a "settlement" meant legally being eligible to the rights of citizenship of the town or city. The seven people profiled above would have known the ramifications of their status well. By this measure a different look at poverty can be gleaned. For as long as Bridget Ferguson lived with her husband, who had a settlement, and as long as Kate Joy lived with her father who had a settlement, they would not be denied town assistance. John Wyman had a settlement in Michigan, but when he came to Massachusetts, he had none. David Ring had a settlement in Salem, but Frank Cross's father did not pay enough taxes to have a settlement when Frank was admitted. While seemingly arcane, the legally ascribed nature of poverty is critical to examining poverty in America before the 1930s. The harsh stigma of pauperism, as well as the implications of the denial of those few social benefits available as well as the rights of citizenship were critical facts of life.

Regardless of definition, the most important point is the very difficulty of separating out a class of poor people as an entity apart from that of "worker" or "average" citizen. This argues for a fluid and situational definition of poverty. Until, perhaps, the relatively brief period following World War II through the early 1970s, the American economy could not sustain the level of "middle class" existence it proclaimed, and large numbers of people were in material want at any given point. As we shall see below, during the Gilded Age, the majority of people were in need at times, and this reinforces the idea that our seven individuals and their families were "ordinary people." (Having said this, please see Box 1.1 on Annie Sullivan, the famous teacher of the blind and companion of Helen Keller, a Tewksbury inmate who would later become famous.)

Box 1.1. Tewksbury's Most Famous Inmate

On February 22, 1876, a fairly routine form (shorter than many) records the admission of two young Irish American children:

Reg. 48457-458 Age: 10
Name: Annie Sullivan born Agawam
James Sullivan Age 5 Hip Disease
Admitted from Agawam Feb. 22, 1876
Condition: Weak Eyes
Examined: March 29, 1876

10 [years old] born July 1866, Agawam, and always lived there till sent here. Father Thomas Sullivan born Ireland. No estate, can't tell if naturalized or paid taxes, or in service in [Civil] War. Now lives in Agawam, working as a farmer for Stephen O'Hearn. Mother Alice died about two years ago in Agawam. Sister Mary, three years old, [is] with [her] aunt Mary Clarey in Agawam. Sore eyes, and James has hip complaint. Neither ever went to school.

One of the ordinary people admitted to Tewksbury was Annie Sullivan, who would earn fame as the teacher and life-long companion of Helen Keller, who also be a brilliant teacher and advocate for the blind (as well as other causes) for nearly seventy years. In her biography of Anne Sullivan, Helen Keller describes her as having had "trouble with her eyes" as far back as she could remember. When Annie was eight, her mother died, leaving the three children. Her father abandoned them two years later and Annie never learned what became of him. Keller describes the reason she and Jimmie went to the almshouse but her sister Mary did not as being "because [Annie] was difficult to manage and too blind to be useful," while "Jimmie . . . was becoming helplessly lame with tubercular hip." Indeed, Jimmy would die at Tewksbury only three months later on May 30.

According to Keller's memories of Sullivan's story of her life, despite her future talents no one paid the uneducated, sight-impaired young girl much mind at the almshouse. "She had no friends but her fellow paupers. It was one of them who told her that there were special schools for the blind and as time went on . . . her desire for an education grew." This school was the famous Perkins School for the Blind then in South Boston, Massachusetts, the first school for the blind in the United States. In 1880, Sullivan prostrated herself before the visiting agents of the State Board of Charities and Corrections, a monitoring group set up by the state:

> To escape from the pit of degradation and disease in which she lived seemed impossible until the stench from the almshouse rose so high that the State Board of Charities ordered an investigation. The investigators did not discover her. The inmates knew the name of the chairman and when the committee members arrived she flung herself towards them, unable to distinguish one from another, and cried out, "Mr. Sanborn, Mr. Sanborn, I want to go to school!"

This was a historic meeting. Here was Anne Sullivan, the young pauper who would grow up to be a very famous American, facing Franklin Benjamin Sanborn, known as an abolitionist, transcendentalist, and a founder of the American Social Science Association. Perhaps ironically, the famous charitable and social welfare reformer Sanborn was also an expert in the new fields of "pauperism," "vagrancy," and charities, who seemed to see little contradiction between running large almshouses and his other reform efforts. Across from him was Sullivan who would become a socialist later in her life. In any event, Sullivan was transferred and accepted into the Perkins School that year.

ORDINARY PEOPLE AND THE GILDED AGE

This book attempts to capture the historical experience of one of America's most turbulent and significant times, the "Gilded Age," which lasted roughly from the end of America's Civil War to the beginning of the twentieth century. Of course this period was named for the vast accumulation and conspicuous display of wealth in America that made the "robber barons," such as J.D. Rockefeller, Cornelius Vanderbilt, Andrew Carnegie, J.P. Morgan, and others, so rich and famous. Yet as the United States rapidly industrialized and urbanized and began to overtake Great Britain as the center of the Industrial Revolution, poverty, disability, and early death marked the underside of "progress." Capitalizing on the largest migration of people the world at that time had seen—the immigration of millions of Europeans and others to this nation—cheap labor served as fodder for the growth of the railroads, steel, textiles, mining, construction, and a host of other industries.

The seven people described above—Frank Cross, Robert Delaney, Bridget Hennessey, Augustine Jacquoit, Kate Joy, David Ring, and Frank Wyman—were ordinary people whose circumstances forced them into one of America's largest poorhouses or almshouses, the Massachusetts State Almshouse in Tewksbury, located a few miles outside of the booming industrial city of Lowell, Massachusetts. As many as 3,500 people a year came into "Tewksbury," whose notoriety was such that, like "Bellevue" (the hospital in New York City), it was uttered as a single terrible word that needed no clarification. Since the State Almshouse specifically served those "unsettled"—e.g., lacking a town or city settlement in Massachusetts—it included a highly varied population. For example, so many immigrants who arrived in Boston came to Tewksbury Almshouse, it may be said to be the Boston area's equivalent to New York's Ellis Island. Additionally, thousands of Americans and Canadians on their way to cities like Lowell, Lawrence, Lynn, and Boston, or heading west to New York, Ohio, Illinois, even California stopped off and stayed. The next chapter describes in more detail the setting of this book and the nature of the data that it is based on.

Importantly, however, even though the seven were stigmatized as "paupers," at least for a time (for Cross, Delaney, Hennessey, and Jacquoit, not very long), the lives of the Gilded Age period in America that most ordinary Americans lived are reflected in the above profiles. It seems that almost everyone was "on the move" at this time. In this sense, Oscar Handlin's famous book title of the "Uprooted" applies not only to the millions of immigrants like Bridget Hennessey, Augustine Jacquoit. Kate Joy, and David Ring above, but to the millions of displaced native-born Americans as well. Frank Cross's father left rural Maine to join millions of his peers in hoping to do better in urban America; Frank Wyman traveled west seeking a future; and Robert Delaney, along with thousands of other African Americans, fled the South to come north, seeking more freedom as well as economic opportunity. Though immigrants to the New World were the largest component of the low-wage workforce, they were joined in their toil by millions of native-born Americans, many of whom had left their homes for work in new places.

If so many people were "uprooted," separated from families of origin and the traditions of their ancestral villages in Europe or rural homes in America, they also were at the mercy of a boom/bust economic cycle and the new industrial economy, which sharply contrasted with farm life. No doubt the massive depression of the 1870s, one of the worst in American history, affected the lives of Delaney, Hennessey, Ring, and Wyman, who came to the poorhouse in the midst of this terrible period of suffering. The next major depression began in 1893 and lasted for half of that decade. Both depressions flooded the almshouses, as well as relief rolls (known then as "outdoor relief"), police stations, and lodging houses, which were used to house the homeless, and the roads filled with what people began in the 1870s to call "tramps." The work that was available was harsh, with little or no safety protection, low remuneration, and few unions, leaving those like David Ring not only unemployed, but disabled in a society without disability pensions or workers' compensation. For women like Bridget Hennessey and Kate Joy, the major employment options of the time were domestic servant or mill "operative." For many women, domestic work represented a surrender of autonomy and dignity, and the field was left almost entirely to the Irish, and sometimes African American and non-Irish foreign-born women. While factory jobs may have been attractive at first to some women, those who were unable to leave through successful marriage or other mobility faced unhealthy working conditions, poor living conditions in their overcrowded tenements, and a reduced life expectancy.

The seven profiles illustrate other issues that characterize the "laissez-faire" period of unfettered capitalism and lack of social welfare provision of the time. Frank Wyman is representative of the large number of downwardly mobile people who fell from stable farm families in New England and the Middle Atlantic in the period which this book explores. His and David Ring's experience also points out the harshness of a system which often served its elders by moving them into poorhouses. Frank Cross represents the other side of the lifespan and the tragedy of foundlings left on the streets, homeless children, millions of orphans and so-called "half-orphans" (children missing one parent) institutionalized in large facilities, and the process of "binding out" children as workers. Neither the early nor later years of life had a high survival rate for average Americans. Life was often short and brutal, though those who did survive to an old age faced abandonment by their families and such indignities as being warehoused away more than today.

Family conflict and violence is, of course, represented in the cases of Bridget Hennessey Ferguson and Augustine Jacquoit. While hardly unique to this era, Victorian Americans acknowledged domestic violence and believed they saw an increase in this behavior compared to previous times. Added to this were the extremely high rates of desertion and separation, husbands leaving wives, wives abandoning husbands, and sometimes both leaving their children. Although sometimes forced by the transitory nature of work and long distances men, in particular, traveled to work, no doubt the collapse of traditional extended families and Old World norms also led to severe problems in family life in the period. The move from the small rural communities in which every one knew everyone to the great anonymous cities of the late nineteenth century impacted behavior as well.

As we have seen with the profile of Kate Joy, social policy and dominant institutions including the Massachusetts State Almshouse added to women's woes by policing sexuality and meting out punishment. While not unique to this period either, the confrontation of immigrant women with predominantly native Protestant officials marked a paternalistic and maternalistic system which often extracted a high price from immigrant and low-income women in particular. While many immigrants and other poor could not afford to marry, and with no easy divorce available for those with problematic marriages, little sympathy was forthcoming from social welfare officials who saw all "out of wedlock" sexual activity as immoral. "Out of wedlock," or "criminal contact," as the Tewksbury officials referred to any sex outside marriage, was a status conferred even on those who were separated from spouses for many years. While as we shall see, the charitable agents punished men as well as women, this only served to increase the overall policing of sexuality as well as other behaviors of the poor and working classes.

The seven profiles also suggest the need for writers and scholars to view life holistically. Many historians and social scientists have described the Gilded Age in terms of its economic and industrial changes. Some literature has developed, though still to a lesser degree, on the family, social welfare, and personal lives of people in America of this time period. And yet as we see with each of the people profiled, the social and economic system of any period interacts for each of us, not only at the level of work or unemployment, but also at the family and individual level where the "personal" resides. It is hard to tease apart the lives of any of the seven and mark what is "economic" and what is "personal." It is my hope to put real people into the historical record, who for many reasons (including the lack of available historical information for the poorer parts of the population) are often still missing from the literature.

THE PROBLEM OF "ORDINARINESS"

How to represent the "ordinary," past or present, is not an easy task. Certainly great progress has been made since the 1960s, when the "new social history" began to replace the earlier sole focus of history on the powerful or political elites. In the social sciences and humanities, scholars influenced by the social movements of the 1960s and 1970s began not only to explore the history of labor, women, immigrant groups, African Americans, Native Americans, and other previously excluded groups, but to work consciously to bring forth the voices of the excluded, past and present. Yet the stubborn fact that those at the lower levels of socioeconomic status leave behind few written records still presents problems in representation. On the one hand, much writing on the excluded focuses on the well-known people within the groups (such as women, African Americans, immigrants, or trade unionists) as a source of pride. But these leaders often themselves came from higher classes and may or may not reflect the lives and thinking of the majority of people in the represented groups. The lives of Frederick Douglass or Sojourner Truth or Joe Hill or Mother Jones or Susan B. Anthony are still *exceptional* ones, not ordinary stories.

On the other hand, another possible distortion is a tendency of writers committed to, for example, ethnic history, to leave out the "warts" of their group and present a more glorified picture. As the early focus of historians moved from dramatic events, such as great labor strikes, to less dramatic areas, such as the day-to-day lives of the Irish or Franco-American immigrants, they provided descriptions which can sometimes be bland in nature.

Statistical data, of course, provide some antidote to anecdote or making the ordinary too extraordinary. The work of Stephen Thernstrom and his followers on nineteenth-century American mobility is an example of how census data can be used, not only to develop a "snapshot" picture of American life, but also, by using longitudinal data, to provide measures of change over time. Most good social science and history uses at least some statistical evidence to ground its explorations. Of course, as all scholars note, statistical data may have its weaknesses, particularly the very partial data that we have from the nineteenth century. Statistics are critical in order to know how many laborers there were, how many domestic workers, how many Irish immigrants, etc. But censuses and other official documents not only tend to leave out the poor and highly mobile, they don't portray well the fluidity and changing nature of people's lives. To take an example, knowing the gross number of laborers in 1880 may obscure the fact that many of our subjects described themselves as "laborers" at one point in time that year, but "peddlers" later, were on relief rolls later the same year, and then identified as a "hostler" (a major nineteenth-century immigrant occupation of caring for horses, later also a low-level rail employee) the next year.

The use of archival data in addition to statistical data helps the historian or social scientist add "flesh and bone" contemporary observation to the broader historical data. Various types of documents have now been used by scholars for many years. The use of case records has been a growing pursuit in those fields such as family history and sociology, social welfare, and feminist scholarship that have attempted to explore family life and the poor. As noted by its best practitioners, such as Linda Gordon, this data has its own drawbacks as "cases," whether collected by early social workers or agents or officials are still not primary data from the pens or mouths of actual poor or working-class people. Although, in this case, most of the data written down by officials were clearly from interviews conducted with the poor people, and often does use quotations from them, clearly both officials and "clients" knew at least to some extent what the other wished to hear and this script shaped the interaction between the poor person and the agent. These accounts require caution, especially when making generalizations.

There are no easy resolutions to these problems, and neither reliance on any one form of methodology, such as the use of statistical data and official records or content analyses of diaries or contemporary newspapers or magazines or other strategies, can ever fully capture a time and place. Questions of representativeness affect every study since no scholar can study everything and must make a selection that limits its applicability. Still, I believe that studies such as these which focus on poor and working people are important, not only to recapture the history of the majority of American people, but also because so much historical and sociological theorizing is based on the counted, housed, and stable part of the population which, particularly at certain points in history, did not necessarily capture a majority of the poor.

As will be discussed in the next chapter at greater length, this book cannot escape the dilemma. To avoid sole reliance on the written description of interviewers, I added a genealogical research component so as to follow "inmates" before and after their stay at the poorhouse, which was sometimes quite brief. I was able to find (see Chapter 2) a good subsample of some of those who passed through Tewksbury who did make the U.S. Census records, city or town Directories, or town or city Vital Statistics (births, marriages, deaths). Still, unlike the seven profiles here, many poor and working people do not appear in census data or in other records. Or they have names so common that a confident judgment on what happened to a specific "John Smith" is impossible. Secondly, in choosing to examine "ordinary" people, I do so through a quite *extraordinary* setting, admission to a large almshouse. On the positive side, this setting adds drama and interest to most every story, as having to give up one's freedom and declare oneself a pauper was no easy matter for any of the people studied. On the other hand, exceptional events in people's lives may not typify how their day-to-day life is lived. For example, going to an emergency room for a serious injury is not exactly a "typical" day for most people, and one's actions and behavior at the ER may be far from one's usual behavior. A further problem that I share with all scholars has to do with sorting through masses of data (some of it repetitious and dry) and then attempting to engage a readership in parts of it. Again the very mundane nature of most data, not to mention its bulk, would frighten the bravest reader. In telling "ordinary" stories, I too have selected those possessing some interest, either because of the manner or quality of the individual's story or in some cases the fact that the inmate's life sparked the keener interest of the interviewer and hence led to a fuller write-up.

I have tried to occupy the middle ground between those who describe mostly the extraordinary persons or events (the great strike or great battle) and those who tend to dwell on the specialized areas of history or social science which are extremely particularistic, to highlight what seem to be the main themes relevant to adding to our knowledge of poor and working people in the Gilded Age. We still lack any real history of poor people in the United States, though we have much work in some subcategories within it, and I hope this work contributes to enlarging this understanding.

* * *

TWO

The Context: The Massachusetts State Almshouse at Tewksbury, Immigration, and Industrialization

> "In many ways the Gilded Age (was) a period of trauma, of change so swift and thorough that many Americans seemed unable to fathom the extent of the upheaval ... "
>
> —Alan Trachtenberg, *The Incorporation of America*

To place ourselves in a very different time is not easy. In seeking to capture both a part of our past and the experience of being poor in America, much context has to be drawn. First I will sketch out the contours of the American Poor Laws, which not only shaped life for those at the bottom of society, but also served as a powerful and frightening specter to all who were not affluent throughout America's history, at least until the 1930s. Secondly, we will examine the broader social context of the massive immigration that was the impetus for the decision by the state of Massachusetts to build three state almshouses in 1854 (the largest of which was Tewksbury) for their "unsettled poor." New England's early start in American industrialization is a context that also needs description. Finally, the materials used for this book, the *Inmate Biographies* and genealogical resources, will be further described and a statistical portrait of the inmates provided.

POOR RELIEF IN ANGLO-AMERICAN HISTORY

Neither the American Colonies nor the independent United States were the least bit innovative in the area of social welfare, but rather took the English Poor Laws, developed famously by Elizabeth I, in complete form into law and practice. While the British system must be acknowledged as the first formal recognition of a governmental role in social welfare, there is little controversy that the poor relief system was a punitive, niggardly system whose purpose often seemed to be keeping local budgets low, and potential recipients off the rolls. For 300 years or more, America would exist without a federal social welfare system such as Social Security or unemployment insurance, and, with the important exception of aid to veterans in the decades after the Civil War, it would be the twentieth century before any major innovations would come.

Structured locally, a town resident who was in need approached officials known as the "Overseers of the Poor." Although relatively low-level officials of towns and cities, still, at least until the twentieth century, these were ordinarily men of some wealth who on a part-time, unpaid basis handled the problems of the poor. Overseers were responsible to their towns for ensuring first that indeed the potential recipient was a settled member of the town, second, that the recipient was without assets, and third, for deciding whether recipients were "deserving" or "worthy" poor, or "undeserving" poor. These tasks were not at all insignificant since from the origin of America great hostility existed toward the poor. As New York social welfare historian David Schneider recounts, by 1650 settlers in some Long Island towns "took the matter into their own hands and organized military companies to protect their villages against the approach of unsettled people and vagabonds." As early as 1636, cities such as Boston made it illegal to have visitors for more than two weeks without the permission of officials. Unless it could be proven that such visitors would not become a public burden, permission to visit could be denied. Later (and extending throughout U.S. history) ships were prohibited from discharging paupers onto American shores. Settlement laws served as an economic protection for towns and cities against a rise in cost which could be directly seen by citizens through their poor tax, but also combined with religious and cultural fears of strangers. Originally, settlers who were not of an approved religious denomination were excluded, while later it was those of different ethnic or national groups. Those who were "unsettled" or in danger of becoming paupers were often "warned out" or served a summons to leave town under the threat of arrest if they ever returned. Even more dramatically, anecdotes of the dumping of poor people, particularly the mentally ill ("insane" as they were then called) are legion in American history. Often moved in the dead of night, such paupers were placed in adjoining towns, with the hope that upon their discovery, the next town would accept that their town was indeed the home of the pauper. Settlement laws were so stringent that some towns and cities spent as much (and in some cases, more) in litigation than they did actually relieving poverty.

Overseers and communities were concerned, of course, with more than settlement, but also with the worthiness of prospective charges. For generations, people in need had to take a "pauper's oath," declaring they were without support or assets. By law, officials could demand parents of children (including adult children) and adult children of older parents to support each other, and in most states more distant relatives were also held obligated by law. Should someone receive aid, their future wages, property, or farm crops could be taken as reimbursement. One inmate of Tewksbury, for example, lost his home to finance poor relief provided to his father when the latter was infirm, helping in turn to impoverish the son. Male paupers were often given a "work test" in which they were asked to demonstrate their fitness by breaking a pile of stones with an ax or mallet. Somewhat surprisingly, overseers complained that applicants sometimes intentionally failed the work test, yet given the awful conditions that able-bodied men were forced to undergo (such as the workhouse), who could blame them? Although decisions on worthiness were profoundly local, several major trends can be discerned throughout history. Generally widows, orphans, the elderly, and the infirm were seen as "deserving" and more generously aided while men who were apparently able bodied (including many who by today's standards were disabled, such as the mentally ill and the developmentally disabled) and women who were sexually active outside of marriage (having sex out of wedlock or committing adultery) were treated harshly. Along with these groups, unworthiness surrounded those judged "intemperate," "delinquent," runaway children, and large categories of people who were judged deviant or irreligious ("all rogues, vagabonds and idle persons ... persons feigning themselves to have knowledge of physiognomy, palmistry, or pretending that they can tell fortunes, or discover where lost or stolen goods may be found, common pipers, fidlers [sic] ... common night-walkers, pilferers, wanton and lascivious persons ... common brawlers and railers ... ").

In the original intent of the Anglo American Poor Laws, those who were "deserving" were rewarded by "outdoor relief," which was usually the provision of food, wood, and other aid, sometimes cash or services by people in the community (such as transportation, medical costs, or store credit). The "undeserving" were to be given "indoor relief," or institutional care—in other words, the workhouse or poor-house (later in history, such facilities were also known as poor farms or county farms or homes).

Although the poorhouse originated in Europe, until the nineteenth century relatively few institutions of any kind existed in the New World (not only poorhouses but also prisons, jails, asylums, or orphanages). The major colonial cities such as New York, Philadelphia, Boston, Albany, Portland (Maine), Hartford, Baltimore, and some others did develop workhouses into which they crowded a combination of non-settled paupers and those they judged unworthy. In both European and American history, the workhouse was a distinctly punitive insti-tution meant to discipline the miscreants with work. The poorhouse, as we shall see, was a less clear institution which held both aspects of punishment and succor, and changed over time in many areas to an almost forgotten home for various poor people who sometimes managed to exert a modicum of control.

ENTER THE POORHOUSE

By the third decade of the nineteenth century, prominent Northern reformers were already out to "end welfare" as they knew it. As the nation grew and began the early process of urbanization, affluent observers were aghast at the rise of costs of poor relief, the begin-ning of social and ethnic diversity, and the decline in the acceptance of hierarchy that seemed to characterize the young Republic. Famous investigations of poverty in New York and Massachusetts concluded that the poor law system was too generous, as John Yates, the author of the influential Yates Report in New York State opined:

> The present poor laws tend to encourage the sturdy beggar and profligate vagrant to become pensioners upon the public funds. These provisions operate as so many invitations to become beggars.... Outdoor relief [had] blunted his proper instincts, or in the words of various overseers of the poor, served to relax individual exertion by "unnerving the arm of industry," and weakened the "desire of honest independence."

Reformers of the Jacksonian period turned to almshouses or, in less archaic English, *poorhouses* as an efficient, catchall institution that would group together all the poor in one place, and, as importantly, provide a Spartan regimen of discipline including work, bible readings, and stern supervision so the poor (evidently worthy and unworthy) would not become slothful and dependent. Beginning in New England and the Middle Atlantic states, hundreds of almshouses began to be constructed in the third through sixth decades of the nineteenth century, crowding a wide array of children, elderly people, disabled people, unemployed men, pregnant women, the mentally ill, and the developmentally disabled with delinquents and criminals.

Because in many places poorhouses would be subject to public scandals throughout the nineteenth century, and well into the mid-twentieth century, and further because of the merger in historical memory with the Dickensian system of workhouses built throughout Great Britain around the same time, the actual intent of the poorhouses needs further attention. No doubt some of the abuses of the poorhouse were built into the idea of erecting buildings to house so many numbers and types of people. However, as so well documented by historian David Rothman, poorhouses—like asylums, prisons, and orphanages, which emerged at the same time—were not viewed by their founders as punitive or repressive institutions. Nostalgic for an earlier time, not familiar with the ways of work (which necessitated most working men and women to find a place to live in the winter when most work which was seasonal ended), and hardly aware that industrialization was already changing their way of life, politicians, ministers, and newspapermen who championed the institution saw poverty as a flaw like insanity, disease, and criminality, and equally subject to quick remediation with the proper training and supervision. On top of their ignorance and misguided optimism, their historical descendants' miserliness, as well as prejudice against the increasing number of foreigners who swelled the ranks of the poor, would make not only poorhouses, but such reform institutions as insane asylums and orphanages into potential snakepits. It must be noted that often-lauded reformers such as Dorothea Dix and other "progressives" were as guilty of this blind naivety as was Yates.

A further important caveat is that fortunately reformers' objectives never really succeeded. First, "outdoor relief" was never abolished. Most towns and, later, big cities, particularly those flooded with immigrants or home to developing institutions such as labor unions and political machines, agreed to assist some people, including those who left poorhouses or refused to enter them. They found themselves begrudgingly still assisting the poor with food, fuel, or other aid while living at home. The more power lower and working-class people secured, the less the poorhouse or "indoor relief" was enforced as the sole manner of aid. Secondly, since the poor were not prisoners and could leave the almshouses after a night or two or a week or a month or two, reformers themselves quickly expressed unhappiness with the very system they imposed. As early as 1834, Massachusetts officials noted:

> Almshouses are their [the poor's] inns at which they stop for refreshment. Here they find rest, when too much worn with fatigue to travel, and medical aid when they are sick. And as they choose not to labor, they leave these stopping places, when they have regained strength to enable them to travel; and pass from town to town *demanding* [original emphasis] their portion of the State's allowance for them as *their right* [original emphasis] ... In winter, they seek the towns in which they hope for the best accommodations, and the best living; and where the smallest returns will be required for what they receive ...

Ironically, at the very time poorhouses were being erected, their failure to control the poor and "cure" poverty was evident to any close observer. Still, throughout the century, other than the occasional increases in outdoor relief or the granting of public works jobs during depressions (particularly the 1890s depression), a combination of powerful forces which had a vested interest in a low-wage labor force, the fear that any more generous aid would be socialistic, and perhaps simply a lack of social and political imagination would preserve the poorhouse as a major way to treat poverty.

What the poorhouses might have been like varied (like the poor laws themselves) from town to town, year to year, and, to some extent, by inmate condition and expectation. On the one hand, the scandal-plagued terrible conditions for which some became well known were evident even to early observers such as the New York State Senate's Investigation in 1856:

> Common domestic animals are usually more humanely provided for than the paupers in some of these institutions; where the misfortune of poverty is visited with greater deprivations of comfortable food, lodging, clothing, and warmth and ventilation than constitute the usual penalty of crime.

On the other hand, in my own book about the history of the poorhouse with a focus on New England, I stress that despite the harsh rhetoric of the reformers, for over a century poor people did find solace and sometimes comradeship there. American writer Sarah Orne Jewett in a fictional account of a local Maine poor farm echoes some stories I heard from elderly people who remember poor farms in New England:

There was a cheerful feeling of activity, and even an air of comfort, about the Byfleet Poor-house.... The inmates were by no means distressed or unhappy; many of them retired to this shelter only for the winter season, and would go out presently, some to begin such work as they could still do, others to live in their own small houses; old age had impoverished most of them by limiting their power of endurance; but far from lamenting the fact that they were town charges, they rather liked the change and excitement of a winter-residence on the poor-farm.

Although the focus of this book will not be on the actual conditions of almshouses such as Tewksbury, it is likely that the first several decades of the state almshouse lived up to the more negative reputations of the "poorhouse." Tewksbury suffered several scandals and had a reputation as a place to die (for nearly thirty years *almost every one* of the many hundreds of foundlings sent to Tewksbury died!). It likely suffered from the neglect of physical infrastructure, health care, food, and sanitary conditions, which did improve later in the century. No doubt people who were not desperate avoided "Tewksbury."

IMMIGRATION AND THE DEVELOPMENT OF THE STATE ALMSHOUSE SYSTEM

Though the development of poor- or almshouses had preceded the massive immigration of the nineteenth century, no other factor contributed to both the growth in numbers of the poor and the widespread panic about poverty that would grip the nation. While America is indeed (except for Native Americans) an immigrant country, the relatively slow but steady pace of immigration into the nation prior to the 1840s, as well as its somewhat homogenous ethnic nature, kept racial and ethnic antagonism toward immigrants at a relatively low level (excluding of course the forcible enslavement of Africans). The Irish potato famine and its aftermath changed this and led to the arrival of two million Irish migrants who were almost entirely destitute. Boston was the second largest port of disembarkation in the United States and came to see itself as overwhelmed with new immigrants. While prior to 1847, typically 3,000 to 4,000 immigrants would enter through Boston annually, in that year over 37,000 people would pass through. Keeping in mind the city as a whole had only 125,000 occupants, and the entire population of Massachusetts was well under a million, the arrival of hundreds of thousands of poor was a shock to the political system and public infrastructure, although it would contribute mightily to the low-wage labor force that led to an industrial economy. Diseases and health problems rose. Jails and prisons, orphanages and asylums, as well as almshouses would fill with Irish immigrants. Nativist sentiment sharply rose in New England and nationally, leading in the 1850s to the brief ascendance of the "Know-Nothing" Party with an openly anti-immigrant platform. In Massachusetts, the Know-Nothings would gain power statewide in 1854 under the slogan "Temperance, Liberty, and Protestantism." To give some idea of their hostility to the newcomers, they demanded a "21 Year Law," requiring someone to have lived in the Commonwealth for 21 years to be eligible to vote! While they did not succeed with this proposal, the new state Legislature mandated the reading of only Protestant Bibles in the school system, began the infamous "Nunnery Committee" to investigate charges of kidnapping and debauchery at Roman Catholic institutions, and mandated a new literacy test for voting. Some people known for their abolitionist sentiments expressed no hesitation in condemning the Irish. The nativist *Vox Populi* in Lowell, for example, fumed "against these ignorant and filthy thousands who come up among us like the frogs of Egypt, around whose homes gather their filth and stench that invited a pestilence."

Although, of course, not every foreigner disembarking in New England remained there (as we shall see, there was considerable migration between the Middle Atlantic and New England states as well as the Maritime Provinces of Canada where many Irish immigrants also landed), the sheer number of "unsettled paupers" caused the Poor Law system to totter near collapse. In 1850, the Governor of Massachusetts noted a doubling in state paupers (those without settlement) and a near trebling in foreign paupers. The Legislature approved creation of a Board of Alien Commissioners to check all ships for paupers. In 1852, the House and Senate of Massachusetts passed the bill that would establish the three state almshouses for paupers, including Tewksbury. The harsh tone of their report clearly links monetary concerns with anti-poor and anti-foreign sentiment:

> The evil [of foreign paupers] is a not a temporary one. These expenses go on increasing from year to year—have nearly trebled within the last ten years—and we see no reason to believe that the tendency to increase will be checked under our present system. It should be a settled principle that the mode of subsistence for public paupers should be lower than what any industrious man can earn ... The community should be satisfied, therefore, that they have done their whole duty to a foreign pauper when they have made provision for him sufficient for him to preserve his health, and that the

coarsest and cheapest food, and the humblest clothing and shelter consistent with this primary object, are all he has a right to claim.... It is another evil of the present system, that under it our own native poor cannot be separated from the foreigner. The difference in their habits and former associations is likely to require a difference in the mode and system of treatment, which is impossible now to make, and thus we must do injustice to our own citizens or more than justice to aliens.

State officials would never succeed in segregating the foreign and native poor. While in theory, perhaps, officials and laymen may have believed native-born Americans had a settlement in some New England town, even before the rise of industrialization this was not the case for many people. Large numbers of native-born Americans never had a settlement in their towns since they had not paid property taxes and poll taxes in one town or city for the set minimum years preceding the request for relief. Complicating the factors of immigration was the beginning of a massive migration of native-born Americans as railroad lines (which began in Massachusetts in the 1830s and made it the state most fully served by railroads by the 1850s) spread. Northern New Englanders began leaving their farms for cities, while natives of previously rural Massachusetts as well as New York and southern New England left for cities and factory towns as well. Some went not only to Boston or Lowell or Providence (Rhode Island), but to New York, Philadelphia, and then west to Ohio, Michigan, and Illinois, and later still further west. The Gilded Age would see another surge of immigration and a massive uprooting of native-born Americans caused in part by depressions, by industrialization, and by the American drive for opportunity and geographic and economic mobility. While the demographics of the inmates of Tewksbury (explored later in the chapter) would show a predominance of the foreign born, their percentages were little different from the "settled" poor of local (e.g., town or city) almshouses and outdoor relief rolls.

In theory, "indoor relief" was to be cheaper than outdoor relief. After all, grouping together thousands of poor people with admittedly "the coarsest and cheapest food" and "the humblest clothing and shelter" would seem to be quite frugal, and the state almshouses were sold to the public that way. But the American system of social welfare has always included strong disputes between institutional supporters and non-institutional supporters over cost as well as morality. Outdoor relief in the days prior to the federal entitlements of the 1930s, while certainly preferable to most poor people than an almshouse, did not always require great expense. Towns often provided a "one shot" payment for medical care, food, or fuel. Strong deterrents were present in many towns to receiving any relief. No process existed to ensure necessarily a week-to-week payment, as in some modern social welfare programs, unless the town overseers deemed someone an especially deserving resident. Yet once the state almshouses arose along with the population growth that accompanied the second half of the nineteenth century, indoor relief had its own costs. The state, unlike towns, could not refuse admittance to any person based on settlement. More and more expensive cases, which involved medical treatment and long-term residence at the almshouse (the elderly and disabled, for example), became common. Towns often intentionally, in fact, sent their paupers there in the same way that states, not localities, gradually had to absorb the costs of the "insane" by admitting them to state lunatic asylums

And so in their first report in 1864, the Massachusetts State Board of Charities and Corrections admitted "the most severely criticized" and "least agreeable" of its institutions were the state almshouses, which were apparently accused of being a vast drain on the Commonwealth's taxpayers. Under the title "The Great Cost of Almshouses Explained," the Secretary of the State Board argued defensively that the three state almshouses (Tewksbury, Bridgewater, and Monson) had been built for 500 inmates each, but instead had soon become home to many thousands. In particular Tewksbury, the largest and nearest state almshouse to the population centers of Massachusetts, was admitting over 3,000 and was averaging at any given time twice the number of inmates that the facility was supposed to accommodate. Neither financial stringency nor segregation had in fact been achieved by the state almshouse system.

MASSACHUSETTS AND NEW ENGLAND AS THE LEADING EDGE OF INDUSTRIALIZATION

According to historian Alexander Keyssar, even during the period between the War of 1812 and the Civil War, Massachusetts was the "cutting edge" of the Industrial Revolution. While Samuel Slater's stolen British plans for a factory system turned up first in America in Pawtucket, Rhode Island, near Providence, the large textile mills of Lowell with their famous "mill girls," followed by the growth of such Massachusetts textile cities as Lawrence, Fall River, New Bedford, and Taunton, and Manchester, New Hampshire, made the corridor running south to north from Rhode Island to southern New Hampshire the center of American industrial development. Economists see the American contribution to industry and eventual ability to catch up and overtake Great Britain as centering on the United States' development of interchangeable parts, pioneered by Eli Whitney in Connecticut and by the Springfield Armory in western Massachusetts in their skilled gun-making processes. With the needs of the Civil War, the Springfield Armory, along with the machine tool plants pioneered by Colt around the Hartford, Connecticut, area, and Brown and Sharpe Company in Providence, Rhode Island, were key contributors to the American "take-off" in mechanization. The New England region from southern Maine to Connecticut also developed a lead in the boot, shoe, and leather industry by the early nineteenth century. The invention of the sewing machine in the 1850s moved the industry from primarily a home production cottage industry with skilled workers to a larger shop industry, with many workers crowding such cities as Haverhill, Brockton, Holyoke, Chicopee, and Lynn, Massachusetts. By 1880, 80 percent of the national textile industry was located in New England, as was 67 percent of the boot, shoe, and leather industry. Massachusetts itself was the per capita leader in 1880 in industrialization, and only trailed New York and Pennsylvania in capital and value of manufacturing, though both of those states were made up of much larger populations.

While the growth of industry brought great wealth to its financial backers, the social problems of a developing capitalist economy were first felt dramatically in New England and the Middle Atlantic states. As Massachusetts urbanized ahead of other states, going from only 30 percent of its population living in cities in 1830 to 75 percent in 1880, observers from conservative elites to radical agitators complained about squalor, overcrowding, disease, homelessness, and rises in crime and prostitution. Early solutions to industrialism's problems relied on the establishment of urban police forces and laws against tramping and vagrancy. The Civil War and expansion of railroads brought new ideas to many a Northern boy, a desire to leave the declining farmland of New England to, on the one hand, go west, but, as often, to try his luck in the growing cities. Certainly for many people, increased opportunities of an urban life with new excitements and rewards came to pass. But for the army of laborers following whatever seasonal work they could get—on railroad lines, or constructing new buildings, bridges, canals, and factories—work was temporary. Paid poorly, with no fringe benefits and subject to gruesome accidents, men often died early, leaving widows and orphans. Factory workers—first known as "mill hands," later as "operatives"—fared not much better. Working long hours, including many children who worked twelve or more hours a day, they toiled in poor conditions, as large families crowded into poor housing. Even in the absence of major depressions, they might be unemployed a good part of the year.

The post–Civil War era of massive moving around which accompanied industrialization helps explain why the Tewksbury Almshouse became the largest institution in New England, and, at times, the largest facility in the United States. The state of Massachusetts embraced the inevitable in the post–Civil War period, having Tewksbury serve as the reception point for all paupers and the home for all of those who were not classified as miscreants (who were sent to Bridgewater, which was located thirty miles south of Boston) or children who as of 1866 were to be sent to Monson, some eighty miles west of Boston. Tewksbury, located next to the highly industrial city of Lowell was less than twenty miles from Boston. The major flows of people of the Gilded Age through Boston (and New York) were European immigrants: millions of Irish, British (English, Scottish, Welch), Scandinavian, German, and, by the late 1880s, Italian and Russian immigrants. Another flow that has been less discussed was the large number of Canadian immigrants. A massive depression in the Maritime Provinces began in the 1870s, and brought hundreds of thousands of emigrants through Maine and New Hampshire (some walked!), many of whom came to work in the mills. Many of these migrants were immigrants from Ireland who had settled in the Maritimes. Others sailed in through Boston and settled in New England or headed elsewhere through New York City. Some returned home seasonally or went home to stay. Beginning somewhat later, the failing farms of Quebec led to a large influx of French Canadians, who settled almost entirely in New England. French Canadians were less likely to return to their native land. Equally numerous were both immigrants and native migrants who jumped trains elsewhere, particularly in New York and Philadelphia, and came to New England. Often having tried their luck in Massachusetts or elsewhere, they left to move again. Similarly, while the migration west is much discussed, many entries in the almshouse notes document men who had gone west and come back. Many had sought gold in the California, for example, only to end up as paupers, at least for a time. Finally, a moderate flow of freed blacks came from the South to New England, particularly in the immediate post–Civil War decade. They were joined by Maritime freedman who had earlier been fugitive slaves.

THE "INMATE BIOGRAPHIES"

Despite reams of literature on social research, much of what leads to interesting results in all the arts and sciences happens by chance. In 2004, upon completion of a book on the poorhouses of New England focused on town or city almshouses in six locations, I became interested in studying the largest institutions in American history that housed the poor in the nineteenth and twentieth centuries. "Tewksbury" was frequently mentioned in my reading of the historical literature, often as a kind of negative worst case, as with "Bedlam" (Bethlehem) Asylum in Great Britain. Still it was only one of several places of interest. When I phoned the current Tewksbury Hospital (the facility still exists, serving as a medical center with substance abuse programs and a chronic disease facility), I was referred to the Massachusetts Public Health Museum located on their grounds, in fact in one of the few surviving nineteenth-century almshouse buildings, the old administration building. There I was met by the effervescent and engaging Chet Kennedy who, as the museum's founder and voluntary director, had put many years into the wonderful small museum on the history of health (and mental health) care in Massachusetts history.

Near the end of the tour with Mr. Kennedy, he opened an old wooden slide door with a little key, revealing shelves of books. These books were old binders, some quite fragile, which contained handwritten biographies of inmates which had been saved quite by chance a number of years ago by a Public Health Museum volunteer. Although in my research over the last several years in New England I have found ledgers of inmate names, their native countries, age, and very short labels ("intemperate," "insane") this was the first time I was able to find material with any descriptive information. Later in my research I would find a similar, though not identical, series of "inmate biographies" that had been archived by the State of Massachusetts and was available on microfiche at the State Archives in Boston, and in Lowell, Massachusetts, at the Center for Lowell History affiliated with the University of Massachusetts at Lowell (see Box 2.1 on "The Two Sets of Books").

The inmate biographies are not exactly what we today would call a "biography." They are a sort of cross between a doctor's examining notes we might see in a hospital record and the more lengthy case records that social workers might keep today. Neither the Archives, the Center for Lowell History, nor the Museum could answer who wrote these entries, and it was left to me to develop a theory. It was clear

Box 2.1. "The Two Sets of Books"

The existence of two similar, but not identical sets of archives, as noted in the text, set up a little local mystery and competition in the Lowell, Massachusetts, area between the Center for Lowell History and the Massachusetts Public Health Museum. The Massachusetts State Archive of the Tewksbury *Inmate Biographies*, which is available at the Center for Lowell History, is made up of shorter entries and is available on microfiche. A set of bound copies of inmate entries found (from 1873 on) at the Massachusetts Museum of Public Health, located in the old administration building of the Tewksbury Almshouse, is hard copy and contains more information. In the entry below for Elizabeth Summers, an 1875 inmate, we see the exact information contained in both, except for what is bolded. Although not drastically different, the bolded copy from the bound volumes of the Public Health Museum does give us a sense of who Summers' lover was, their relationship, and that she was now "heart broken." The note of her due date ("she will be sick in February") may reinforce my belief that the medical personnel at Tewksbury added to the original information now in the Archive.

#45288 Elizabeth Summers 35 years old from Chelsea admitted on January 2 [1875] [record then says she is] 30 [she was] born in England, [and] landed in Quebec on September 11, 1873 on the steamer "Circassian." went **direct to Ottawa,** Canada until November 16, 1874, [she] then came to Boston via [the] Vermont Cent[ral] and Lowell [Railroad] **and** [has lived] **in Boston and Chelsea since. A spinster.** Single, domestic, pregnant by Stephen Ball, **an Englishman and a stone cutter** in Ottawa, Canada, **She became acquainted with him in Ontario 'as it were' they were engaged but the ceremony was deferred from time to time because of his absence. She is now quite heart broken.** The criminal contact [began?] in May 1874 two or three times after [that] under an engagement of marriage. Received a letter from him asking her to meet him in Boston at the "female home" but she has failed to find him [there]. Her father William is in England, her mother **Esther** is dead, no friends in this country. **She will be sick in February,** [she was] discharged to Boston **by [the] General Agent** [on] April 2, 1875. [Her] son Stephen [was] born [on] March 3 (inmate #45649).

from reading them that all potential inmates of the state almshouse were required to undergo an interview and gain a permit to be admitted. (Occasionally the biographies indicate an individual or family simply arrived at the almshouse door, which usually brought a great deal of consternation.) The permits were issued at the Massachusetts State House where a representative of the State Board of Charities and Corrections was present or by the local Overseers of the Poor of the particular town the person or family sought aid in. Many biographies cite the permit, sometimes quoting from them, but at other times it is clear that the notes went well beyond the data quoted from the permit. In the early years of the biographies (the 1860s) notes were generally short (about a paragraph was common), and after the presenting information of name, age, location (including sometimes where they had lived over a long period), occupation if any, family members, and settlement (did they pay taxes in such-and-such town?), there was often a follow up by a "Mr. Nash," evidently the state agent who investigated cases. Nash, a precursor to a social worker, was often quoted in detail, verifying or disputing the inmate's story of his or her condition, and Nash's judgment often led to discharges, transfers to the workhouse or insane asylum, or other decisions.

By the 1870s, both sets of "inmate biographies" were expanded markedly, averaging at least one handwritten page, and in the Public Health Museum, often averaging two pages (the books at the Museum begin only in 1873, with earlier ones lost). Frequently, in addition to the presenting information, detailed information about the individual or family's life was included. This was especially the case for out-of-wedlock mothers, whose sexual intimacies were actually recorded in great detail. Another group that received much attention was those long-term New Englanders who lost their properties or incomes in the long depression of the 1870s. The tone of the biographies changes sharply from warm characterizations of "a deserving old man" and "a girl who is quite bright" to damning words of hostility: "He is a bummer and is a lazy. Does not want to work," was not uncommon, or "she is strumpet. Send to Bridgewater [the state workhouse]!" But while judgmental attitudes and prurient glimpses at sex lives certainly characterize the archives, the writers (who were most likely the clerks of the state almshouse) were quite careful to complete the biography and usually cite the inmate opinion and quotation before adding their own assessment. Sometimes when a particularly troublesome inmate returned, some of the detail was dispensed with to simply assert they were "drunkards," "bummers," or other negative characterizations. But usually a considerably intimate glimpse is provided into the lives of the poor.

The inmate biographies change again in the 1880s and early 1890s. Perhaps because of some greater sophistication or the impact of several investigations and scandals at Tewksbury, most famously in 1883 (which did include at one point a controversy over an inmate entry, See Box 2.2 "Tewksbury's Biggest Scandal"), shorter notes with less negative labeling dominate. Possibly an order went out to the clerks to include "just the facts" in written material. Yet by the depression years of the 1890s, an increase in length occurs, and while there is far less negative name-calling, there are again more stories told from the inmates point of view. Obviously depressions caused the poor to be seen as more "deserving," as people more like the clerks and other officials of the almshouse crowded in and many a "worthy" old man or even white-collar worker was forced into the almshouse.

Box 2.2. Tewksbury's Biggest Scandal: Governor Benjamin Butler and the Investigation of 1883

"It is paupers' skins that are tanned now for the slippers of the aristocrats."
—Benjamin Butler

No scandal rocked Tewksbury or perhaps any other state institution in Massachusetts as much as the nearly year-long battle of 1882–1883 in which populist governor and Civil War hero Benjamin F. Butler made dramatic charges against the superintendents and staff of the state almshouse. Butler, an interesting historical figure, had started his career as a conservative Democrat, became a Radical Republican and ally of Ulysses S. Grant, and then turned into a Democratic populist and Greenback Party politician. He served just one year as Governor in 1882–1883 and clearly hoped to gain the support of the mass of voters by his dramatic investigation. Beginning with charges of financial malfeasance, nepotism, patient abuse, and theft of inmate clothing and monies, and moving to the excessive deaths of newborn babies and poor surgical instruments, the biggest headlines trumpeted by the state's Democratic Party papers were those of trading in bodies of dead paupers and transporting them for a profit to medical schools. Tanned human flesh converted to shoes or other objects was said to have come from Tewksbury paupers, and popular pamphlets displayed ostensible pictures of the use of such flesh. Banner headlines in other papers, of course, denounced Butler as a demagogue lacking in the least bit of proof.

In late July 1883, the majority of the State Legislature rejected the Governor's charges and found "the main charges of the governor, groundless and cruel." The minority report representing the Democrats, while not supporting the finding of tanning of human flesh, did find serious fault with the institution and recommended considerable changes. Butler was defeated for reelection and most historians have discussed the investigation as not Butler's finest moment. The most dramatic charges (body snatching and tanning) seem now to be scoffed at. Nevertheless, many of the "lesser" charges seemed reasonable, and the publicity, as in the case of many almshouse investigations (and later mental asylum and orphanage scandals) did improve the management (which for one thing ended the twenty-five-year reign of Thomas Marsh and his sons). It also brought new health precautions, financial and other forms of accountability, and rules about disposal of cadavers. Also, as noted above, since the scandal involved the almshouse register's biographies of several inmates, it is likely to have had the effect of changing the way cases were entered into a shorter, more "professionalized" form.

We cannot be certain though why some years provide more detailed notes than others.

As with any discovered history, the archives are both exciting, yet fragmented and limited. We must know the rules of the settlement laws and almshouse to understand what inmates were asked and know the dominant Yankee, male, Protestant values of the time, particularly as the likely writers of the texts appear to be the almshouse clerks. This position was always occupied by men who were middle class, and, for most years of our study, were actually one of two sons of the superintendent of the almshouse! At the same time, knowing the culture of the potential inmates and what they gained or lost from certain answers is equally important. Other factors limit their usefulness. While the inmate biographies on microfiche at the Archives and Center for Lowell History begin in 1860, they are nearly unreadable at first. Their condition combined with the very rough form of recording and the very circumstances of the Civil War period led me to discard the 1860–65 period from my study. Poor handwriting though at times made even some later case records difficult to read. Moreover, why the clerk wrote two or three pages on one person and a paragraph on another is never totally knowable. Some short ones might indicate boredom with "another typical Irishmen" in slightly different words. On the other hand, the exotic (Native Americans and certain immigrants or sailors from Asia or Africa aroused interest), the sexual (lengthy records, for example, of those who came from "houses of ill fame"), and the sympathetic (this poor old man used to own many acres of land) warranted greater length.

Nevertheless, the presence of such detailed notes about a population whose general historical record has been reduced to either statistics or anecdotes, I judged as being very significant and helpful with the caveats mentioned. I needed a strategy to read what were initially over 100,000 biographies (later approximately 85,000 with the elimination of the 1860–65 period). I chose to sample the archives, copying several months at marked intervals of every other year. I was able to eventually develop a record of approximately one-fifth of the inmates (or 17,000) who stayed at Tewksbury between 1865 and 1895. These statistics are used below to provide a general portrait of the inmates. Since, however, the 17,000 cases contained many routine as well as notable interviews, and quite a repetition of stories and circumstances, I chose to transcribe verbatim transcripts of about 10 percent of the inmate biographies to serve as a qualitative data source for this book. This sample of 1,450 cases, or about 1,700 people (some were families), will serve as a detailed source of data. Subjectivity, of course, is involved here. Certainly there might be cases in the excluded ones that would interest another scholar. Research of this sort appears to me as being as much art as science, though we can use some objective elements such as sampling to structure our projects.

Having discovered that the two sets of books, those archived by the State and those at the Museum, did not differ markedly for the 1880s and 1890s, I was able to arrive at a compromise in which I did much copying from the microfiched archives in Lowell, and through the aid of the Museum volunteers, was able to obtain copies of the handwritten notes for a sample of the 1870s, which often added to the record of the inmates considerably. It is my theory that while the official archives was written by the clerk at Tewksbury, the inmate books that came into the Museum's possession appear to be either physician or nurse examinations, since, for example, they all contain a health status such as "well," "has syphilis," "pneumonia," etc. They also on the whole appear more sympathetic and knowledgeable about the inmate than the clerk's notes. (See Box 2.1.)

Prior to moving on, it is important to note the populations that are less documented in this book than others. Tewksbury maintained an insane asylum, but these records do not seem to be incorporated into the biographies. Often there are one- or two-sentence notes about an "insane" inmate being transferred to another facility. As a whole, however, the record does not treat in detail the issue of insanity. Similarly, by approximately 1870, more and more "drunkards" and certain criminals were sent to the State Workhouse at Bridgewater. Hence, less information is provided about some of the inmates identified as "deviants" by authorities. I suggest that even if more records were available, the labeling of inmates as "insane" or "drunk" is profoundly unhelpful except in obtaining demographic information, as these inmates often were granted no opportunity to tell their story, and we learn little of value about them as real people. Although as noted in the "Who Were the Inmates?" discussion below, children were gradually removed from the almshouse, going from making up nearly a third of the population in 1865 to only about one in fifteen in 1895; still there were more than enough children in the almshouse in my overall sample (about one in six inmates was under 15) to develop some interesting data.

As will be discussed further below ("Who Were the Inmates?"), the sample reflects the demographics of New England. The number of African Americans north of the Mason-Dixon line, for example, was small in the latter third of the nineteenth century, and peaks in the inmate population at 7.2 percent (at least three times higher than the general population of New England) in 1872. Irish and Canadian immigrants are more numerous, for example, than German immigrants, who never had as large a presence in New England as they did in parts of the Midwest and Middle Atlantic. Still other groups are underrepresented in the almshouse as compared to their New England population, particularly Italian Americans and French Canadians.

Supplementing the Biographies with Official Records

I am in debt to a National Endowment for the Humanities seminar held in the Summer of 2005, and particularly to the facilitator, Professor Richard Brown of the University of Connecticut, for encouragement and some practical assistance in developing a second form of research data to supplement the inmate biographies. In order to both verify some of the data either self-reported by inmates or noted in the record by clerks, as well as to find out what may have happened to the inmates after they left the almshouse (again remembering stays were often short), I did a genealogical search on some of my sample from the *Inmate Biographies*. Generally these databases consisted of the well-known Church of the Latter-Day Saints (Mormon) Family database, vital statistics (usually births, marriages, deaths) available through the New England Historic Genealogical Society (NEGS), and through Ancestry.com, a commercial but the most extensive of the sources, which included the most detailed census information, occasional directory listings from cities and towns, and even family trees. Because the inmates not only came from all of Massachusetts but all over the world, it was not possible to visit libraries or town halls in every town they came from; however, I did compare a list of names of inmates from Lowell and Lawrence, two of the larger cities around Tewksbury. I was able through these sources to gain data on 361 individuals or families (again far more people than actual cases). In some cases, the detail might seem small (a date of death) yet could in the context of the write-up be crucial. In about 200 cases, I was able to get extensive material including numerous census appearances and/or directory or family tree information.

As anyone familiar with trying to research their ancestors knows, such research is fascinating but very difficult. Those with very common names, the Browns, Johnsons, Sullivans, O'Briens, Smiths, for example, were often too common to find. Also, because the sample of inmates came from all over the world, some only "passing through" Massachusetts, and others living in the state from the northwestern tip of the Berkshires to the far eastern coast of Cape Cod, it was not practical to do what some relatives are able to do: go to one particular town to view its hard copy records to locate their ancestors. For this reason, I was limited to the Internet searches above. These records have expanded in availability in recent years and allow us to examine, for example, U.S. census enumeration sheets which recorded much personal information and town and city vital statistics records for births, marriages, and deaths.

Genealogical records themselves require much interpretation. First, even with only a moderately common name such as my own, several candidates for one's search will emerge. Fortunately the biographies frequently had ages (sometimes dates of birth), towns of residence, occupations, sometimes names of husbands or wives or relatives past or present, and other information. Still, at times a judgment call had to be made whether a "Dave Wagner" married in 1880 in a small town in Massachusetts was the particular inmate or a man with the same age and name who married that year in Boston. Records of vital statistics (births, marriages, deaths) and census records are subject to their own errors, omissions, and occasional illegibility as well. At times I found the inmate biographies and official information to differ even where I was certain I had the right person. Often a male identified as single by the inmate biographies had actually been, or was married. A man identified with one trade now had another. In some cases, it seemed lazy census takers might be to blame when whole pages of people were marked off as born in Massachusetts, particularly in many institutional settings. In other cases, individuals themselves likely presented themselves and their history differently. Finally, while the inmate biographies are rich in detail, if requiring caution in use, the official records are dry in themselves and, without other information, would tell us less than we hope. Census data is available only on a ten-year basis, and many people, at least in the nineteenth and early twentieth century, appear in every census. Poor and mobile people in particular are frequently not available. Much of the data on certain genealogical collections are about the stable old Yankee families of America. On the occasions where I researched an inmate who was a long-term New England resident, a great deal more data, including family trees and burial inscriptions, were sometimes available. Immigrant and long-term poor families were far less likely to be found, and information was more sketchy.

Still, as shown by the examples at the beginning of the last chapter, the combination of inmate biographies kept by the state almshouse along with census, vital statistics, and other data available from genealogical sources can come close to providing a human dimension for poor and/or working-class people in New England during the Gilded Age. Given the paucity of any "history of the poor" in the United States, I believe this is a start for one period of time.

Who Were the Inmates?

As advocates and fundraisers would put it today, poverty can affect anyone. The inmates were men and women, newborns and very elderly, white and nonwhite, laborers and clerks and even some physicians, ministers, and merchants. Yet, just as today's rhetoric can be misleading, poverty generally is a close cousin of working for low wages and not typically a fall from way above. The inmates who were admitted to Tewksbury resemble in most ways the masses of the time period, and specifically, the data about other inmates in almshouses in America.

Tables A1–A6 available in the Appendix provide detailed information on the sex, age, marital status, nativity, and (current or former) occupations of the Tewksbury inmates between 1865 and 1895. These include both figures for sample years, and a comparison of the inmates with Massachusetts census figures to give a sense of difference or similarity with the overall state population. Although some caution must be used for certain measures due to problems and inconsistencies with the censuses of those days, generally we are able to support U.S. Census conclusions about almshouses and other supporting literature about the poor at this time.

In terms of sex, except for the first two samples taken during and shortly after the Civil War in which women predominate, men constituted the majority of inmates, as was true in most almshouses nationally. While overall the average of nearly 64 percent men among adults may not seem dramatic, it may obscure some of the years (particularly depression ones) in which about four of five inmate admissions were men. Such a ratio is not surprising if one understands the social roles of the time. It was men who often left Europe ahead of their families to find work; it was men among native-born families who ventured far away to find construction or other laboring work. Few women were ever labeled "tramps" and, in fact, Massachusetts law for sixteen years defined the "tramp" as male. As some historians have pointed out, families also may have been more willing to care for their aging or disabled mothers more often than their fathers, but since at this time (see below) the elderly were not as dominant in the almshouse as in the early twentieth century, this seems to be a secondary explanation.

Except for the admission of children (see Table A.1B), the age structure of the inmate population was not dramatically different from the state population, though it tended to be younger, and especially so for women. Because of state policies, children declined from one-third of almshouse inmates in 1865 to under 10 percent by the 1890s. Adding marital status information (Tables A.3A–3B) provides an even clearer picture of typical inmate populations. As with most almshouse populations, averages show inmates far more likely to be single or widowed than married, which is reasonable enough given the absence of a supporting income plus a secondary possibility of some populations such as the disabled or very poor generally tending to not marry. However, when the data are broken down by sex, a more divergent path is seen. Women, except for widows (see Tables A.3A–3B), who were always well above the state average, tended to reflect the state's population, with many married. It is the male population in which the absence of marriage is dramatic. So in 1875, married males at Tewksbury were less than half the percentage of married males in the state, and in 1895, the gap was greater, with the inmates being two-and-a-half times less likely to be married. Though these findings support other studies, a caveat is in order. Men were often admitted to the almshouse after traveling (or "tramping") for work. Many men may not have been queried intensely about marriage, whereas women no doubt were because of Victorian ideas about gender and sexuality. As I shall discuss in later chapters, marriage was a very different institution in the nineteenth century, particularly with the absence of the easier divorce laws of modern times. Many people remained legally married years after one of the partners had gone off, hence creating separations without divorce. It may well have been that the women were more likely to describe themselves as married or widows than men, at least some of whom may have been on the move from former families.

Tables A.4A–4H on nativity of inmates will bring few surprises to specialists either. Keeping in mind that "nativity" means only nation of birth and not ethnicity, the vast majority of inmates were foreign born, with those born in Ireland being the single largest group. On average, nearly three-quarters of the inmates were foreign born. Just as people of color are today far overrepresented in poverty compared to Caucasians, foreign-born immigrants bore the brunt of low-paying jobs and unemployment at the time. Keeping in mind that many ethnic Irish came to America from Canada (particularly through the Maritimes) and Great Britain (particularly through the ports of London and Liverpool), the Irish-born category, as high as it is, understates the actual number of ethnic Irish poor. As it is, Irish-born inmates were nearly four out of nine admissions, and ranged from being nearly 60 percent of the population in 1865 to lows of about three in seven in the 1882 and 1890 samples. Table A.4C shows the dramatic difference between the percentage of Irish immigrants and the Irish-born population of the state. In 1875, the percentage of inmates was nearly three times as high, and by 1895 when many Irish were now second generation, Irish-born inmates were 40 percent of the inmate population, but only a little over one in ten citizens of Massachusetts.

While all foreign-born immigrants were overrepresented in poverty, there are some differences. The British, interestingly, joined the Irish in being highly overrepresented in poverty. The British and Canadian immigrants both constituted (Table A.4A) more than one in nine inmates each; however, in Tables A.4D and A.4E, we can see the British born were four times greater in the inmate population than the Massachusetts population in the years sampled, while Canadians were only slightly overrepresented. Many Canadians, particularly from the Maritimes, went back and forth to their homes, and so, though some fell on hard times, many were apparently able to return to families or neighbors. The numbers of Scandinavian, German, Italian, Russian, and other immigrants (Tables A.4F–4H) at Tewksbury while small, appear in most cases to vastly exceed the state averages. However, due to the small numbers it is hard to judge the significance of the findings.

Perhaps the most interesting data, because of the tendency of many Americans to associate poverty with being a nonworker, are the occupational data presented in Table A.5. Several cautionary statements need to be made. First, the data (as all above) were self-reported and may or may not have been subject to verification by agents at Tewksbury. Secondly, these occupations were not always current occupations, since an elderly man, for example, might have been a loom fixer at one point but was no longer actively working. Hence a comparison with contemporary Massachusetts data provides only a very crude measure. The time lag in occupational data is often evident, as for example, many seaman and sailors, a declining occupation in New England, ended up in the almshouse in the 1870s and after. Thirdly, the vast

number of occupations precludes a meaningful comparison for many
job titles (whose names themselves kept changing). I have rather as-
sembled the most common occupations of Tewksbury inmates in Table
A.5: laborers, domestics, textile operatives or mill hands, shoemakers
or workers, seamen or sailors, skilled craftsmen, and farmers, which
constitute about 82 percent of those inmates for whom occupations
were listed over the entire time period. Data for professional, white
collar, and sales or small storekeepers are not presented, nor are some
other occupations such as teamsters, hostlers, charcoal burners, long-
shoremen, waiters, barbers, and hatmakers. Finally, for convenience
sake I have compared the numbers with the Massachusetts census, but
because many inmates were born or lived elsewhere, the comparison
serves as a rough measure only.

Not surprisingly, some occupations or former occupations such as
laborer, domestic servant, and seaman were overrepresented among
almshouse inmates. As in other studies of poverty, "laborer" was the
single highest category, representing nearly two of seven inmates. Domestic service was the most common women's job in this period, and
was particularly common for Irish immigrants, and to a lesser extent,
Swedish Americans and African Americans. Better than one in six inmates were domestics. Here we find a more complex relation though.
In some years, domestics were nearly one-third of the inmates (1867) or
one-quarter of all inmates (1887). Yet in the two depression years shown
(1875 and 1895), when they are compared to the residents of the state,
domestics were less likely to be in the almshouse (see Table A.5B). The
complexity of this relation is the fact that most domestics were live-in
servants, who may have gained considerably from this status at a time
of depression. They had a residence (assuming the employer did not
discharge them), and certainly many affluent people may have been able
to weather the depressions and still kept at least some of their servants.
Seaman and sailors were on the whole about one in sixteen inmates,
but in several sample years of the 1870s they were well over one in ten
inmates. Here their overrepresentation clearly parallels the decline of
New England's shipping industry in the post–Civil War period.

One of the more interesting findings is how many skilled craftsman
(or former skilled craftsmen) found their way into the almshouse. Bak-
ers, boilermakers, carpenters, carriage makers, firemen (locomotive
firemen, not firefighters), machinists, mechanics, moulders, painters,
plasterers, and plumbers are examples. On the whole, more than one
in six inmates was listed as having a skilled trade. However, here we
find a more economically cyclical relation, with the crafts workers ris-

ing to over one in five inmates in the 1870s and in 1893, for example. It is a good reminder that while few merchants and doctors fell into poverty, many skilled workers did.

Textile workers, as employees of one of Massachusetts' largest industries, collectively were the fourth largest percentage of named occupations behind laborers, domestics, and skilled craftsmen, accounting on average for about one in ten inmates. Their numbers, though, were highly variable, as they represented only one in sixteen inmates in 1887, but nearly one in five in the depression year of 1875. Overall (see Table A.5B) textile workers were slightly overrepresented that year, but in the 1895 sample, they are underrepresented to their overall percentage of the population. Workers in Massachusetts' other leading industry—the shoe, boot, and leather industry—were present consistently *less* than their numbers in the state population. They averaged only 2.4 percent of the inmates over time and were well under their presence in the population. This is not surprising, because they were on the whole more highly paid than textile workers. Also, it should be added that while many inmates did traverse many miles in coming to Tewksbury, still the almshouse was closer to the textile centers of Lowell and Lawrence, and a little more removed from the shoe cities such as Lynn and Brockton. Finally, farmers or former farmers were nearly 3 percent of inmates, although they were a far higher number in the 1870s. Farm comparisons are difficult because Massachusetts censuses did not make clear how many farm owners eked out a full living from such work, but it appears (see Table A.4B) that farmers (though not farm laborers) were underrepresented in the inmate population compared to the state.

Despite the cautions noted, the trends are consistent with nineteenth-century studies of poverty and working-class life which showed laborers and domestics as the most vulnerable populations, and factory operatives next. It does remind us however that skilled craft workers and farmers, for example, were not immune from poverty.

Finally Table A.6 notes the small numbers of those inmates labeled "colored." Despite the archaic wording, this label is important since the term was applied not only to African Americans, but also to Africans, Asians, and Latinos and various people labeled as mulatto or dark, including for example Portuguese and Cape Verdian people. As the table indicates, people of color were a small part of both the inmate population and the state population. But people of color were overrepresented in the almshouse, particularly in the post–Civil War period when many Southern freedmen came North.

THE BOOK'S ORGANIZATION: TOWARD A HISTORY OF POOR PEOPLE

The book's overall purpose is twofold: to serve as part of an ongoing effort to document further the lives of poor people in America, and also to help those who are students of the Gilded Age to further understand life at this time. As a result of this dual focus, some of the material in this book will be known to some specialists, such as historians and social welfare scholars, while other material provides new information and insights to continued scholarship.

Part I of the book focuses on a long-time topic of historians and sociologists, mobility—both geographic and economic. In Chapter 3, "The 'Uprooted': Immigrants and Migrants," I use the documentary evidence of not only immigrant inmates, but also the large number of inmates who were migrants from around the United States to support the general notion that this time period was, as the Trachtenberg quote at the beginning of the chapter suggests, one of massive trauma. Oscar Handlin, the popularizer of the word "uprooted," as well as his followers, have come in for some criticism for the broad stroke of this term, and perhaps an implication that all immigrants suffered trauma. The more nuanced studies of immigration are important, and certainly show that most immigrants were voluntary departers from their native soil, and in the case of many immigrants, they had some assets to enable them to come to America to begin with. Still, the experiences of the many people who became homeless, impoverished, ill, or disabled that are documented in this book should remind us of the trauma of moving, even if such a move may have been "voluntary" in origin, and even if moving, "on average," brought improvements (*ultimately* in any event) over the economic or political conditions prevailing in Cork, Ireland; Halifax, Nova Scotia; Vilna, Lithuania; or even in some small towns in Maine or New York State.

In Chapter 4, titled "Falling Down: Yet a Surprising Resilience," I combine the *Inmate Biographies* with a considerable amount of census material to explore economic mobility. Although only a relatively small number of inmates fell from "on high," it is important to tell the stories of men (and some women) who fell into poverty. While the average inmate was a working-class person who fell into poverty, perhaps what is the most interesting finding in the chapter is that among those we can identify, many who left the almshouse after a short stay were able to return to either their previous economic pursuits or (dependent on both age and economic conditions) to sometimes achieve some upward mobility.

In Part II of the book, I use the considerable data available in the *Inmate Biographies* about family life, family conflict, and sexual relations of the time. People of the post–Civil War era and throughout this period believed, as many interestingly came to believe a hundred years later, that there was a "crisis in the family." Chapter 5, "'Criminal Intimacies': Out-of-Wedlock Births," uses the phrase of the almshouse records in the title for extramarital relations, and reviews some of the many narratives about sexuality in the Gilded Age. Such narratives swing erratically over the decades between accounts of punishment of women who were sexual to accounts of punishment of men who were "predators," from pleading the innocence of women to a prurience about all areas of sexual behavior. The almshouse biographies say, of course, a great deal about the author(s) and the dominant norms of the time. But, importantly, they also give some sense of the consequences of nonmarital relations at different times, which could be devastating. Nevertheless, some follow-up data here does show, as today, most out-of-wedlock mothers went on to lead, as far as we can tell from official records, fairly normal lives. In Chapter 6, "Family Conflict and Desertion," I draw on the extensive notes on the many separated or deserted families who entered the almshouse. Separation from family was so common that it is sometimes difficult to interpret whether men were off at work or permanently gone. Was "desertion" really separation without available divorce? Census data here do help as well in confirming that there was indeed much permanent separation in this period, and much conflict in the families of the poor and working-class immigrants. It appears too that when women became pregnant or had an infant that there was a high likelihood of male desertion.

Chapters 7 and 8 look at the early and late stages of the life cycle to examine children ("Being 'Put Out': Children In and Out of the Almshouse") and elderly people ("'We Can Do Nothing for Him': The Fate of the Elderly")—two other major population groups in the state almshouse and in poverty generally throughout much of nineteenth-century (and twentieth-century) history. Long before "orphan trains" became well-known, poor children were routinely "bound out" with families, some of whom certainly were kind and caring of the charges, while others were most certainly not. Although the data do not always present enough follow-up to evaluate the placing-out system, they do provide us with some hints as to the future lives of some bound-out children. Similarly, in Chapter 8, I discuss the plight of the older person. They were sometimes among the first to be abandoned. Many stories of the almshouse biographies are sympathetic to the elderly, who were often claimed to have been deserted by family.

Finally, in Chapter 9, "From History's Shadows: Partial Views of the Poor," I return to the issues and dilemmas of reporting and exploring the lives of ordinary people, particularly those who fall into poverty. The strengths and limitations of the approach used are discussed, and areas for future research explored.

PART ONE

MOBILITY: GEOGRAPHIC AND ECONOMIC

[A] group of permanent transients, buffeted about from place to place, never quite able to sink roots and to form organizations ...
—Stephen Thernstrom, *Poverty and Progress,* 1964

One of the major consequences of the factory system was the creation of a floating population composed of people who moved about from city to city like vagabond peddlers of labor.
—Allan Dawley, *Class and Community in Lynn,* 1976

Most historians would agree that American society went through a period of tremendous change in the last third of the nineteenth century with massive immigration, internal migration, and the rise of industrialization. To those living at the time, the large crowd of laborers and poor families must have seemed like "permanent transients" and a new "floating population." In towns and cities of the Northeast, it must have seemed as if "strangers" were everywhere. Two famous observers of the massive processes of immigration, spatial mobility, and economic mobility were Oscar Handlin and Stephen Thernstrom. Handlin's classics such as *Boston's Immigrants* (1941) and *The Uprooted* (1951), and Thernstrom's *Poverty and Progress* (1964) and *The Other Bostonians* (1973) drew widespread attention to the issues of immigration and economic mobility of the period. Their books, to some extent, have fallen out of fashion, yet the lives of many of the thousands of people who passed through the Tewksbury Almshouse lend support to some of the major themes of these prominent authors.

As each generation of historians reinterprets history through the prism of their own times, the meaning of such important events as mass immigration, migration, and industrialization changes. Handlin, in *Boston's Immigrants, The Uprooted* and other works focusing on immigration, in particular the Irish experience, represented a critical view of America's pre-1960s version of the "melting pot." Very much a liberal historian, the sufferings of the Irish and other peasant people transported to America were of key concern to Handlin, and he looked back with pain, and perhaps some nostalgia, to peasant culture. Similarly, Thernstrom's work, particularly *Poverty and Progress,* debunked the then-prevailing historical and cultural view of industrialization and "progress" as solely positive change, noting how many victims fell downward and wandered from place to place. The losers in the economic game of industrialization were very much also "uprooted," cast off to the highways and streets of America. His more optimistic *The Other Bostonians* showed Americans gaining some mobility not through Horatio Alger's "rags to riches" but in smaller steps, or as he put it, moving from "rags to respectability."

The tremendous changes in history and the social sciences brought about by the 1960s and 1970s make these older works seem somewhat anachronistic to some. Handlin's work in particular was criticized as overstating the isolation, suffering, and the impoverishment of immigrants, and for not stressing the many strengths of immigrant networks and communities. By the 1980s, immigration studies moved to a more cross-national focus (rather than a narrow American one) and tended to stress the cultural adaptations that immigrants make, and how they are able to develop diverse cultures without necessarily assimilating to the dominant culture.

Many of the changes in immigration research are to be applauded. Handlin's work, for one thing, overgeneralized the experience of one particular ethnic group, the Irish, and one particular time period, the famine and post-famine Irish diaspora of approximately the fifth through eighth decades of the nineteenth century. As a general proposition, later immigrants came to America (and other parts of the Western Hemisphere) more planfully, had stronger social networks, and were able to save money to bring relatives or to return home. Later immigrant groups, with some exceptions, were not the poorest among their countrymen, but had some savings and privileged location relative to the vast population of peasants in their countries.

Still, as in all trends, intellectual movements can overcorrect and lead to historical forgetfulness about the suffering and difficulty of immigration. As Chapter 3 will suggest, many of the immigrant inmates of Tewksbury were very much "uprooted" in all senses of the term. Many had lost loved ones on the passage to America, some were mistreated on their journeys across the ocean, many were lonely and nostalgic for home, and many lost loved ones once in America through death and desertion. While, to some extent, this work may parallel Handlin because it takes place in Massachusetts and includes many Irish immigrants, nonetheless these issues were not restricted to either the Irish immigrants or to those who came from New England. Perhaps, if there is a general criticism to be made of the new immigration literature it is that it may have replaced the focus on the individual or small family (which was a criticism of Handlin) with an "oversocialized" conception of people. In a parallel to the new communitarianism, historians and social scientists may overstate social networks and resources and miss the loneliness and pain that many individuals suffered, particularly among those groups who have gone through poverty.

Thernstrom's work found a complex pattern of movement, both spatially and upward, downward, and laterally in terms of socioeconomic status. It too has come in for criticism. Several authors now criticize the "mobility research" that followed Thernstrom's work (and tracked issues of "persistence"—i.e., who stayed in one place and who left) as somewhat of a "dead end." It is not, after all, very sexy research to say some people move up, some down, and some sideways. In debunking the Horatio Alger myth, Thernstrom certainly did not present a radical critique. Other critics remark that in fact Thernstrom's *The Other Bostonians* (1973) did not fit with the changed times of post-1960s academia.

New historical writing also has some valid criticisms of Thernstrom. Census data are limited, and its few comparable categories, for example, occupation, are open to question as to how much they elucidate. Moreover, while Thernstrom imputes much change to the process by which an individual may be listed as a "laborer" one year, and a "carpenter" the next (or moves from a "carpenter" to "clerk") he does not support his judgment of mobility with people's subjective judgments at the time. The latter is particularly problematic when Thernstrom asserts that the mobility people found in the mid- to late-nineteenth century, while not dramatic, was somehow "enough" to prevent the development of more class consciousness or social unrest. I, like other observers, tend to believe he is certainly "on to something," but he offers no concrete proof.

The criticism of Thernstrom, as with that of Handlin's work, may be primarily the result of newer and different biases. Like Handlin's work, Thernstrom's work was postwar liberal. He critiqued the excesses of Horatio Alger's "American Dream" that "everyone" could make it in America. In the context of the post-1960s infusion of "the new social history," labor studies, and other academic studies of the "Other," this became a rather obvious point. Moreover, that there was so much mobility in both directions (upward as well as downward) certainly contradicts the focus of much new social history and much social science, which sometimes focuses on just downward mobility. Clearly Thernstrom's faith in American mobility, even if less dramatic, and his use of the already older sociological categories of social class status (low white collar, high white collar, etc.) may have seemed anachronistic not long after its publication. Still, as with Handlin's, there is much truth and perception to Thernstrom's work. Outside of the mass depressions, when vast numbers fall, a complex pattern of movement marks American history in which there are many winners as well as losers. Again, as with immigration research, I would argue that perhaps an oversocialized view exists which tends among some historians and social scientists to deny the profoundly localistic and individual family nature of economic mobility.

So, interestingly, as I examine this particular historical sample, while I find support for "uprooting" and, of course, for downward mobility, in the almshouse, of all places, I also find support for some of Thernstrom's complex realization that people are constantly moving in each direction (and perhaps, most particularly, laterally). As rough as the measures are, as we shall see in Chapter 4, comparing the Tewksbury inmates to data available about them at other points in their lives, we find as many inmates left the almshouse to return to the same or similar economic positions (and in some cases to higher statuses) as moved downward. Whether this qualifies as "rags to respectability," I am less sure of, but it does contradict the sometimes popular (in academia as well as the public) broad belief in America that "once poor, always poor."

Like all academic debates, much depends on how one interprets data and what expectations we have of research. Certainly, just as no one disputes the difficulty some immigrants (and I would add internal migrants) faced, I suspect few would disagree that economic mobility patterns are complex as different individuals, families, groups, and communities constantly experience large differences in economic gains and losses (even at times of wide cataclysms such as depressions). Much depends on our expectations and our assumptions of the audience expectations. While my sample cannot provide definitive answers, it does illustrate and, to a large degree, complement Thernstrom's work, in the sense that moving beyond the "snapshot" observations of the almshouse clerks, we do see considerable economic and status flux occurring, and likely this prevented even the "poor" from coalescing in a very coherent form, at least culturally, politically, and organizationally.

THREE

The "Uprooted":
Immigrants and Migrants

There is, of course, not a clear definition of being "uprooted." In talking of real people's lives, the complexity of life and its changes, its risks and rewards, its sufferings and joys, measurements cannot be made of all forms of sorrow, loss, and isolation from familiar places, family members, and friends. Whether the subjects of this book came from across the seas, Canada, or even rural New England or the South, degrees of suffering were involved. This held true too whether the immigrant or migrant's choice to leave home appears to us primarily "voluntary" (that is, the "pull" of the perceived opportunities seems more obvious than the "push") or less so (i.e., the "push" of the famine in Ireland or religious and political persecution of the Jews in Eastern Europe seems more salient than opportunities in the New World). As nicely summarized by James Jasper, "Immigration is not normal action. It is dramatic, unsettling, and costly." So that even when a choice is consciously made to pick up and move, significant degrees of trauma may be entailed.

Another important point is that the perils of immigration and those of migration within a nation have been separated conceptually, but this is somewhat arbitrary. Because of the nature of late–nineteenth-century work and the low-wage positions occupied by most immigrants, whatever sufferings or problems occurred in the passage and adjustment to the new nation were compounded by the routine departures of men (in particular) for all parts of the United States. It is difficult in practice to know how much loneliness, alcoholism, poverty, and other social problems to attribute to one experience or the other. To take two entries made by almshouse clerks about Irish men in 1873, we can see the large number of places these immigrants went following their arrival:

Patrick Forbes 66 [admitted] from Worcester … September 10. He was born in Ireland, County Tyrone, and landed in St. Johns [New Brunswick] in 1825, then [he] went to St. Andrews [New Brunswick] in 1832 and [stayed] there until about 1845. Then he went to Eastport, Maine [and] thence to South Bend, Indiana until 1859 then [he went] to Rochester, Minnesota for a year. Then he traveled all over the country … he left Yankton, [in the] Dakota Territory in July 1873 to make his way to St. Andrews [New Brunswick] and so he had come this way. His wife Mary died in 1860 in Rochester, Minnesota. He's been a blacksmith, he paid no taxes, [although] he owned a house and a shop in Indiana. He has 5 sons in Dakota and 4 daughters in Minnesota. He has no relatives or friends here. …

Patrick Sweeney, 38 years old, [admitted] from Boston with fever and ague [on] June 11. He is a previous inmate here … He was born in Ireland, County Kings, [and] landed in Boston [on] January 1, 1864 per the steamer "Columbia." He then went directly to Dedham, [Massachusetts, outside of Boston], he was there for a few months [and] he [has] since lived in various places in Massachusetts, Rhode Island, Connecticut, New York, Pennsylvania, New Jersey, Ohio, Illinois, Indiana, and Kentucky. He had been working on railroads principally. He hasn't been in any one place but a few months at a time, [he is] not naturalized, [he owns] no estate and [has] no [military] service, [he is] single and [a] laborer, [he has] no relatives or friends. He last worked on the Delaware and Lackawanna Railroad, and he came to New York to go to the hospital but he was refused admittance as he lived in Boston, he then came here …

In addition to the compilation of a whirlwind of travel which can certainly be described as "uprootedness," both men were described negatively by the clerks at Tewksbury. Forbes, though a widower and a blacksmith who had owned property, was labeled a "professional bummer." The note taker arrived at this judgment evidently because Forbes "ha[d] 163 coppers that he had begged on the street and he looks like a tramp." In the case of Sweeney, although his movements (like many Irish men) were very much required by railroad employment, which was unsteady and mobile, and one would think his unemployment in the depression and rejection by a hospital might evoke some sympathy, he was characterized as "a shiftless fellow" and sent to the workhouse. Whatever problems these men had, they no doubt were not assisted by the negative attitudes they encountered at the hands of this charitable institution.

Despite the arbitrariness of separating out the populations, for convenience sake, I will divide the overseas immigrants from the Canadian immigrants and American-born migrants for purposes of this chapter's organization. I will then review some of the many sojourns taken by our subjects, with an overview to the many hardships they may have encountered. Of course this is not meant to convey that all immigrants and migrants had the same degree of suffering. As most observers have noted, a series of factors—including improvement in the technology of overseas travel, the availability of better communications systems which in particular led to a system of "remittances" in which American immigrants could wire money to their kin to travel to America, and, importantly, the fact that the class system and economic environments differed dramatically between home countries (for example, the famine experienced by Irish immigrants as opposed to Swedish or Italian immigrants)—all made for some important differences between groups. Nor, as will be clear, did Canadian- or American-born migrants suffer anywhere near the trauma of overseas immigrants, both because of the conditions of travel and because of the occupancy of most of the lowest positions in American society by immigrant labor rather than native-born or Canadian migrants.

EUROPEAN-BORN INMATES AND THEIR TRAUMAS

The ships that carried the massive number of immigrants across the Atlantic, particularly in the years before the Civil War, were often known as "coffin ships." Various estimates put the deaths from typhus, cholera, dysentery, yellow fever, and other diseases, which came to be known collectively as "ship fever," at between 10 and 25 percent of the occupants. Sail ships were poorly constructed and large waves frequently took their toll on overcrowded ships. Often unable to afford even the steerage fares, many Irish immigrants were crowded aboard fishing boats headed from Liverpool to Nova Scotia or Newfoundland. Here they were crushed in with the fishing stocks in conditions without space or any waste removal. The ships bred disease and death. While the worst conditions were associated with the 1840s and 1850s, Herbert Gutman notes the campaign of Joseph P. McConnell in the 1870s in which he charged in *The New York Herald* that "better accommodation is provided for cattle ... than ... for human beings." Partly because of the continuance of bad conditions, and greatly because the inmates told their stories of the pain and suffering of their arrivals years earlier, the *Inmate Biographies* of Tewksbury are full of stories of deaths on the passage to America:

Hannah Donahoe from County Cork, Ireland landed in Boston in 1848, but [her] two brothers she came out with both died just after [they] landed.... (1866)

Julia Ryan [is] a 45 year old woman who landed in New York on July 7, 1870 per the "Queen of the West." Her husband died on the passage, she gave her three children away the day before she came here, to a priest to find [a] home for [them] with Irish people ... (1871)

John Day left Ireland, County Waterford, and [he] landed in New York in March 1868 on the steamer "City of New York." His wife Bridget and their nine daughters and two sons were all lost on the passage to America in 1873 . . . (1875)

William Wilson, a 33 year old Irish immigrant, [was] admitted to the almshouse on January 27, 1880 ... He landed in Boston on January 1, 1880 per the S.S. "Marathon" ... He was taken sick the second day after landing, [he] is suffering [from] the effects of being wet through on the passage over, which was very rough. He has a cold and trouble with his legs ... Lung disease ... (1880)

Johanna O'Connor admitted from Cambridge on January 6, [is] 42 years old, she was born in Ireland. She landed in New Orleans when she was still an infant and [her] parents died six weeks after, she was taken to the Sisters of Charity and [was] in their charge until she was brought to Boston by her brother ... (1893)

Anne Lee admitted from Boston on June 3 [is] 54 years old [and] was born in Ireland ... she landed in New York when she was thirteen years ... her Parents Thomas and Rose Ruddy, her mother died in Ireland, her father drowned on passage to the United States ... (1895)

If the trauma of losing parents, husbands and wives, children, and brothers and sisters was not enough, the passages were full of exploitation. As noted by Handlin, the captains of these vessels "often harshly mistreated the passengers," sometimes by misleading them about the length of the trip, by profiting from sales of necessities such as water to the impoverished passengers, and by actual violence. One issue that several admissions to the almshouse allude to, over a number of years, was sexual advances and perhaps rapes aboard the vessels:

Annie White, a 15 year old girl admitted on March 9, 1875 ... [was] born in England and landed in Boston in October 1874 per the S.S. "Marathon".... She was thought to be pregnant when she came here as she was seduced on the passage out by the Captain's boy who took her to his berth and attempted to have intercourse with her but was interrupted ... (1875)

Eva Dorr 22 years old from Boston admitted on February 18. She was born in Nova Scotia and left there in May 1879 and came to Providence, Rhode Island on a vessel. Captain Joseph Harrington seduced her on board and is the father of her child. [She is] pregnant.... (1880)

Sarah Boyle, a 33 year old born in England ... landed in Boston per the S.S. "Bohemia" on August 26, 1894 ... she is pregnant, sick in eight weeks, [the] father of [her] child [is] Bob [the] head baker on the "Bohemia" [The] child [was] begotten during the passage out.... (1895)

Once in America, a large number of immigrants could not locate their loved ones or found themselves abandoned or mistreated by them:

Mary Butler nee Geary, a 28 year old Irish immigrant who landed in Boston on November 27, 1869 per the S.S. "Samaria." She bought her ticket for New York and went there ... she was there for two months then the Samaria Company paid her fare back to Boston. Her husband came over last June [but she] doesn't know his whereabouts. Her parents died in Ireland.... She has no friends ... (1870)

Michael Murray a 16 year boy who had came from Ireland and landed in Boston per the ship "Tarifa" on June 20, 1870 ... He [had been] taken from a poorhouse in Ireland and sent to an uncle in Charlestown [Massachusetts] who thought him [to be] an older boy. Finding him young and stupid, he brought him here [Tewksbury Almshouse] as he could get no work for him ... (1875)

Mary Peterson and her son Charles, 26 years old and 6 months old [respectively, were] admitted from Boston on February 28. She was born in Denmark and landed in Boston [in] August 1878 and has lived there since. Her husband John came over with her, but left her in June 1879 and she has not seen him since. Her parents [were] never in America. Her father [is] dead. Her mother is living in Denmark ... she would like to go back to Copenhagen when she is stronger.... (1880)

Jane Duxbury a 29 years old English immigrant with her children Herbert, 7, Annie 5, and Henry 2 landed in New York in October 1889 per the SS "Servia," Cunard Line ... she wants to go [back] to England, she came out [to America] with a man who was to marry her but [he] deserted her in Philadelphia ... she was sent to New York.... (1890)

Marital desertion is more complex to interpret than may first meet the eye. For while Charlotte Erickson is certainly correct in noting "sometimes emigration was a means of escaping from an unhappy domestic situation," and Hasia Diner makes the important point that Irish men suffered from a greater loss of status in the New World than did women, the fact remains (see Chapter 6) that desertion and separation rates were tremendously high among all parts of the population, not just immigrants. No doubt the new circumstances of America, both its opportunities and its sufferings, caused discord and desertion. But it is also true that couples and families scattered across the country quickly, with men often leaving the ports of entry to find whatever work they could. In some instances, as will be further discussed, families used the almshouse as a survival strategy, not because the men had left their families on some sort of permanent basis, but because the men were away at work, and, as charged by the founder of modern social work, Mary Richmond, many poor people "worked the charities"—i.e., women appeared with children in hand, stating they had no husband or that the husband had deserted them. The almshouse records again and again note the men were "off," but there is an ambiguity throughout as to whether the husband had left the relationship or only the immediate area. And if he was "off," was it for a week or for months or years? Some biographies state the specifics, others do not.

Scholars of immigration have long realized that complicating any discussion of immigration is the fact that large numbers of immigrants returned to their homelands or even commuted back and forth. Estimates vary, depending on both the particular years and the national group. Walter Nugent, for example, estimates the overall "return rate" at a low of 30 percent and "quite conceivable" at as high as 40 percent for the entire period of mass immigration. Yet interestingly, while immigration scholars tend to note returns as an indication of immigrants' possessing material resources or stronger family networks than previously thought, many of the inmates of Tewksbury were the ones left behind and sometimes they experienced this abandonment as a shock, inducing despair and loneliness. For example:

> Ellen Whittaker, a 21 year old woman with a ten month old son Thomas ... an immigrant who was born in England and landed in Boston on April 17, 1875 per the S.S. "Parthia" with her husband Squire Whittaker. [They went] directly to Fall River and have been there since ... Her husband returned to England a month ago. Her parents [(previously arrived) also] returned [to England in] October 1874. She [was] left to shift for herself.... (1875)

> John DeGraaf, a 19 year old ... admitted to the almshouse on February 3, 1877. He was born in Holland and landed in Boston 1871 on the S.S. "Siberia." His mother Mary, [and his] brothers and sisters were with him ... in August 1876 ... his mother returned to Holland. His father died in Holland. His uncle ... in Lowell ... will do nothing for him ... (1877)

Rose Harpp, a 21 year old German immigrant admitted to almshouse on January 31, 1895 with her son Carl, an infant.... She landed in Boston in 1888, [with her] father Henry and stepmother Lillie.... then [her] father returned to Germany and [he] died there. Her stepmother then went to Providence, Rhode Island and died there three years ago ... [She now has] no relatives.... (1895)

As we can see, among the many immigrant inmates "left behind" were women, young people whose parents or elders did not find the New World suited them, or people who were disabled in some way and would perhaps be a drain on the family.

None of this is to deny that some immigrants who found themselves in the almshouse for brief periods had available social networks. Two groups that stand out and generally had shorter stays at Tewksbury than others were Swedish immigrants, who often had contact with Swedish communities in Massachusetts or elsewhere or with labor agents, and Polish immigrants, who in Massachusetts clustered in the southern Worcester County areas of Webster and Dudley. Victor Swenson, an inmate in 1876, for example, arrived directly at a Swedish colony in Aroostook County in northern Maine. For some reason, he was "sent by [the] Swedish Consul" to Portland, Maine. He later came to Massachusetts to work on the railroads and was in the almshouse briefly with a note that he "appears well disposed." Ida Johnson, a 22-year-old inmate in 1885, was pregnant and had an eleven-month-old son with her. The record immediately noted that "her friend Mrs. Caroline Johnson in North Easton, Massachusetts and Mrs. Julia Murphy [in] Chelsea will give her a home." Two Polish immigrants admitted to the almshouse in 1890 clearly had established networks:

Joseph Rynkella, 25 ... landed in New York in the company with the family of John Glonjena [now in Webster, Massachusetts] at a date which enabled him to arrive in Webster by the Harwich Line on March 16, 1890. He has some money, also has friends and countrymen in Webster ...

Victoria Voski ... [a] 25 year old Polish immigrant landed in Boston on July 11, 1889 ... went direct[ly] to Webster and [has been] there since ... Father Chalupka of Webster says she landed in Castle Garden on April 20, 1889 and has a brother in Thorndike. She was sent to him in Webster on June 7.

Although there are other examples of such networks among Irish, British, and Central and Eastern European immigrants, they are rarer, keeping in mind, though, that the almshouse seems to have had little or no resources for interpreters and certain inmates were simply listed as "does not speak English!"

What European immigrants had most in common when compared with other almshouse inmates was their level of devastation and destitution. Over and over, children with Irish (and later, to a lesser degree, Italian) surnames were described in the almshouse records as starving or seriously ill foundlings left to the poor-relief system. The agents of the state Boards of Charities frequently labeled the immigrant families as "poor," "destitute," or "too poor to care" for someone, as in the case of Johanna McCarty, a 65-year-old Irish immigrant admitted in 1873. They reported "this old lady has been entirely neglected by her relatives and children and has been living alone supporting herself by picking up rags and junk." (Ms. McCarty died twelve years later at Tewksbury.) Although it is, of course, difficult to compare levels of suffering, and the agents' statements were subjective, some of the most heartrending accounts were of European immigrant families:

Two orphans, Anna and Charles Razoux, 12, and 9 respectively, were admitted to the almshouse on January 1, 1872 from the town of Chelsea ... [their] father [was] born in Germany or Switzerland [and] died in [a] hospital in Boston [in] November 1871 [while their] mother was born in Holland [and she] died of starvation in Chelsea [in] September 1871. [The] children [are now] in [the] family of Mrs. Kimball of Chelsea who proposes to adopt them ... (1872)

Ellen Doherty 27 years old.... born in Ireland, County Donegal, and landed in New York on June 17, 1870 per the S.S. "Brittannia." [She then went] to her husband Neil on 53 Cooper Street. Her husband [had] landed in Quebec in 1868 and went direct[ly] to Boston. [He was] there until May 25 [then he] went to look for work [but the] family [was] ejected from tenement for non payment of rent.... She thinks he has committed suicide as she saw in [the news] paper that one Neil Doherty of Boston committed suicide in Vermont on May 28th ... (1875)

Michael Collins 25 years old admitted from Boston on November 30. He was born in England and landed in Boston on August 30, 1871 per the S.S. "Malta." His family came with him and [they are] now here ... he is a slaters tender.... they sold all their furniture and household goods to buy food for family. They tried to ship back to England and failed. (1875)

Michael McGuire ... 48 years old, born in Ireland, a widower, shoemaker, he landed in Boston in 1868 [and was] there until 1875, [then] New York and New Jersey until 1878, then back in Massachusetts, Boston and vicinity since ... [his] wife Jane died in England, [his] parents died in Ireland, [he has] no relatives. He was out of work in Milford [Massachusetts, a small town in Central Massachusetts], [he] got low spirited and tried to cut his throat ... (1885)

Virtually all cases of starvation, hunger, and suicide attempts in the sample taken from the *Inmate Biographies* were from European immigrant families. The sympathy the cases sometimes evoked may be surprising given what likely was the clerks' general attitude toward immigrants, which was certainly far from positive. Yet, of course, they were not absent compassion. Also, the vast majority of the families and children (as opposed to single adults) who entered the almshouse were European born, and this certainly helped evoke sympathy. On the other hand, it is possible that some family situations may have been judged as "squalor" or "miserable conditions" because of prejudices such as Yankee discomfort with immigrants' large households and their particular living conditions, which may have repelled the middle-class observers.

In still another horrific category, that of severe disabling industrial accidents, again certain ethnic groups, particularly the Irish and Italian, were overwhelmingly represented:

James Kelley, 34. ... born [in] Ireland, County Mayo landed in New York 1857 ... He has since been working on railroad near Ashland [Massachusetts]. [The] shanty occupied by himself and [his] comrade took fire, [his] comrade [was] burned to death and [he him] self [is] horribly burned on [his] face and hands ... (1872)

Thomas McCalliacut, 35 years old, admitted from Boston January 13. He was born in Ireland and landed in New York in May ... [he has worked] on various railroads in Massachusetts ... [he was] blown up by a blast on Fitchburg Railroad on November 12, 1876. [He is] blind. [He spent] two months at the [Boston] Eye and Ear Infirmary. [He was not discharged until May 21, 1880] (1877)

Gicinto [or Giacinto] Tocchio admitted on February 19, he is 30 years old and admitted from Pittsfield, he was born in Italy, single, laborer. [He] landed in New York about October 1893, he went direct to Pittsfield and has been there since . . . His legs were paralyzed, caused by tree falling on him one year ago, he cannot walk. [S]peaks little English. ("In 1904 he was sent to Torino near Genoa, Italy. Discharged Feb 12, 1904 to Torino near Genoa, Italy.") (1895)

Of course, native-born and Canadian immigrants suffered starvation, destitution, suicide attempts, and deadly and disfiguring industrial accidents. But the numbers are so overwhelming that, even from the almshouse clerks' view, the suffering of early industrialization was borne heavily by European immigrants.

THE CANADIAN DIASPORA

In the period of interest, millions of Canadians came to the United States, some temporarily, but most for good. Because of the unregulated border crossings, migration to and from Canada was "sieve-like" and has been understudied. In fact, the Canadian crossing consisted of at least four flows. One was the usual interchange of travel and departures from what was then called "British North America" (Ontario Province and the Maritimes), and, to a lesser degree from Montreal, to the United States, mostly to the Northeastern and some of the Midwestern states. A part of this flow was seasonal workers such as craftsmen, and later operatives, who came to the United States for a part of the year and then returned to Canada. However, three major flows drove these numbers far higher. Hundreds of thousands of Irish immigrants found passage to the Maritime provinces, some because of cheaper fares, but many because ship masters were trying to avoid the American "head tax" and inspection of vessels. Although many European immigrants did immediately (as we shall see) wander to the United States, many also settled in the provinces of Nova Scotia and New Brunswick for a number of decades. Then the third flow of Canadians started, this one beginning with the economic downturn in the 1870s and including both European-born and native-born people from the Maritime Provinces heading to New England and New York. Finally, the fourth flow was from Quebec and began slightly later (mid- to late-1870s on) in response to crop failures and economic decline in that province. Because census data did not separate the English and French speakers until 1890, the figures on these different flows were often merged together.

The Canadian diaspora played a large role in the swelling of the Tewksbury population because in addition to the large numbers of Canadian-born immigrants shown in Appendix table A.4A, many of the Irish-born inmates arrived first in the Maritimes and lived in Canada for some time. The history of Irish and British immigration is then inextricably linked with both North American "host" nations' history.

I provide only a brief glimpse of the sojourns of some Canadian immigrants—focusing on how and why they came to the United

States—understanding they suffered some of the trauma already addressed, but that more than many European immigrants, they often did return home and had relatives and roots in Canada, particularly the British Canadians. While French Canadians after the mid-1870s more rarely returned back home, still the shorter duration of their travel to the United States, and the frequent movement as whole families into New England seem to have made both the British Canadian and Québécois diaspora difficult, but not as devastating as it was for some other groups who experienced immigration. Also, because of the proximity of social networks in Canada, we shall see below that some almshouse inmates were able to tap into these networks for help, far more easily than those whose friends and family were overseas.

One of my first revelations in reading the *Inmate Biographies* was how far immigrants walked in the freezing cold weather of Maritime Canada and New England and other places in the Northeast to arrive at Tewksbury. Though not unique to Canadians, walking appeared to be frequent and longstanding among Canadian migrants. As Handlin and others have noted, many were Irish immigrants who landed in the Maritimes and simply started walking down the coast. John Bohen, an 1871 Tewksbury inmate, born in County Cork, Ireland, recounted landing in St. Andrews (New Brunswick) in 1839 and then walking through the countryside to Boston, a distance of at least 300 miles. An 1865 entry notes that the Shaw family (George, 61, Mary, 39, and their four children ages 3 to 13) from Nova Scotia, Canada, had left there two years before and walked from the Halifax area to Bangor, Maine (a distance of 254 miles); they then "took the cars" (railroad) to Buffalo, New York. After eighteen months in Buffalo, they came "most of the way on foot" to eastern Massachusetts (at least 450 miles). The authorities of Lynn, Massachusetts, must have taken pity on them in the late fall of 1864 and sent them to Tewksbury for the winter, although on January 26, 1865 (hardly far into the winter), they were sent to Portland, Maine, presumably to get them back to Canada, but perhaps simply to get them out of Massachusetts. "Frozen feet," sometimes leading to amputation of the limbs, was a frequent notation in the almshouse records. But, of course, walking was not the only route. Also typical was 20-year-old Edward Poor, born in St. John, Newfoundland, who landed in Boston on the schooner *Captain Stanton* as a "stowaway" in 1865. Later in the almshouse records, the exact manner of travel is difficult to trace as the ever-present word "tramping" became a shorthand term for all traveling. We find out, for example, in 1890, that Arthur Archibald "tramped from Nova Scotia to Lawrence [Massachusetts]," another long distance, but he may well have arrived through a combination of walking and taking "the cars" or "beating the fares."

If many Irish and British immigrants and native-born Canadians could not wait to come to America, it is also true that, as historians note, like many European immigrants, they were also drawn to the United States by labor recruiters. A.L. Eno's history of Lowell, Massachusetts, for example, notes the mill owners' dismay at losing the "mill girls" of New England who were their original labor supply for the new textile factories. In 1865, Eno notes, they began sending recruiters to Canada, including French-speaking ones, who promised young girls the allure of good wages and secure jobs at Lowell's massive textile factories. The almshouse notes directly parallel this account with several young women who seemed to have been lured to the area. Three cases in the sample of inmate biographies of 1865 and 1867 mention labor recruiters in rather negative ways, as the Canadian women were all pregnant, and one had syphilis:

> Rachel Stannes, 19 years old ... and her son Kenneth ... [she is a factory] operative..[who had] lived with her father and mother in Prescott, Canada. She lived with them until five months ago when a man brought a lot of girls to work on the Pacific Corporation [a large textile company] via the Manchester and Lawrence [Railroad]. The father of [her] child [is a] Kenneth Mckenzie, a boatman, [who] lived sometimes in Ottawa and sometimes in Prescott ... (1865)

> Josephine Austin, 17 years old ... born in Ottawa, Canada ... she came first to Massachusetts not quite nine months ago [when the] Overseer of Merrimac Mill [another large textile mill in Lawrence] Mr. Watson sent a man after her and she and eight others came down with him. He paid [her] fare down and they had to repay him afterwards. [She] was here about six months before she was touched. [She] went with [a] fellow calling himself Mason, [which is] not his true name. [They] came via Rouse's Point and the West Central [Railroad]. [She now has] syphilis and [is] pregnant ... (1867)

> Louisa Sweeney, 18 years old. She was born in Sherbrooke, Canada, single, operative ... Mr. Arnold sent for her and paid her fare down. Many others came with her. [She] worked in Salem one and a half years, [but they] didn't give her hard wages. She came after July 1865. [She is] pregnant by Hugh [illegible]. [The] child [was] made in Salem eight months ago, he is a shoe-maker [who] did work in Lynn and Marblehead....[She] is a good girl, [she] came to [Tewksbury Almshouse to] have [her] baby ... (1867)

The entries are intriguing. Clearly the clerks and agents did not approve of the recruiters bringing down from Canada the above women. In the case of Josephine Austin, we can see her fare was paid, but she was in debt to the recruiters for it. The note that "it was six months before she was touched" gives us the impression that either sexual favors were expected of the young women or that at least the almshouse agents found this method of entry into the country put the women in some sexual danger. Louisa Sweeney did not even receive "hard wages" but may have worked off her debt and been paid through provision of room and board. Again, while the putative father here is a shoemaker, that she is described as a "good girl" suggests perhaps (in the clerk's mind) that the recruiting led to such sexual predation. Unfortunately, we do not have enough information or many other cases to probe labor recruiting practices further.

Canadian emigration and shorter trips to the United States were so different from each other in character and in result that, even in the poorhouse, a place of suffering, it is hard to make generalizations. Some who came from Canada to work in the mills are clearly cases which were sad:

Ann Scott, a 43 year old woman born in St. John, Nova Scotia first came to Massachusetts about two weeks ago from Portland, Maine by [the] boat "Montreal." [She] had been in St. Johns Lunatic asylum [for] one year and seven months [and then she] came to Lowell to work in [a] mill but [she] found it too hard ... (1870)

Mary Green, 30 years old.... has one arm ... born ... in St. George, New Brunswick and landed in Portland, Maine in the fall of 1873 ... She first came to the United States in the fall of 1870 via a boat to Calais, Maine. [She was] there [for] over a year and lost her right arm in a mill there on May 20, 1871 and [she then] returned to St. George to her parents. [Her] parents William and Sarah are both dead in New Brunswick.... [She] wants to go back to St. George, New Brunswick. (1876)

On the other hand, not every migrant suffered difficulty working or was a victim of an industrial accident, and some seemed to succeed in making some money:

Rebecca Barker, 28, and Augusta, 10 years old [both] born in Carleton, New Brunswick admitted from Lowell on January 3, married. [She] came to Lowell from Houlton, Maine seven weeks ago. Her husband, George A, [is] now in Houlton. They had no trouble between them, but he went into woods to work and she thought she might earn some money in the mills ... (1887)

Some came for medical care and, from what we can tell from the almshouse records, quite a few came to have their children, who like most of Tewksbury's births were out of wedlock. Many of the women were desperate to hide the birth from their families:

> Celia Brown admitted from Lynn on January 26. [She has] "weak eyes"[and is] 35 years old. She was born in Newfoundland, [is] married.... She came to Boston to have her eyes treated [but ran] out of money, [and then she] came here ... (1885)

> Ada Sanborn, 27 years old was born [in] Yarmouth, Nova Scotia. [She] is single and a nurse ... She landed in Boston on October 1, 1866 per the steamer ... [she is] pregnant. The father of her child is Alfred Johnson. They had a connexion [sic] in Yarmouth, he came to Boston one week before she did. She came here because if her mother knew about it, "it would kill her." (1867)

> Mary A Boyce, 22 years old, admitted on May 12 examined May 2 ... She was born in St. John, New Brunswick and landed ... in Boston in April 1875 per the steamer "New Brunswick" under the name of Mary A. Murphy ... [she is] single, [a] domestic, pregnant. The father of her child is Edward Boyce of St. John, New Brunswick. He is a single man, he used to visit her at her father's house and [had] criminal contact in August or September and continued from time to time after New Years. Boyce's family lived in a portion of her father's house and young Boyce visited her room in the night. Boyce knew her condition but would do nothing for her. Her [parents] Patrick and Mary Manning [are] in St. John. [Her] father doesn't know her condition. She says her father would kill her if he knew it. [Her] mother discovered her condition and sent her to Boston. [She] says [her] friends and her mother are going to send her money every month ... [She] is now in terrible distress.... (1875)

It is quite interesting given the unsavory reputation of the almshouse that women sought it out in some circumstances for childbirth. As we shall see in Chapter 5, this was not by any means true only of immigrant women. The fear of family and community scorn must have been great indeed for women like Sanborn and Boyce (above) to come from so far away to have their children. They also very likely faced the prospects of having no hospital nearer to them that would admit unmarried mothers, since most private hospitals rejected unmarried mothers from admission, and, in any event, all charged patients money. Public hospitals—aside from the almshouses—were almost nonexistent in Canada, as well as much of the United States (this began to change in the Northeast in the 1890s).

Besides coming to the United States for any sort of work which would help them survive and to have children, frayed relationships between families led some into the almshouse after arriving. Where one partner, usually the man, left Canada to earn money, which he or she would then promise to return to the family, obviously family members were extremely dependent on contact with their loved ones. Below are two examples of women attempting to find their husbands:

Marie Duroche, a 32 year old woman with her daughters Adelaide, 11, and Erzula, 3 years old ... came from Canada to Boston [in] July 1874 via [the] Grand Trunk Railroad to find [her] husband Nelson Duroche who [had] left her 2 months [previously] ... [Her] husband [is] intemperate and shiftless. [He has been] in the United States [for] six years. [Marie has] two children with her mother in Upton, Canada. [She is] pregnant. [Her] friends ... [have] raised $215.00 for her ... (1875)

Jenny Smith was admitted February 1. She is 20 years old. This woman came to the United States to find her husband. She was born in Nova Scotia, [she is] single [and] pregnant. The father of her child is a Ham Price, she met him in Saccarappa, Maine and she came to Boston to find him last Friday.... (1890)

And finally, according to the *Inmate Biographies,* a woman trying to leave her husband:

Elizabeth Green, 25 years old, admitted from Boston May 18. She was born in St. John, New Brunswick and landed in Boston in January 1880 on the S.S. "City of Portland." She has been in Boston since. Her husband George is now in St. John, where his mother also now lives ... She is pregnant [and] came to Boston to get rid of her husband.... (1880)

The old English settlement laws bound the two nations together, and since localities were held fiscally responsible for their poor, the state of Massachusetts frequently clashed with Canadian officials over the poor who crossed borders. Massachusetts officials had no compunction about sending poor people to Canada, such as Thomas Maxim in 1873, who had been knocked down and robbed in Boston. Yet they also complained when they perceived someone was mistreated by the Canadian Poor Law officials. In 1871, for example, 62-year-old Daniel Lewis, though a resident of the United States for many years and a government employee during the Civil War, was sent to Quebec by the Massachusetts State Board of Charities officials, as he was born in Hatley, Quebec. The officials complained, however, that the "authorities would not provide for him but took him to a place twenty miles from Hatley and left him, and from there the same way, and [then] gave him $8.00." Citing the man's age and blindness and even his status as a "knight templar" and Mason membership, the agents appeared angry. Just as a tug of war existed between American cities and towns over settlement, and, in the case of the state almshouses of Massachusetts, between the state and adjoining states and towns, a great deal of the writing in the files is about finding the legal settlement for poor people whose circumstances were frequently complex and ambiguous.

RURAL MIGRATIONS IN THE UNITED STATES

Although there was no movement of native-born Americans which can be called a diaspora or can be compared with the uprooting of immigrants, historians note that most of the so-called "tramps" wandering the roads and streets of late–nineteenth-century America were native-born white men. Walt Whitman, in fact, wrote with shock at seeing American-born poor men wandering the streets, for this scene, more than the immigrant poor, must have threatened the American notion of success:

> If the United States, like the countries of the Old World, are also to grow vast crops of poor, desperate, dissatisfied, nomadic, miserably-waged populations, such as we see looming upon us of late years—steadily, even slowly, eating into them like a cancer of lungs or stomach—then our republican experiment, notwithstanding all of its surface-successes, is at heart an unhealthy failure.

Though the Tewksbury State Almshouse would provide shelter for poor people born in all the states of the Union and most of its territories as well, the largest share of inmates was from the New England states and New York, with other Middle Atlantic and Midwestern states following further behind. In turn, the most common places of birth for the native inmates were the rural areas of New England and New York. As noted by Raymond Mohl, the urbanization of the Northeast came about from the "tremendous release of the rural population," and this point was made as well by Stephen Thernstrom, who suggests these former rural dwellers were essential as part of the workforce for American industrialization. The movement away from rural areas, particularly the northern New England states of Maine, New Hampshire, and Vermont, had started long before this time period. Many rural towns in northern New England were already losing population by the 1850s as the railroad expansion both weakened New England's advantage in shipping farm products, while at the same time leading many of its own youth to jump on the same rails to improve themselves and see the world. They went to the large cities of the East and then in increasing numbers to found new cities and towns of the Midwest, many modeled after their old New England villages.

But while the depopulation of the rural areas of New England had started long before, Harold Wilson is likely right that it was the Civil War that "marked the beginning of the decline in rural life." He notes, for example, that the small state of Vermont sent 34,000 troops to war, but that not one-half would ever come back to their home state. Historian Peter Knights locates the migrants who headed (at least at some point in time) toward Boston as being initially "residents ... of an area extending from the coast of Maine across New Hampshire and Vermont, then contracting south to include Massachusetts east of the Connecticut River, a sliver of Northern Rhode Island, and the peninsula of Cape Cod." With some additions, later on, such as western Massachusetts, the upstate New York counties near New England, and northern Connecticut, this description seems to fit about two-thirds of the native-born inmates of the Tewksbury Almshouse in the 1865–1895 period.

Unlike most immigrants, many of the traveling rural migrants came from families who owned homes or farms. While a fuller discussion of economic mobility awaits in Chapter 4, one difficulty we can note is the problem that small farmers of New England (or craftsmen in some cases) had in passing on to their descendants what wealth they had while ensuring their own modest survival. Generally inheritance was not necessarily by primogeniture in the Northeast, and, in fact, sometimes it was the youngest son who inherited the farm. However, along with this ownership came the obligation to support, not only parents in their old age, but any unmarried aunts and sisters, at the very same time when many farms were no longer very profitable ventures. The offer of the farm was not particularly an incentive for some ambitious sons, and the farms were too small to allow them to support more than one son. Further, many skills learned in the country were not transferable to the city. Knights notes that many low-paid jobs like teamsters, stablers, and other animal management jobs went to young men born in rural areas, but not necessarily the more highly paid jobs.

Although we have insufficient data to document the success stories of New England Yankees who became, many of them, white-collar workers or proprietors, there are many examples of those who fell down. Webster Powers, a 19-year-old young man admitted to the almshouse in 1873, had already been homeless and "tramped all over the country." Born in the small town of Orfand, New Hampshire, his mother died when he was four. He went with his father to White River Junction (Vermont) until about 1870. Then he went to work on the Erie Canal (in the) summer, "and [lived] in poorhouses and station houses ... arriv[ing] in New Bedford three or four months before" he entered Tewksbury, and he had previously been sentenced to New Bedford's workhouse. Webster charged that his father, Abner, had "abused him and [that he] ran away" from home. In this case we have some limited additional data. Abner Powers, 40, was listed in the 1860 census in Orfand, New Hampshire, with a wife, Polly, 35. He had a modest $663 in personal property (likely for a rural family to be livestock or farm equipment). Webster had four older siblings (two of them farm laborers), and one younger sibling. There was also a boarder in the house. Webster was found again in the 1900 census in Strafford, Vermont, where he was now 47 and a boarder himself. He was single without a listed occupation. He *may* also be the Webster Powers of New Hampshire listed in the 1880 census as an inmate of Boston's House of Industry, although his birth date is somewhat off. Despite the bare information we have, likely Powers was downwardly mobile from his rather modest background. Clearly he did not gain any property from his father. Although his status as a single 47-year-old boarder without an occupation is hardly definitive, it does indicate he was probably a man of little social status in the small Vermont village he had returned to. Meanwhile, his oldest brother, Chandler, came to own a farm in Vermont, perhaps helped by the capital inherited by his father. The only other male in the family, Webster's younger brother Jacob, also left the region and was later a single boarder working for a logging company in Washington State.

Many other rural New Englanders followed trajectories that led them into poverty and the almshouse. William S. Pennock, the son of Cyril—who owned property in Norwich, Vermont, and was a mason—left Vermont for Massachusetts in the 1850s. After fishing off the coast, he settled down in Boston as a teamster and a moulder and married Sarah D. Smith in 1857. He was 43 when admitted to Tewksbury in 1875 and was described as "intemperate." He must have died shortly afterwards as his wife is listed as a widow by the 1880 census. Additionally, in this case we can find that his family resided for a long time in the small Vermont town, with his father accumulating a bit more personal property until they moved to Minnesota around 1880. Pamela Billings (née Allen), admitted to the almshouse in 1876, had also been from a property-owning family from East Windsor, Connecticut. She married Jabez Billings and, like many native New Englanders of the time, went West. After ten years in Iowa, Pamela went back to Enfield, Connecticut, in 1858, but her "husband has not provided for much for her support." She was further charged with bearing several illegitimate children. She had spent four months in the Springfield almshouse and was now "blind for eight years"; she died at the Tewksbury Almshouse on April 22, 1879. Her separated husband did remarry and was found in three further censuses in the West (Iowa and then Colorado) and was recorded at one point an affluent "dry goods merchant."

Other examples of New England rural migrants included Stuart Robinson, admitted to the almshouse in 1885 at 36 years old. He was born in Calais in northern Maine. He had come to Massachusetts when he was three years old with his parents. He was described as a spinner, a semiskilled textile worker. "He [had been] all over New England since [he was] 20 years old," a fact that appears consistent with his trade, which was marked by continual layoffs and closings. Charles Feeney was a 40 year old admitted in 1890 to Tewksbury. He was born in Blackstone, a small Massachusetts town at the edge of Worcester County. Also working in the textile mills as a weaver, he had "resided in Maine for the past four years, [in the] West for five or six years, [in] Fall River for seven years steadily, [and then in] Taunton for four years, New Bedford [for] two years, [and then] worked in Mt. Hope Mill in Fall River for seven years steadily." His father had owned property in Blackstone. To take another New England migrant from 1895, Peter Burns was admitted at age 33. He was born in Maine and came to Massachusetts in 1882. He was a laborer who had come to Lawrence, Massachusetts, "for a year and a half, [then to] Providence [(Rhode Island) for] one year, [then to] Lewiston [(Maine) for] two years, [back to] Providence [for] one year, [then] Southbridge [(Massachusetts) for] two years, [then] Philadelphia [for] two years and Lowell [(Massachusetts) for] one year." Burns ended up at the Tewksbury Almshouse after suffering an industrial accident "injuring his left arm in the Lowell Bleaching and Dying Company Mill five months ago. [His] arm is useless, [and he] has [a] suit against the company [going on] trial in April."

Despite the very different circumstances that brought these people to the almshouse—some, for example, arriving in depression years, some not, some came for help from what surely were "personal problems" like drinking or family separation, some primarily because of poverty caused by unemployment or industrial accidents—the New

England rural migrants shared a history of mobility throughout at least wide stretches of New England, if not further, such as the West or Philadelphia and New York. While we will further examine the complexities in exploring economic mobility, many seem to have left behind the property their fathers had held.

Finally, another rural migration that requires attention was that of African Americans, some newly freed slaves who came North after the Civil War. During the War, it is estimated that 180,000 African Americans served in the Union Army and that another 500,000 poured behind the Union lines. Only a small percentage of these numbers headed to New England, but still during the 1865–75 period there were significant numbers of Southern-born blacks joining their Northern counterparts. Some wanderers came directly out of the wartime experience in the army:

> Riley Carr, 21 was born in Missouri [as] a slave, his father Richard Roberts [had] run away to Iowa [and he lived], there five years. [Riley] came to Massachusetts in 1863 and enlisted in 55th Company "H" in Boston. [He was] discharged [in] September or October ... having served about two years and seven months, [He] enlisted two days after arriving in Boston. [His] parents [are] in Iowa. [He has a] sore leg ... (1865)

> Daniel Rooker ... 21 years old [was] born in Alabama. His parents were born there, they were never in Massachusetts. His father is white, his mother [was] a slave. He enlisted in Williamsburg in Company "C" 55th Regiment on August 23, 1864 and was discharged in Boston on August 29, 1865. [He then] came to Boston via steamer. [He was] never wounded [but has a] sore leg, in Boston since. [The] town owes him $100. [He] was previous[ly] six months in Haydenville with Josiah Hayden, [where he] was [a] servant to Adjutant James Hayden, son of Josiah. [He is] here by glass in [his] leg ... (1865)

> Nelson Williams ... 45 years old [was] admitted from Pittsfield [on] April 27. [He was] injured by [the railroad] cars.... He was born in Culpepper Court House, Virginia as a slave, sold and went to New Orleans and was freed by the war. He came North with the troops in 1863 or 1864 on a transport to New York and from there [he] went to New Haven, he was there a few months and then he was arrested in New Haven for breaking and entering and committed to State Prison in Wethersfield for seven years. [He] served six years and then was pardoned ... (1875)

But other Southern African Americans came North after the war ended:

> Rachel Hodges ... 21 years old admitted from Boston on February 10[.] She was born in Richmond and came to Massachusetts last July with a

Mrs. Dickson [colored] of Newburyport ... [She?] first lived with Mr. Fitts in Haverhill. [She was] there [for] 4 months [and] then [came] to Boston and went to Abington [and was] there [for] 2 months. And [she] came to Boston because she was lonesome without colored folks, and was sent there. Her father is dead, [her] mother [is] in Virginia, [she] has no friends, [is a] domestic.... (1870)

John Andrew, a 13 year old boy from ... North Carolina ... came to Boston on [a] steamer from Norfolk about three months ago. [He had] came from Adair County with his cousin Martin to look for work. [He] says [his] people and his uncle William Davis gave Martin money to bring to Boston [but] shortly after reaching Boston, Martin abandoned him. He [John] strolled out to the country to Hyde Park, there [he was] doing odd jobs for various persons until he was sent here ... His mother Hagar Jarvis is dead. [He has] no relatives [or] friends ... [he was] sent July 11 to State Primary School [in Monson] (1873)

It is quite difficult to tell how the many migrants from the South fared. Between 1865 and 1880, the small black population of Boston doubled. At the end of the Civil War, African American men held a small niche in certain employment areas such as barbering, chimney sweeps, porters, and service jobs in restaurants and hotels, while some drove carriage vehicles and hacks, and some were hod carriers or janitors. Women worked as cooks, maids, washerwomen, seamstresses, and nursemaids. Thernstrom's detailed portrait of Boston's labor force suggests that as poorly as all African Americans fared in the economy, Southern migrants trailed behind Northern-born black workers. Further, by the turn of the century, some of the jobs traditionally held by African Americans in Boston, such as barbering and waiting, were being taken over by white immigrants.

The little we do know is negative. John Andrew (above) died two years later in 1875 (at only 15 years of age) from "gangrene of lungs." Nelson Williams who had come North in 1864 had (as noted) already served seven years for breaking and entering in the Connecticut state prison. He had additionally served two and a half years in prison in Hartford for stealing, making his terms fill almost the entire period between his arrival North and the 1875 admission. He was called "a thief and [a] vagrant" but later in the same note "insane, but apparently harmless."

On the other hand, some New England–born blacks were described with more respect, not only than the Southern-born population, but at times than the Irish. For example, the following two "deserving" cases of poverty were both of African Americans:

William L Baronett, 68 years old ... born in Providence, Rhode Island. He first remembers living in Bangor, Maine. He was there about twenty years, then [he] went to Portland [Maine, for] 15 or 20 years, then [he went] to Chelsea [Massachusetts?] where he has lived since. His wife died last May. He once owned a house for 6 or 7 years in Bangor. He has paid taxes in Chelsea all the time he was there, for 8 years. He is a laborer and ship carpenter. His father owned property in the [Canadian] Provinces. [He] seems like a worthy man ... (1870)

Frances Day, 46 years old from Chelsea [Massachusetts, was] admitted on February 9. She was born in Portland, Maine. [She] has been to and from Boston and Maine several times. She last came to Massachusetts a year and a half ago and [has been] there in [the] vicinity since. [She] married Ed Day in Boston ten years ago. He [was] born in Philadelphia. [Her?] parents belonged to old settler family in Portland. [They are?] dead.... [She has] cancer. [She] last heard from her husband two years ago ... [She is] reported as a worthy, temperate woman ... (1880)

Because of the age and rootedness of the above inmates, we can secure more information than with the Southern migrants. Baronett was born in 1802 in Providence and married in 1856 (rather late) to an Abigail Hussey, probably a white woman, in Bangor, Maine. He died at Tewksbury on February 20, 1870, from gangrene. Frances Day and her husband Edward (listed as mulatto) were in the 1860 census in Boston. Edward was 25 years old and a barber who was born in Pennsylvania. She was listed as "Fanny" and was 27 years old, born in Maine. In the 1870 census they were now in Easton, Massachusetts, and she was listed as Harriet. Her husband was now listed as "Black" and was still a barber. Harriet had $1,000 personal property in her own name. Her 1880 death certificate from Tewksbury does indicate she was 46 and died of cancer.

Above all, the almshouse clerks and agents were record keepers of social class, and they most definitely sat in judgment to find the "deserving" cases of all races and ethnicities. Those who owned homes or were from "old settler" families were afforded some respect, but most of the passing migrants, whether from Europe, Canada, New England, the rural South, or elsewhere, had no claim to such "worthiness."

FOUR

Falling Down:
Yet a Surprising Resilience

[He was] in [the] coal business [with the] firm [of] Fowler and Tapley.
[He] was one of the first citizens of Lynn ...
—Tewksbury record for William Fowler (1880)

He owned several houses and land, horses and stock, [and was a]
subcontractor under the name J. B. Winn ... He lost his property
three years ago, became crazy, pushed his hands through the window
and was badly cut rendering his hands useless ...
—Tewksbury record for James Dooley (1874)

The almshouse was certainly a place of crushed hopes and disap-
pointed dreams, and when I first read some of the *Inmate Biographies,*
I was struck, as I believe many middle-class readers would be, by the
stories of downward mobility. For William Fowler, once "one of the
first citizens of Lynn," a wood and coal dealer worth over $13,000
in 1860, and James Dooley, an Irish immigrant who had done well
as a subcontractor and owned several houses, the loss of property,
job, or home must have been devastating, and in some cases, such
as Dooley's, led to severe grief. For a number of reasons, while these
cases constitute a minority of the Tewksbury inmates, these accounts
are important to describe. They cast a needed cautionary corrective
on the "American Dream," showing the potential of both economic
events (depressions, unemployment, technological change) and personal events (divorce, disability, old age, etc.) to bring down people
even from the upper middle class.

Still, as these cases were not typical, this chapter will move on to
review two other sets of cases which exemplify other paths in and out
of the almshouse. The first is the more typical "fall" into the poorhouse,

which was not from a great distance, but was from the working class to pauperism. As Alan Dawley notes of the Gilded Age, most workers were "caught up in an oppressive cycle of low skills (and) low wages … [and] as some individuals escaped the cycle, others were ensnared to take their place." Struggling to survive, but barely having what some in the period referred to as a "competence" (ownership, savings, or other security to survive a financial hardship), ordinary workers sometimes found themselves forced into the poorhouse. Finally, this chapter will examine the large number of inmates who were temporarily poor but whose long-term paths can be characterized as either relatively stable or even, in some cases, on an upward trajectory after the period they were in the almshouse. This discussion will reinforce the notion of the fluidity of poverty raised in Chapter 1.

FALLING FROM ON HIGH: DOWNWARD MOBILITY INTO THE ALMSHOUSE

That the fairly affluent were not immune to pauperism is suggested by Table 4.1 below, showing the number of inmates in a subsample that had property ownership prior to their admission to the almshouse. Table 4.1 was developed by using the United States Census enumeration sheets from the years 1850, 1860, and 1870, in which citizens were asked about the value of their property, both real estate and personal (usually in this period personal property would include not only savings and investment, but household items such as carriages or furniture, farm equipment, tools, and livestock). Of the approximately 1,470 cases chosen as a more intensive sample (see Chapter 2), I was able to locate some supplemental information beyond the *Inmate Biographies* on 361 cases. Of the 361, 186 were listed in at least one of the three above censuses. Of these, more than half (91) had some property. Table 4.1 lists only the smaller percentage (less than a quarter, or 44) that had more than $1,000 in property. Although any cutoff point is arbitrary, given the use of $500 by Alan Dawley as a measure of "a competence" in 1860 and 1870 Lynn, Massachusetts, and the average yearly wage in the state during the Gilded Age that hovered around the $400–$450 a year range, $1,000 in property would be equivalent to more than twice the average annual wage and the corresponding starting house prices.

It should be noted that there were ambiguities to the censuses' placement of the values next to certain family members or individu-

Table 4.1 Property Ownership for a Sample of Tewksbury Inmates and Their Families

(Total sample = 186, total property owners = 91)
*ambiguous cases

Property ownership over $3,000 (n=20)

George Ball (1872) 1860 (father) $4,000 personal property, father a grocer, George a clerk, a carter

Pam Billings (1876) (husband) 1870 $3,000 personal property, husband a dry goods merchant, she "keeping house"

*Solomon Conway (1880) 1860 (guardian) $2,500 property and $1,350 personal property, guardian a farmer, Solomon a farm laborer

James Dooley (1874) 1870 (self) $4,000 real estate, $2,000 personal property, a subcontractor

Augustus Flint (1890) 1860 (father) $2,500 real estate and $1,175 personal property, father owned hotels, Augustus a harness maker
    1870 (father) $11,000 real estate and $6,000 personal property

William Fowler (1880) (self) 1860 $8,250 real estate $3,000 personal property merchant
    (self) 1870 $3,000 real estate $2,000 personal property

*Agnes Goddard (1876) (adoptive family) 1870 $4,800 real estate and $4,000 personal property, adoptive father a dry goods merchant

Charles Hand (1870) (mother) 1850 $3,000 real estate, father had been a government worker, mother a housewife, he was disabled

Elbridge G. Hardy (1877) (father) 1850 $5,000 real estate property, father a tavern keeper, Elbridge a hostler

Charles Hatfield (1895) 1870 (he and wife) $15,000 in real estate and $500 personal property, wife wealthy, Charles a seaman

*Cordelia Hathaway (1873) (group of farmers) 1850 $5,000 real estate farmers, she a housewife

*John Mann (1875) 1870 (adoptive family) $2,500 real estate and $650 personal property, adoptive father a painter

Ruth May (1880) (she and husband) 1850 $10,000 real estate, husband a farmer, she a housewife (she and husband) 1860 $6,000 real estate and $1,200 personal property

Frederick Merritt (1865) (self and another farmer) 1850 $4,500 real estate, a farmer

William Mullen (1895) (father) 1870 $3,000 real estate and $500 personal property, father and son were blacksmiths

Charles Razoux (1872) (father) 1870 $8,500 personal property, father a liquor dealer

Elizabeth Sandford (1874) (husband) 1870 $3,000 real estate and $150 personal property, husband a farm laborer, she a nurse and seamstress

Delia Stafford (1880) (father) 1870 $5,000 real estate and $3,000 personal property, father in "marble works," she a domestic

Jane Thompson (1895) (she and husband) 1860 $3,500 real estate and $300 personal property, husband a farmer, she a housewife

*Alfred Williams (1877) (adoptive family) 1860 $8,000 real estate and $1,000 personal property, adoptive father a physician

---

Table 4.1 continues on next page

Louisa Arnold (1895) 1860 (father) $1,600 real estate value
Olivia Clark (1893) 1870 (she and husband) $2,000 real estate and $100 personal
property
John Conlin (1895) 1870 (father) $1,500 real estate and $800 personal property
Philip Cook (1890) 1870 (self) $1,000 personal property
Frances Day (1880) 1870 (self) $1,000 personal property
Dexter Gigger (1895) (with friend) 1850 $1,600 real estate
Patrick Good (1877) 1870 (he and wife) $600 real estate and $400 personal property
Charles Hand (above) (mother) 1860 $2,000 real estate and $500 personal property
Harvey Harridon (1890) 1860 (father) $800 real estate and $420 personal property
*Abigail Hayford (1865) 1870 (she and partner?) $1,500 real estate and $250 personal
property
Lyman Holden (1882) 1860 (father) $1,800 personal property
Ann Howe (1877) (she and husband) 1870 $1,400 real estate
William Jones (1893) 1850 (father) $500 (?) real estate
    1860 (father) $1,052 real estate and $190 personal property
    1870 (father) $100 real estate and $2,000 personal property
Ella Johnson (1875) 1860 (she and husband) personal property worth $2,000
John Naughton (1874) (self) 1870 $1,000 real estate
George F. Perkins (1876) 1860 (father) $1,000 personal property
Laben Phetteplace (1880) 1850 (parents) $1,800 real estate
    1860 (mother) $350 real estate and $800 personal property
Anna Pooler (1872) 1850 (father) $1,000 real estate
Emily Powell (1874) 1870 (father) $1,500 in real estate and $500 personal property
William Prescott (1890) 1860 (self) $500 real estate and $1,000 personal property
Elizabeth Sandford (above) (1874) 1850 $1,000 real estate property
    1860 $1,000 in real estate
Frank Silk (1880) 1860 (father) $1,440 real estate and $100 personal property
Issac Simmons (1875) 1850 (parents) $1,000 property
    1870 (parents) $1,200 real estate and $500 personal property
*John Thornton (1882) 1870 (adoptive family) $1,950 real estate and $450 personal
property
Ellen Whipple (1877) 1870 (mother) $900 real estate and $375 personal property
John Wyman (1874) (self) 1850 $1,500 real estate
    (self) 1870 $1,500 real estate and $400 personal property

---

* Solomon Conway was described as "simple minded" and having a guardian, but as
having earned money, so his part if any of the property listed under the guardian's
name is unclear; Goddard, Mann, Williams, and Thornton were all bound out youth,
see Chapter 7. Hathaway was part of a group. Hayford was listed as a housekeeper
with a male of her age; it is not possible to determine if they were lovers or if she was
an employee.

als in a household. For example, although usually the male head of household had the listing of property, sometimes a ditto mark was placed next to the wife, and sometimes women had their own property listing. Some of the asterisked entries in Table 4.1 are complicated either by group living, where it is unclear if the group was actually sharing in the value, or by the uncertain line in the nineteenth century between "boarding out" of youth (which I will discuss in Chapter 7) and adoption, which was unregulated.

Another rough gauge of downward mobility is the occupational titles of various inmates. Among the more highly placed occupational statuses were a chemist (Kernt Fundin, 1890); a clergyman (Joseph Thompson, 1873); a hotelkeeper (Henry L. Joy, 1873); an overseer of a mill (Henry Morris, 1895); an "owner of a small factory" (Thomas Graham, 1874); four physicians and a phrenologist (Solomon Pollock, 1893, Frank L. Wyman, 1893, Edward Monroe, 1885, John O'Flaherty, 1865, and William Johnson, 1880); a reporter (Robert Fraser, 1893); five teachers (John Perkins, 1893, Joseph Farrell, 1880, Hugh Donahue, 1880, Mary Burke, 1875, and Frederick L. Taylor, 1874); an underwriter (James W. Ross,1890); and a fair number of merchants and owners of small businesses, including Fowler and Dooley above. It is noteworthy that the most affluent families in Table 4.1 were not those who were professionals or other high-status occupations, but grocers, tavern keepers, farmers, blacksmiths, and painters, of which there were numerous inmates who also fit that occupational label.

While not large in number, the cases of drastic downward mobility are interesting in several ways. First of all, as opposed to the overall sample, they are overwhelmingly native-born "Yankees," many from old New England families. Second, the cases cross both depression eras and more prosperous years. Third, they indicate, on the one hand, the fact that property or savings within a family could not predict the future course of any particular family member. Yet, on the other hand, in most cases in which we can obtain adequate information, some family members were able to continue the economic legacy and come out relative "winners." Rarely were entire families downwardly mobile.

In two of the cases of sharp downward mobility, it would appear that old age was a primary cause, although we have to be careful not to assess "causes" in a deterministic way. William Fowler, born of an old Yankee family, who then married into the Ingalls family of North Andover, Massachusetts (whose family tree has several M.D.'s), as we saw, had a large amount of money in 1860. His business may have been declining, however, as in 1870 the census record lists him as worth $3,000 in real estate and $2,000 in personal property, down from $8,250 and $5,000, respectively, in the previous census. Fowler was 65, and in his biography, the clerk opines that "he probably has wandered away from home, [he is?] a little demented." Whether this should be taken at face value is open to question, and it begs the question as to why he stayed in the almshouse for one month. His wife Harriet had died in 1876. It seems by 1880 his children were doing well, notably the oldest son, Charles, who was an attorney in Washington, D.C. The second oldest son, William H., was in Hyde Park, Massachusetts, working as a machinist. With the daughters being harder to find and other information missing, it is difficult to speculate as to either Fowler's medical condition or his family's caretaking. I was unable to find any date of death for Fowler. His sons, though, clearly did well. In 1910 William H. had his own business as a "proprietor of a machine shop" and his own home and family, and, as noted, Charles was an attorney. So at least in the case of the older males, the family was able to pass on its economic and human capital.

Ruth May, also an 1880 inmate, illustrates how money was no barrier to ending up in the poorhouse in old age. As Table 4.1 shows, Ruth and her husband Thomas, a farmer, had property worth $10,000 in 1850 (a considerable sum) and a not insubstantial $6,000 in 1860, along with $1,200 in personal property. Thomas May passed away in 1863, leaving Ruth a widow. Here again we have a family mystery in that in 1870 William, their oldest son, is found in Dedham, Massachusetts, as a flour dealer with $11,000 in real estate and $2,000 in personal property, yet his mother is nowhere to be found in the census. In 1880, prior to entering the almshouse she has found succor (by this time she was 70) with her sister Joanna and brother-in-law Timothy Phelps in Northampton, Massachusetts. They owned a farm, but of far less value than Ruth's son, who was also listed in the 1880 census as a flour dealer, now moved to West Roxbury, Massachusetts. No doubt, as we shall return to in Chapter 8, the elderly had plenty of reason to fear going to the poorhouse. Whether family members could have been more helpful in caring for her is a matter of speculation.

Family estrangement was clearly at work in the case of another elderly and formerly affluent man, Charles H. Hatfield, an 1895 inmate. As Table 4.1 reveals, his property in 1870 was the second highest recorded in this subsample, with $15,000 in real estate and $500 in personal property. Importantly though, the property was listed under his wife Ann Louisa's name, and the almshouse biography too stresses

"Ann Louisa owned property in Boston and Medford; [when] she died in Medford in 1871, [the] property went to [the] children." Indeed, Charles's occupation was that of seaman, usually not a very lucrative occupation. Interestingly though, as the 68-year-old Hatfield ended up in Tewksbury (he would die there that year), his son Charles Edwin worked as an attorney and in 1910 became a bank president living in Newton, Massachusetts. Again since wealth and poverty are distributed through families, winners and losers are clearly visible.

Physical and mental health problems seem key in the cases of Charles F. Hand, an 1870 inmate, and Delia Stafford, an 1880 inmate. Hand, also from an old New England family from Connecticut, impressed the almshouse clerks with his background:

> [He] went to Phillips Academy in Andover. [He was] there [for] 1 year ... [then] at school [for] 2 years at Amherst ... [then] Williams College 4 years [graduating] in class of [18]"59." Three years at Andover Theological Seminary. [He] enlisted at Madison in 14th Connecticut regiment. He served [illegible] transfer to 22nd US Cavalry. [He] served 1 5/12 years [and] made [the] 63rd US ... Infantry. He served until the close of the war, then returned to Madison [Connecticut]. [He was] there about 5 months ... [His] father owned some property there but for last thirty years of his life was in Government employ at Washington where he also owned property ...

The almshouse biography stated that "Charles has been wounded in the head at 'Gettysburg' by a sabre stroke," and implied he had what we would now call post-traumatic stress disorder as it was written that he "calls himself a minister [though we] think [the] sabre stroke [has] affected his brain." Again this was itself a subjective judgment as Hand did after all attend seminary school. He remained at the almshouse for only a few weeks, but died four years later (at the age of 37) in Washington, D.C. His mother maintained a home in Madison, Connecticut, according to the 1850 and 1860 censuses, and Charles's sister Elizabeth was a teacher. Unfortunately, further data on them is not available. For Delia Stafford, her loss or estrangement from at least a moderate level of property is complex. Her father John who was "in marble works" (see Table 4.1) and had a fair amount of property in the 1870 census ($5,000 in real estate and $3,000 in personal property). Yet her father had some sort of mental breakdown. Here the census confirms the almshouse notes that in 1880 John was a patient in the Mclean Asylum (later to be a world-famous private psychiatric institution near Boston). But at the same time, Delia was in the almshouse having a child whose "father ... [was] her cousin Clarence Stafford of

Orange, Massachusetts." Her brother, N.M. Stafford of Cambridgeport, had agreed to "settle her bills." In this case, whether the wealth was carried on to anyone is unknown. Delia is recorded in the 1910 census in Waltham, Massachusetts, at 64 years old, with no occupation, living with a niece. Her brother Norman Meade sadly also had a mental health breakdown and was a patient at Worcester State Hospital until he died in 1911.

Relatively young and ostensibly healthy men also fell into the almshouse from families with money. Two examples are Augustus Flint, 41, an 1890 inmate, and George Ball, 35, an 1872 inmate. Augustus's father Josiah owned a hotel in Maine in 1870 (see Table 4.1). His property listing was the highest in the sample, with $11,000 in real estate and $6,000 in personal property. Interestingly, already in that year, Augustus's older brother George H. had quite a bit of property, being himself listed in Lewiston, Maine, as being in "dry goods" and worth $6,000 real estate and $7,500 personal property. However, Josiah died in 1872, and then George died at the untimely age of 32 in 1879. Augustus was by trade a harness maker and married Christina Atkinson from New Brunswick in 1882, but I was unable to determine their wealth, as he is not in the census (which ceased cataloguing wealth at this point in any event). He died in 1891. Similarly, George Ball came from a moderately affluent Boston family, his father, Nahum Ball, being a grocer worth $4,000 in 1860, while George was already a clerk. Nahum Ball died in 1866 of "old age." Here in this case, the "Inmate Biography" describes the settlement of the estate as such: "when he [Nahum] died his [George's] mother came in possession of a part of the Washburn estate [the in-laws' estate]. He [George] was an heir to a portion of said estate but [he] sold his claim to [his] uncle Henry Washburn [who was the] secretary of [the] Boston Insurance Company, Boston." According to the records, George joined the exodus to California, and he may be the George Ball in the census records who was residing in San Francisco in a lodging house in 1870. He was a carter born in Massachusetts, with a small $150 in personal property. In both the cases of Flint and Ball it is a bit hard to make out what happened and one can speculate on all sorts of personal, familial, or other issues which may have intervened.

Importantly, while each story is unique, the presence of so many inmates in the subsample who came from families with property suggests obviously that there were likely many more in the total admitted inmates of Tewksbury who came from similar circumstances.

THE USUAL "FALL": FROM THE WORKING CLASS

While it is interesting and important to note that those who came from families with significant property and sometimes higher-status occupations fell into poverty, more usually, the people who became inmates of Tewksbury had started only several steps above poverty. Observers of the Gilded Age such as Alan Trachtenberg place the number of workers "who barely held on above ... the poverty line at 45 percent ... while about forty percent lived below the line of tolerable existence." Although it is always true that those most at risk for poverty are working-class people, economic conditions in the Gilded Age were far worse than for most of the twentieth century, with the notable exception of the Great Depression. As immigrant and farm families entered cities and factory towns, they clustered in the ranks of laborers and factory operatives whose pay even official observers noted was insufficient to support a family. They depended on child labor for a large part of their survival, some studies citing as much as one-third of their family incomes. Of course depressions caused the number of inmates to soar at Tewksbury and all other poorhouses, and also led to the rise of outdoor relief. To take just a few examples of the devastation of the depressions of the 1870s and 1890s, we quote from several "inmate biographies":

Mary Loftis, 20 and daughters Mary, 2, and Katie five months old ... [Her] husband ... worked in the Rogers Mill, [he is now] out of work, when [he was] off for a job [he] got on a [drinking] spree [and was] sent to House of Correction in Boston for three months ... (1875)

Thomas Gallagher 60 years old admitted from Lowell on August 12 ... He lost his earnings by failure of contract and returned to Lowell [on] August 6 [and] has been in search of work, finding none, his wife upbraided him. He [then?] attempted to cut his throat with a razor. [He] says he has not eaten for three days. He had not been drinking ... In no institution [before] ... (1875)

John Ellis and Albert Ellis both admitted February 14, they are 9 years old and 13 years old, admitted from Boston ... [Their father] Luther B is a brakeman who worked for the Fitchburg Railroad and boarded with these 2 boys at 41 Wall Street in Boston. [He] was discharged by the Railroad and deserted the children ... (1895)

Rob Rawson admitted [on] February 2. [He is] 23 years old born in England, a machinist ... he landed in Montreal on June 20, 1894 per the SS "Sardenian" and tramped to Boston from there, arriving in September and has done no steady work since.... (1895)

But many working-class people also arrived at the poorhouse in years when the unemployment rates were not as high as in depression years. For women, absent available opportunities for skilled work and most legal rights of property ownership, the death or separation from a husband or the birth of a child out of wedlock were often sufficient to throw them into poverty. One example of downward mobility is the case of Ellen (O'Harry) Aldrich in the 1860s. Ellen, born in Ireland, married John H. Aldrich, a bricklayer from rural Hopkinton, Massachusetts, in 1858. John grew up in a property-owning family who later lost their house to foreclosure. In 1864, having joined the Massachusetts 29th Company in the Civil War, he died at the age of 28, his death certificate listing the cause as "inflammation of lungs." Ellen was left with two children and entered the poorhouse. Sadly, she is listed as an inmate of the Ashland, Massachusetts, poorhouse in 1870 and as "insane" and having no occupation. In 1880 she appears as one of many boarders of a farmer in Ashland named George E. Grey and is again marked in the census as "insane." One possibility is that in addition to her husband's death, Ellen may well have had an illegitimate child while her husband was at war. A child, Ellen, was born in 1863, and listed as illegitimate; the mother was Ellen and the father listed as in the U.S. Army. Ellen died a pauper in Ashland in 1887.

Matilda (Quince) Connors provides another example of falling into poverty. Born in Durham, New Hampshire, in 1839, the daughter of a farmer who owned property, she was married on May 15, 1859, to George Connors of Hampstead, New Hampshire, also from a family who owned an estate. George was a shoemaker with no property who served in the New Hampshire Volunteers in the Civil War. According to the inmate biography, George was "intemperate" and Matilda was "criminally intimate" with a Philip Grinnells of Haverhill, Massachusetts. Grinnells was a shoemaker as well and evidently Connors stated she was "drunk when [the affair] first commenced." The biography is silent on what became of Connors or Grinnells, but Matilda appears in the 1880 census still in Haverhill "housekeeping" with her son Franklin W., 22, who "works in a shoe shop," and Melinda, 18, Franklin's wife, also appears in the Haverhill city directory as a laundress in 1894. She is also probably the Matilda Connors who ends up in the Haverhill poorhouse in 1920. Here we have a very ordinary case of poverty in which the almshouse usage in the first case (Tewksbury) is necessary for having an out-of-wedlock child, and in the second case (Haverhill's poorhouse), probably for old age and/or infirmity. Mary (Jones) Bennett provides another example of a woman who ended up in the poorhouse. Born in 1844 in Sudbury, Massachusetts, to a farmer who owned property, she married a Nathan G. Bennett who was born in Maine. We learn he owned no property, although he paid his poll taxes. At some point around 1870, they separated. Unfortunately, I was unable to find Mary in the censuses after 1870 and before 1900 when at 56 she was an inmate in the poorhouse of Marlboro, Massachusetts. Though she was only 56, it is not terribly surprising that she came to Tewksbury and then the Marlboro poorhouse given how difficult it would have been for her to support herself, possibly in conjunction with lack of extended family support, and other issues such as infirmity.

Men of very modest means fell each year into pauperism as well. Often the almshouse clerks explain their decline as due to personal problems. John F. Conlin, 44 years old, an 1895 inmate, was a mason who had paid fourteen poll taxes, and whose father was also a mason. They had held a small amount of property. Now a widower, the clerk stated Conlin had been "here before many times on account of alcohol." In the 1910 census, in fact, John is in the state workhouse at Bridgewater. Simon Davis, a 57-year-old inmate in 1890 who had a history of small property ownership as a farmer, a keeper of a fish market, and a fisherman was evidently ill as the clerk wrote "debility" at the end of the write-up. He died at the almshouse later that year.

The relatively prosperous (as compared with other decades) 1880s give examples of numerous men who entered Tewksbury, often for short periods of time. In 1882, Henry Turfey, a 41-year-old laborer who had come over from England and served in the Navy during the Civil War, spent two and half months in the almshouse. In 1885, George A. Wells, a 35-year-old African American barber born in Boston, spent two months at Tewksbury. In that same year, James H. Arnold, a 49-year-old English-born bookkeeper who had recently returned from England, spent less than two weeks, and Hubert Brooks, 19 years old and also recently arrived from England, had a brief stay. William Meek, a German-born 46 year old, who was one of the "German recruits" brought over to assist the Union in the Civil War and was now a brewer, stayed at the Tewksbury Almshouse for an undetermined period. In the 1887 sample, Thomas Shea, a 40-year-old Irish-born laborer and a widower, had a two-month almshouse stay. He had owned a house and land for seven years in Lawrence, Massachusetts, but evidently fell on difficult times and lost the property. Virtually all the men mentioned were widowers with no nearby family or friends to help them.

For many poor people the admission to the poorhouse represented tragedy, not just in the loss of any pride and autonomy, but in the loss of their home and family. Approximately one in six of the inmates I can document (hence much likely many more) died at Tewksbury. This does not count those who may have died at other poorhouses, such as possibly Ellen Aldrich (Ashland), Matilda Connors (Haverhill), and Mary Bennett (Marlboro), and possibly John F. Conlin at Bridge-water Workhouse. Of course, many inmates were elderly and/or ill, but certainly the high death rate reinforced the widespread perception that the almshouse was a place to go to die.

LIFE AFTER THE ALMSHOUSE:
THE RESILIENCY OF THE POOR AND THE FLUIDITY OF POVERTY

By no means does it detract from the tragedy of poverty or horror of the almshouse to note that for most inmates, especially those not elderly or ill, the almshouse was by no means the final stop of their lives. In fact, follow-up data suggest that as many people did as well after their stay at Tewksbury as before, and some did better.

It is important before going further to admit the many method-ological problems inherent in any effort to trace the poor (or, for that matter, most nineteenth-century citizens). The combination of many poor people avoiding official records (they often did not pay taxes, vote, marry, or appear in city and town directories) with the general problem of common names, which in turn were probably subject to a certain amount of changing as well, makes any definite effort to make powerful historical or social science statements difficult. Moreover, studies of economic mobility confront a difficult conceptual issue since they combine exploring people through developmental time and broader historical time. That is, studying where a person is in 1880 or 1890 is to a large degree dependent on what is going on in the life of the nation, state, and city he or she lived in, but is equally dependent on his or her own age and the human and social issues that age raises. In other words, what are our expectations for mobility? In attempting to assess even a small sample I ran into this issue immediately. If a young orphan was in the almshouse and ten years later was a laborer, was that upward mobility of a sort? In a sense, yes, in that being out of an institution and working is a better life alternative. But in another way, we can answer "no," as we would expect a healthy child in ten years time to move on, and being a laborer was the lowest status of work. Or take the case of Ruth May earlier. Her entering the almshouse at age 70 seems tragic to us, and betokens downward mobility. Yet given that there were so few places for the elderly to go, particularly if infirm, perhaps it does not betoken much of a fall. There are many other conundrums. Occupations continually change as do their status and pay. Homeownership and other property-owning becomes more common or rare over time and implies different statuses at different time periods. And in a sense the whole endeavor of mobility study (as some have criticized Thernstrom's research) is infected by a time bias. For example, since the economy of the Northeast was far better in the first three decades of the twentieth century than in the 1890s, we would expect many people would gain status in these years.

In many ways, economic mobility is a social construct which has a great deal of subjectivity to it. Realizing this, I struggled with whether and how to calculate economic mobility.

Still, I would argue that studies like this do have importance despite their imperfections because of the stereotypes about poverty and poor people which are embedded in both scholarly inquiry and the public mind, sometimes crossing political perspectives. If the idea that "once poor, always poor," is not contested by study and discussion then serious misjudgements may be made. It is not necessary, on the one hand, to be a Panglossian believer in the "American Dream" that everyone will succeed to study those who move out of poverty, but neither will it do to impute a sort of frozen class system to American history which might better describe a caste system.

For a nonrandomized sample such as this, I suggest that there are enough instances of occupational stability and improvement to support the thrust of mobility research that began in the 1960s. Because I can't provide thousands and thousands of cases, the power of this argument from a quantitative perspective can only be suggestive; still, further study of this and other populations can lead to fruitful results.

I began with the 361 cases for which I could find additional data. Keeping in mind again that many inmates were deceased or not located in future censuses or other records, I still found 167, or nearly half, after their initial location at Tewksbury. Twenty-five inmates, like Aldrich or Bennett above, were at other almshouses, homes for the aged or disabled, hospitals, and asylums. These were in themselves more of a diverse lot than they may seem, as some former inmates were patients at well-known health facilities. But, discarding these cases, I still had 142 inmates. I have presented in Table 4.2 58 cases (actually slightly more individuals) who, in my opinion, made out relatively well following their discharge from Tewksbury. I based this judgment, as Table 4.2 indicates, either on occupational attainments, family occupational attainments (usually husbands or grown children), and/or in terms of property ownership. I also decided to limit my table to those for which data could be easily conveyed—for example, there were dozens of others who could be viewed as having had interesting career patterns, but whose job titles or other status made it too difficult to convey in a table.

The data gathered about the lives of inmates after they left the institution provide a few interesting ironies. While hundreds if not thousands of inmates who passed through Tewksbury were servants at some points in their lives, four of the people above *had* servants later in their lives. Bernard Roesing (recorded as Werner Rusing by the almshouse) was found in 1880 as a brewer in Chicago. He was married, with two live-in servants. James Waddington, an 1880 inmate, had a servant in his family in 1900 Boston, where he was a music teacher. Similarly, John Batchelder, an 1877 inmate who was an elderly farmer in New Hampshire by 1920, had a servant; and Frank Briggs, an 1895 inmate as a child, had a servant in his house in 1930 in the state of Washington.

What is certainly another poignant story is that of Frederick Briggs, Frank's brother, and one of four Briggs children who were state wards and were placed out from Tewksbury. While in the early decades after his admission, he was a cloth finisher, and moved to western Massachusetts, in the 1920 census (after serving in World War I) Frederick moved to the town of Tewksbury and was working as a blacksmith at the State Infirmary, which the Tewksbury Almshouse was now renamed. He lived with his wife Ellen and they owned their home. By 1930, Frederick was now a mechanic at the institution, and had been married for twenty-six years to Ellen. Their home, as shown in Table 4.2, was valued at $5,000, and they had two boarders in the household. What it must have been like for man who was an inmate at 14 in the almshouse and was now a skilled worker at the same facility we do not know. Such transitions, however, are not entirely unusual.

Among the many former inmates for whom the almshouse represented a moment in time of temporary poverty, there were many reasons both for their poverty and for their later mobility. First of all, the almshouse differed from modern specialized institutions in serving a wide variety of needs. It is not surprising that several categories of people—immigrants who landed there immediately after their arrival in the New World, orphans or other children who were in the almshouse,

Table 4.2 Sample of Occupations of Former Tewksbury Inmates after They Left the Almshouse

Year of Admission	Name	Census Year*/ Other Record	Occupation
1875	Mary Alton	Marriage License (1882)	husband mechanic
1877	John P. Batchelder	1880, 1910, 1920	owns farm
1895	Amanda Berquist	1900–1930	owned house $5,000 (1930) son a pressman
1874	Jabez H. Bradbury	1880, 1900	watch repairer, 1900 farmer, own home
1867	Elijah F. Breck	Marriage License (1868)	broker
1885	Michael Boland	1900, 1930	laborer, $500 real estate
1870	Francis Bogan	1880	grocer
1895	Frederick Briggs	1900–1930	blacksmith, mechanic at Tewksbury, owned home valued at $5,000 (1930)
	Frank Briggs	1900, 1930	servant, farm laborer, cook in a restaurant
	Robert Briggs	1900–1920	street car conductor, police officer
1873	Edwin (Frank E.) Cole	1900, 1910	teamster, watchman in a car works
1880	Frank Cross	1900–1920	mechanic of leadline pipes
1875	George H. Davis	1880, 1900	farmer, owned farm
1895	Philomenia DeAngelis	1900, 1920	husband grocer, owned house
1876	Michael Dennison	1880	cooper
1875	Daniel Dunn Jr.	1880, 1900	blacksmith, own home? (illegible)
1874	John & James Duverin		
	John	1880, 1910	census tobacco farmer
	James	1900–30	farmer (1930) owned farm $2,000
1873	Albert Fisher	1880	painter
1893	Charles W. Francis	1910	"ice-man sales," own home
1877	Mary Freeman	1920	manager of a stock ranch
1895	William H Garvey	1900, 1920, 1930	tinsmith, sheet metal worker, own home valued at $2,500 (1930)
1877	David Glass	1900	slate and tin roofer
1877	Patrick Good	1880, (1890 City Directory)	boiler maker
1876	Jennie Grafton	1900	husband farmer, owned land
1872	Mary Hickey	1880	husband cotton dyer, she keeping house
1880	Ida Irwin	1900, 1920, 1930	cashier, 1930 $6,000 worth of property
	Robert Irwin	1930	jewelry salesman, $5,000 property
1893	Augustine Jacquoit	1900–30	ran boarding house, owns home worth $2,500
1874	Edward F. Jelly	1880	machinist
1880	Patrick Jennings	1900, 1910	fireman

Table 4.2 continues on next page

Table 4.2 (continued)

Year of Admission	Name	Census Year*/ Other Record	Occupation
1874	Mary A. Kearns	1881 English census	son a clerk solicitor
1874	Eliza J. Killips	(marriage license, 1878) 1900 census	husband a rail brakeman laundress
1895	Joseph Leadbetter	1910–1930	farmer owned home/farm
1882	Augusta Lee	1900–1920	own property, husband a lather
1874	Margaret Lovett	(marriage license, 1878)	married to a soldier
1890	Laughlan McGilvray	1920	son owned house, salesman for suspender company
1877	Richard McTigh	1920, 1930	farmer, 1930 owns real estate worth $4,350
1895	William Mullen	1900	blacksmith
1875	Cora (Oakley) Pumphrey	(city directory, 1890)	clerk bureau of statistics?**
1865	Lucinda Parsons	1880	son working as plumber
1890	Nelson Peterson	1900–1920	farmer, cutter in a shoe factory, construction foreman
1895	Emma Phife	1900–1920	servant, son a sailor, owned house valued at $2,500 (1930)
1890	Winthrop Pocknett	1900, 1910	farm laborer, rail brakeman
1895	Sadie Polinsky	1910 1930	office girl in a watch factory, father collector debts
1880	Ellen Quilty	1900	nurse
1872	Charles L. Razoux	1880, 1910	clerk in a telephone office, machinist
1885	Ellen Rhodes	1900	music teacher
1895	Joseph Rice	1900, 1910, 1930	coal miner, owns house $5,000 value
1880	Jenett Ridell	1920, 1930	worked for rail shop, janitor, $5,000 real estate
1895	Minnie Roth	1920 1930	1920 husband a rail worker, home owned value $1,200
1885	Eliza Ruffley (Elise Ruefli)	1900, 1920, 1930	nurse, son a lawyer, $15,000 property
1875	Werner/Bernard Rusing	1880, 1910	brewer
1870	Dennison Shoales	1880	machinist
1870	Alonzo Stone	1880	farmer
1880	Charles Tarby	1900–1930	laborer for government, barber, owned home worth $2,500
1895	Carl Tornquist	1910, 1930	ironer in a shirt company, 1930 own property valued at $1,700
1880	Charles Van Patten	1900	U.S. military based in Cuba
1880	James A. Waddington	1900, 1910	music teacher
1877	Alfred Williams (aka Breed)	1880, 1900	laborer, oiler
1895	Elizabeth Williams	1920	bookkeeper in a business office
1876	James Woodbury	1880, 1910	laborer, driver in a box factory

Notes:
* Unless noted otherwise the years listed are census data
** abbreviation in directory is "bur stat" which may be the Bureau of Statistics

and women who were having children out of wedlock or had come to Tewksbury after a separation or being deserted—went on to lead lives which in many cases differed little from other working people. The second-largest category of people in Table 4.2 are workers who were victims of the economic downturns of the 1870s and 1890s in particular, and who were able to return to their occupations or to secure other ways of earning a living when economic times improved.

Two of those who later employed their own servants are examples of recent immigrants who upon arrival in the United States entered the almshouse for short stays. Werner Rusing, age 32, and his brother Clemens, age 19, were admitted to Tewksbury on April 7, 1875. They had landed in New York on March 6, 1875, and shortly after, the "brothers [were] robbed of $240 in an Emigrant House [in] New York. [They had been] bound for Cincinnati [but] got on the wrong road and boot up [e.g., ended up] in Boston. [They have] frost bitten feet." The Rusings were discharged nine days later. Similarly, James Waddington was admitted in January 1880. He was a 47-year-old man who had immigrated from England and landed in Quebec in late 1879. Waddington was a musician who "came to America in search of a position as [an] organist. He [then] spent his money and got to drinking." He was "removed to Boston on March 26, 1880." Waddington, a widower, remarried in Boston on December 22, 1880, to a Helen O. Dunbar. He was listed as a music teacher, so perhaps he had a job already. In the early twentieth-century censuses, Waddington remained married to Helen (29 years as of the 1910 census) and his job was described in 1910 as "music teacher, public."

Many inmates who did well later in their lives entered the almshouse as children. Two examples of young inmates who appear in Table 4.2 besides the Briggs children are the Irwin children and Charles Tarby. The Irwin children, Eddie, 9 years old, Phoebe, 7 years old, Ida, 6 years old, and Robert Irwin, 4 years old, were admitted from the Holden, Massachusetts (near Worcester), poor farm for a little over a week in May 1880, and then transferred to the Monson facility. Their father Edward had died in 1878, and their mother Nora's "whereabouts [were] unknown." Unfortunately we are given very little other information about the family and why the children came into state custody. I was able to find bits and pieces of information about the children later in their lives. Ida Irwin in 1900 was in Boston living with another brother, William, 36 years old, who was married to Catherine, 33 years old. A cousin, Marjorie Jeffries, lived with them. William was a telegraph operator, Ida a cashier, and Marjorie a clerk. Similarly, in the 1920 census, William still worked for the telegraph office, and Ida, 41, was still single and was now described as a cashier at a college office. In the 1930 census, the family was listed as owning $6,000 worth of property. Robert Irwin became a jewelry salesman in Idaho who owned $5,000 in property.

The same year, Charles Tarby, an 8-year-old African American boy, was admitted for about three weeks. Charles was born in Woodstock, Vermont. His mother Julia was dead, and he had not seen his father Charles "for [the] past year." Evidently he came to be cared for by his grandfather Austin Hazzard in Vermont. Hazzard then "two weeks ago sent him to his aunt Mary J. Phelps and she was found to be in jail." Whether Charles was sent to Phelps once she was out of jail or back to Hazzard, or was placed out, we do not know. I was able to locate Charles, however, in four censuses, the first in Lynn, Massachusetts (1900), and the remainder in Everett, Massachusetts. He was married to Erma this whole time, with whom he had at least five children. Described as "a laborer for government" in one census, at age 69 he was a barber and owned a home worth $2,500.

Women inmates often admitted for childbirth or after a separation (see Chapters 5 and 6) were also among those who often did well after the almshouse admissions. Jennie Grafton was the daughter of a Methodist minister who was admitted to the almshouse at age 21 in 1876. Described as "a domestic and a dressmaker," she was pregnant by an "Algernon S. Fuller of Central Falls, Rhode Island, who[m] she had met through a friend of a friend." She gave birth to Lillian Mae and apparently was sent to the workhouse for her sexual transgression. Still she married William J. Jackson in Boston on July 13, 1878, and the daughter took on his name. She remained married to William and moved to Montville, Maine, where her husband was a farmer who owned land. He was 25 years her senior and they had been married as of the 1900 census for twenty-one years. Their daughter Lillian was 23, single, and living with them. Jennie (Grafton) Jackson died on May 12, 1904, in Montville at only 49, while her husband died in 1908 at 78.

Eliza Ruffley (whose real name was Elise Ruefli) provides another example of a woman who entered Tewksbury to give birth to an out-of-wedlock child. She was 21 years old, born in Switzerland and arrived in Boston on November 27, 1883. According to the *Inmate Biography*, the father of her child was a Jacob Walzer of Switzerland, and "she came to America to have her child born." However, she was admitted on March 11, 1885, which appears to present some date discrepancies in her account. In any event, though, she did give birth to a son, Robert. While in 1900 Elise is in the census in Boston as a nurse living alone, by 1920 and 1930 she and her son Robert have settled in New Hampshire. Her son became a lawyer in general practice. His home in Concord, New Hampshire, as Table 4.2 shows, was valued at $15,000 in 1930, which was far above the average at this time.

An example of another inmate who fared well after initially needing help was Augusta Lee, a Swedish immigrant who entered the alms-house in 1882 with her children, Harry and Ella. Augusta (maiden name Anderson) was 29 years old and had arrived in America in 1873. She married John J. Lee, a first-generation Irish American in 1880, and they lived in western Massachusetts where the children, evidently twins, had been born two months before. According to the biography, "her husband is off [for] five months." Whatever happened and however long John was gone for, the future censuses show the two married, as of 1920, for forty years. Her husband remained a blacksmith in Springfield, Massachusetts, who owned property, and in 1920 he was recorded as working "in a machine shop" as a lather. We shall return in Chapter 6 to this question of husbands being "off" but in this case clearly either John was "off" for a relatively short time or perhaps because the family needed help; Ms. Lee presented herself with her young twins as having an absent husband.

Though all the problems noted above, immigration, abandoned or neglected children, out-of-wedlock births, and marital separation, contributed to admissions to the almshouse, the greatest number of people in Table 4.2 were those who were admitted during economic depressions, when work was unavailable. In 1877, for example, David Glass, Patrick Good, and Alfred Williams were all out of work due to the depression. David Glass had "carried on a slater's business" and owned two houses in Boston. But since September 1876 "he [was] idle most of the time" and was sleeping "in station houses for lodging" (during the later nineteenth century, police stations opened their doors to the homeless for overnight lodging). Patrick Good was a boilermaker who had owned a home in Boston, but at the time of his admission "he [had been] out of work [for] most of [the] time [for the] past two or three years." Alfred Williams had worked on the railroads as a fireman, but since June 1875 he was "in various places tramping" for work. Given the depth of the depression of the 1870s, it is not surprising that when some economic recovery came, skilled workers in particular regained their status. When David Glass is next found (not until his marriage in Boston 1896) he was a slater and was a "slate and tin roofer" in the 1900 census. Patrick Good is in the 1880 census as a boilermaker in Boston and is also listed in the Boston directory in 1890 as a boilermaker.

Although Alfred Williams was a laborer in the 1880 census, by 1900 he was an oiler (consistent with his prior fireman job).

Similarly, to take a few examples of the 1890s depression (lasting approximately from 1893 to 1897), William Garvey, Joseph Leadbetter, and William Mullen were inmates who were down on their luck during the depression but appear to have returned a few years later to their prior statuses. Garvey, an English-born tinsmith, was admitted to Tewksbury for about seven weeks in 1895. He later moved to Providence, Rhode Island, and in 1900 was listed there as a tinsmith. He had been married three years with one child. They then moved to Altoona, Pennsylvania, and in 1920 they owned their own home there. Garvey was listed as a railroad sheet metal worker that year, and in 1930 as a "tinner in a rail shop." His home in Altoona, as shown in Table 4.2, was valued at $2,500. Joseph Leadbetter was a 20-year-old man who was the son of a farmer in rural Princeton, Massachusetts. He was also admitted to the almshouse for about seven weeks in 1895. Like many young men, particularly in depressions, he seems to have gone off to secure work or additional income. He was reported to have been "in many different places in Massachusetts." But by the new century, Leadbetter was steadily in Princeton as a farmer, presumably having inherited his father's land. He married in 1910, and in 1930 he and his wife and large family were still in Princeton working their farm. William Mullen, a 35-year-old blacksmith, spent about four weeks at Tewksbury in 1895. By 1900, William was back with his family in Boston, he and his wife having been married for eighteen years. They had four children and William was still a blacksmith.

Like other mobility research based on official records, there is not an exciting flair to this data, particularly in describing those who were relatively stable in occupation or social status, or those who were mildly mobile over the years. Clearly, in some ways, the first sets of stories, of falls from high status into poverty, are more dramatic because they tug at our heartstrings. In this sense, I can sympathize with part of the problem of the mobility research that Thernstrom and others undertook: its lack of drama subjects it to potential shrugs, as large numbers of small changes are compiled for the historical record.

"RAGS TO RESPECTABILITY?"

In his important book *The Other Bostonians* (1973), Thernstrom takes the position that, while the "rags to riches" dream of the Horatio Algers was not the case in American history, nevertheless his research suggests that for many people slow and steady progress, or "rags to respectability," marked the era of the Gilded Age and Progressive Period. Although the research in this book, as already noted, has too small a sample to compare with Thernstrom and other mobility researchers, several comments can be made about this characterization.

First, when closely examining the actual case examples, we find that what appears as the greatest "mobility" is often true by comparing short-term census listings rather then long-term family changes over generations. Rather dramatic changes are sometimes not very dramatic since, in some cases, our subjects appear to be returning over time to a family status they had lost. For example, Jennie Grafton, while an almshouse inmate and for a time a domestic servant, was, after all, a daughter of a minister, and so her becoming a farmer's wife is not a very dramatic move. Both John Batchelder and Joseph Leadbetter returned to their fathers' occupations as farmers. David Glass's father was a slater; Fredrick A. Briggs, father of the Briggs children, was a carpenter who owned a home; and William Mullen's father was a blacksmith (as was his son) who owned property. Many inmates examined above have parents whose occupations were not listed and hence are unknown to us. But we know the Rusing brothers started with cash when they arrived from Germany. Also, many of those examined came from countries whose immigrants were often small farmers or small tradesmen like Augusta Lee from Sweden, Elise Rueffli from Switzerland, and many others in Table 4.2 like Augustine Jacquoit from France; Amanda Berquist, Charles Francis, Nelson Peterson, and Carl Tornquist from Sweden; Mary Freeman from Austria; and Charles Razoux, whose father was a liquor dealer from "Germany or Switzerland." None of this is to suggest that there was no upward mobility within my sample or in the time period examined, but it does suggest that mobility is a complex *family enterprise* in which a focus on short-term census or other data or only on individuals can be misleading. Few of those who rose came from extremely poor backgrounds with no access to some form of a trade or skill or other form of human capital.

Second, studies may underrate the role of chance or what is ascribed as "personal" problems or issues that prevent people from becoming economically mobile. Alan Dawley perhaps puts this best in the paragraph below, in which he interprets life at the time as having a set of unseen rules:

Unless the worker inherited an estate or married a paid-up mortgage, he had to travel an extremely difficult road to get there. Along the way he encountered a set of rules that read like a series of "Keep Out" signs. Don't Get a Disabling Injury; Don't Get a Serious Illness, Don't get too Old to Work; Don't get laid off.

In this sense we might say some of what distinguished the "successful" people from the "unsuccessful" (those who fell into poverty in a long-term way) may be a matter of health, age, luck, and particular occupations, as well as the more frequently talked-of roles of familial human capital and socioeconomic status. Some of this is obvious, as we saw with the role of age in William Fowler and Ruth May's cases, and injury and disability in the case of Charles Hand. But beyond that, the particular occupational settings in our sample seemed to play an important role. For example, there were very few factory workers in Table 4.2 who moved up. Those who appear in Table 4.2 are overwhelmingly either those who inherited skilled trades, such as David Glass or William Mullen, or those who moved from domestic service to more responsible levels of service occupations, such as was the case with Augustine Jacquoit, who came to run a lodging house, and Mary Freeman, who became a manager of a stock ranch. Another category of people were those whose marital choices were upwardly mobile ones, such as Charles Hatfield earlier in the chapter or Amanda Berquist, Philomena DeAngelis, Jennie Grafton, Augusta Lee, and Minnie Roth in Table 4.2. And there are, although they are far less predominant than in other studies, some who moved into low-level, white-collar jobs (Charles Francis, sales; Ida and Robert Irwin, cashier and sales; Cora Oakley, a clerk; Sadie Polinsky, an office girl; and Elizabeth Williams, a bookkeeper). Notably, most of this last category were children in the late nineteenth century who benefited from the rise of white-collar work later in time.

In sum, while I believe the exploration of mobility among the poor is critical to any basic understanding of their lives, and has been severely understudied, I am not convinced that "rags to respectability" characterized American life in the Gilded Age. It may be better expressed that a percentage of those who lack resources may achieve some upward mobility *if* they can *survive* for the period of time that is necessary for major changes to occur in the broader economy and job market. As examples, it was a lot more advantageous to immigrate to America in the 1880s than in the mid-1870s when depression devastated much of the nation, whether this occurred by plan or luck. All other things being equal, a personal problem, from marital desertion to alcoholism, is easier to overcome if the person is young, and times are better. If emotional trauma or disabilities can be overcome, then, if the economy is better, one can move forward with life more easily (of course, we know the stress of poverty and unemployment is the opposite and hits more when times are bad). These rather "commonsensical" comments are meant to remind us that upward mobility may be a matter of being among those "still standing" when better economic times return.

PART TWO

THE "CRISIS" IN THE FAMILY

> For at least 150 years there have been periods of fear that "the family"—meaning a popular image of what families were supposed to be like, by no means a correct recollection of any actual "traditional family"—was in decline ... these anxieties have been particularly projected onto lower-class families.
>
> —Linda Gordon

As Linda Gordon notes, it is hard to read Victorian accounts of the horrible things occurring in nineteenth-century families without being reminded of the "crisis in the family" talk of recent decades as well. It is true that the raw Victorian rhetoric of "bastardy," "seduced and abandoned," "harlots," and "criminal intimacies," which we shall discuss shortly, has fallen out of favor. And some panics, over "fallen women" in the nineteenth century, and teenage pregnancy in the late twentieth are at least somewhat time bounded. But overall conventional observers in the late twentieth century (both liberal and conservative) paralleled the Victorians in bemoaning increased divorce and separation, freer sex which they saw leading to promiscuity and disease, and the specter of nontraditional families, unmarried women, single parents, and out-of-wedlock births.

As Gordon also makes clear, the "decline of the family" rests on the assumption of the existence of a conventional middle-class family which itself was only enshrined as an ideal in the middle decades of the nineteenth century. This bourgeois nuclear family of the male breadwinner and female director of the domestic sphere never fit the experience of the majority of the people studied in this book. Men who were poor or near poor never had the secure "breadwinner" status that the property-owning patriarch had, and women of lower classes have worked outside the home for a century or more. Even in the most conventional of working-class families, young children went to work early rather than attend school, nonrelated boarders lived in the house to help pay the rent, and non-nuclear family members including fictive kin lived with mom, dad, and children. Among those who were poor, the terms applied to them describe their "deviance" and imply a once-fictive middle-class life they never had. In his fine work about how the laws of America operated historically to oppress the poor, Jacobus ten Broek contrasts the majority of poor even in 1971 with the conventional norm:

> Ceremonial marriage is often expensive and also may not be a part of the cultural mores of various minority groups. For many people at the lower end of the economic scale, divorce, the minimum cost of which in California is generally about 200 dollars is a luxury beyond their financial means.

Ten Broek shows how, since the Anglo Poor Laws of the sixteenth century, the poor were held captive to a set of concepts that often had little relevance to them:

> When poor families break down, the husband simply leaves. Desertion has become known as the "poor man's divorce." In this context many concepts dependent upon the legality of the marriage relationship, such as bigamy, adultery, and in part legitimacy of offspring, are robbed of much of their traditional content.

The father who leaves is, of course, a no-good deserter, a "deadbeat dad" in today's terms; the mother is at best a poor parent who deserts her children to work and raises her child alone, or, worse, if she chooses to have sexual relations, to be a harlot or "loose woman." Many children were "illegitimate" and, as "bastards," could be legally removed by the authorities, at least until the twentieth century, with little or no recourse for the parents.

In the chapters that follow we examine the almshouse clerks' narrative about family and sexual relations. Chapter 5, "'Criminal Intimacies': Out-of-Wedlock Births," focuses on the many inmates of Tewksbury who came to the almshouse to give birth, usually in the absence of marriage. In doing so, the women in the early years (prior to the 1880s) risked being sent to the workhouse for their crime of having nonmarital sex. They were interrogated at length (as is true today of welfare recipients) about the father of the child, and, should the father be named and "findable," he was subject to arrest, and if he failed to marry the woman, he could be forced to remain in jail until a judge ordered a bastardy hearing. Yet, interestingly, the data reveal a string of contradictions. First is the well-known contradiction of the supposed sexual repressiveness of the Victorians, which as philosopher Michel Foucault has commented on, is contradicted by the extreme sexual prurience of the times. The entries themselves in the 1860s–1870s log at length the "connexions" of men and women and where they had intercourse and how frequently. Secondly, by reviewing the many cases of pregnancy (241 in my sample), we can also see how the various Victorian myths of "seduced and abandoned" women being preyed on by vicious men, sometimes conjured as upper-class "rakes," were untrue. There are a few cases of exploitation by employers (usually of domestic servants, and then usually by family members, often the sons of the employer) and certainly some cases of rape, but overwhelmingly the cases reported are of consensual sex between young women and men, most of whom met, as today, because they worked together or boarded nearby (in tenements), or met at dances or other amusements. Finally, interestingly, as the years went by fewer and fewer inmates were punished or prosecuted. While the clerks sometimes continued to label the woman harshly ("a harlot") they do not appear to suggest punishment, and while they nearly always seem to favor finding the father, this effort too lagged.

In Chapter 6, "Family Conflict and Desertion," I review almshouse entries about married couples and families. The almshouse was always a place of shelter for victims of family violence. Additionally, many women reported themselves as "deserted," and men, too, were often "separated." I use a sample of 189 cases to explore to what extent we can determine whether a man being "off" meant merely that he was finding work, whether in the absence of divorce "desertion" or separation was an unproblematic substitute, or whether in fact "desertion" adequately describes the movement away from families. While the subject is complex, and the records include many women leaving men, and members of both sexes engaging in adultery, infidelity, and often "intemperant" behavior, on the whole, it appears that male "desertion" was a major phenomenon, particularly at the time of pregnancy or shortly after childbirth. The notes and even official records do not fully allow us to gain all the answers to this phenomenon, but it is likely that both the economic pressure placed on male breadwinners and other psychological pressures of supporting a family were most difficult.

FIVE

"Criminal Intimacies": Out-of-Wedlock Births

"She was seduced by ... and after that was [or became] more or less common."

Stock description of female inmate who had been "criminally intimate," 1870s

"[She] does not appear like a bad girl."

Common almshouse note for some women judged not at fault

All people who applied for poor relief have been subject to negative moral judgments going back to the early Anglo-American poor laws which enshrined the idea that there are "worthy" and "unworthy" poor. But even within this highly moralistic arena, women who entered the almshouse pregnant were subject to labeling as either "seduced," and hence blameless, or as "loose" women who had sought out sexual relations and hence could be punished and vilified. Women who were judged immoral could be imprisoned in a workhouse or house of correction, although gradually reformers created "homes for fallen women" under a variety of names. This chapter will review the Victorian drama, which, in the earlier years of the almshouse (roughly until the late 1870s), shaped both the description and treatment of women and the hunting down of the putative fathers through "bastardy proceedings." I will then describe how the records and other data about the actual relations between poor and working-class women and men tend to be far less dramatic than the Victorian rhetoric. Finally, for women we have information about, we will explore what became of the unmarried mothers who entered the Tewksbury Almshouse.

THE ALMSHOUSE RECORDS AND "VICTORIAN STOCK FIGURES"

It is, of course, easy for twenty-first-century readers to feel superior to the traditional Victorian treatment of sex and gender relations. It is easy to forget how popular with the general public these caricatures were and for how long elements of both the gender and sexual code of the mid-nineteenth century lasted. Michael Grossberg, a scholar of nineteenth-century law, reminds us of the popularity, for example, of the laws of "seduction," which decreed criminal penalties for those men who had sexual relations with women under the "promise of marriage" but did not marry their "seduced":

> By [the] 1840s [there was] strong judicial support for damages for "seduced and abandoned" cases … courts insisted "the female and seducer do not stand on equal ground. She is the weaker party and the victim of his acts, and the seduction has been practiced upon her under the false color of a promise of marriage which he never intended to perform" … An 1845 petition from more than 5,500 Massachusetts citizens to make seduction a crime illustrates popular support for such measures.

At least for the dominant propertied classes, Victorian morality enshrined in law protected the sanctity and security of marriage and was justified as a needed defense of women who were seen as helpless against shrewd men who might prey on them. As Sherri Broder argues, rather than fight this dominant morality, Gilded Age reformers such as the labor leaders and populists used the Victorian caricatures themselves to blame upper-class "rakes" for seduction and bastardy, while citing low wages and poor working conditions as the cause of the problem of "fallen women." Hence, with the exceptions of some radicals,

> all the Victorian stock characters that served to depict the men, women, and children of the poor—the missing father who walks away from his role as family provider and protector (the tramp), the sexually active fallen woman (the prostitute) who irresponsibly conceives a child she never intends to raise and becomes a dangerously unfit mother; the half-orphaned waif well on his way to becoming a thief (the neglected child)—were central not only to scientific charity and organized philanthropy that defined mainstream or orthodox liberal benevolence in the late nineteenth century, but to the organized labor movement that challenged them as well.

It is also interesting when we look at the almshouse notes to observe the snatches, such as these below, which show how an obsession with sexuality accompanied "Victorianism":

She says she complained of him, the child made outdoors, with him many times, always [had sex] outdoors ...

Their first criminal intimacy was in the house of Henry Burrage where she was a domestic and he was a boarder ... they were left alone in the house January last. He came to her room about January 15 and they had intercourse twice and again on January 18 and three or four times after ...

The child [was] made [at] his father's house on June 1, 1871. The criminal contact several times in yard adjacent to house. [There was] no promise of marriage until [she was] pregnant.

Her stepfather and she used to work out in the fields and sometime in January last, Sullivan and she became criminally intimate, first in the Cow House and occasionally after that, in the field's outer buildings and the "dwelling" house until one week before she left Ireland April last ...

Of course, the interviewers and recorders would justify their detailed queries by their need to discover who the father of the child was, to determine his whereabouts, to assess legal blame, and to confirm the date of pregnancy. Yet many of the details contained in these entries of the 1870s above seem extraneous to us, such as where the sex occurred and how many times couples had intercourse. One gets the distinct feeling that the almshouse and state agents were having quite the time doing these interviews!

The Victorian construction of a "good" girl as compared with the sexualized "other" was based on the belief in a kind of "slippery slope" theory of sexual morality that actually reinforced the gap between the social classes by creating a self-fulfilling prophecy. In the case below of Ida Hackett (1873) we see the Victorian fears of the slippery slope—a fall from sexual purity leading to prostitution—presumably coming true:

20 [year old woman admitted] from Boston with syphilis ... She was born in Ohio first remembers living in Rochester when she was 7 years of age then came to Boston and has been living there and Beverly since.... Father Samuel Chase who is a large real estate owner in Beverly. Mother's second husband is Charles Seaman.... Ida says she was seduced by a Nathan Stanley, a married man and church member of Beverly some four years ago and after that was more or less common. In the summer of 1871 she was with child fathered by Albert Preston of Beverly and because of the circumstance the mother turned her out of her house. She was arrested and committed to the House of Correction in Ipswich for vagrancy for six months. Her child [was] born there [in] August 187? child lived for two months then died in Boston on Worcester Street where Ida was a wet nurse. For over a year since then she has been mistress to George Reed

of Boston who she says [was] an overseer of a graveyard. She has been an inmate of a House of Ill fame at 49 Melrose Street that was kept by Fannie Howard. She has also been inmate of the Dorchester Industrial School from age eight until she was thirteen years old. She got syphilis five or six months ago. She thinks she caught it from Rufus McNeil with whom she was for some time criminally intimate. She says she came here from the home of the New England Moral Society of 6 Oak Place. She says that two of the lady managers are her guardians, a Mrs. Smith and a Mrs. John Kilton that also had an illegal child ...

On the face of it, like other cases recorded at Tewksbury, here were the worst fears of the dominant morality of the time realized: a "seduction at an early age" (although today, of course, 18 would not be considered terribly young), leading to other affairs without benefit of marriage (she became a "mistress"), and finally this leads her (inevitably) into a "house of ill fame." Yet the case gives a good example of how the response to her transgression, her expulsion from her middle-class house and her imprisonment, might very well have set the course for her future. An 18-year-old woman thrown from her family support at this time would have had little or no way to earn much of a living. In fact prostitution often paid far more than the most common women's job, domestic service. Compounding her eviction from home was her punishment, being sent to the House of Correction in Ipswich, which indeed would have further decreased her employability and set her on a track to survive however she could. In the House of Correction, no doubt, she made further contacts connecting her to the underworld of prostitution. D'Emilio and Freedman argue in their history of sexuality that "women who did not achieve the ideal of purity were considered to have 'fallen' literally into lower class" since sexual and moral purity were so central to bourgeois respectability. Here we have an example of sexual transgressions moving a middle-class woman into the lower classes at least at the time she was admitted to Tewksbury.

In addition to the cases of women "gone bad," the inmate records also reveal actual cases of other Victorian fears, such as brutal assaults by men, and the exploitation of women by employers and by the affluent. Rapes certainly are recorded, such as:

[1867] Flora Nickerson 18 years old, she was born in Prince Edward Island ... single, operative ... pregnant. The father of her child [is] George Duncan [a] machinist on [the] Lawrence Corporation. The child [was] made about December 1st. [She was] raped by him in lonely place out of city in revenge for refusing to marry him which she did for she heard he was married. [She will be] sick [e.g., due to deliver] in three months ...

[1876] Alice Scott 16 years old she was born in Baltimore, colored ... she came to New Bedford in August 1873 ... There since, working as a domestic except for some two months as a chamber girl at the Mansion House, [she] says while at the latter place doing chamber work she was caught in a room by one of the boarders—a white man—of a concert troupe room, [she] thinks five months ago and he caught her in the room and threw her on the bed and had connection with her. He was with her for two hours, says she has been with no others. She did not mention it to any one.

Although there is no way of knowing how many women were coerced into sex according to modern standards of law, Victorian officials, at least in Massachusetts at this time, seemed to be careful to record allegations of force, and to state them clearly in the records. There were only one or two occasions where officials noted that the woman's credibility might be weak due to earlier allegations of immoral conduct.

Coerced or at least highly exploitative sexual encounters with men possessing economic or social power were recorded in detail in these particular years as well. An entry from 1873, for example:

Josephine Barney 19 from Lowell pregnant admitted on June 16 from Boston. [She was] born in Canada [and] left Quebec on October 1872 ... [she is] single, [a] domestic and operative. She became pregnant by Dr. Moody, a married man. [She?] says her sister Jennie Bermea was a domestic in Moody's family, [and] Josephine was there on a visit to her one forenoon and Moody had criminal contact in a room off the kitchen where he slept. [This was] sometime in November last, she has been with him only once ... She had filed a complaint against the doctor and it [was] tried on June 24, 1873, the case was continued and the defendant must leave the state. Dr. G.D. Moody an [illegible] doctor who resides in Ayer City and is 52 year[s] old with whom her sister resided. Moody told them that Josephine had a womb complaint and nothing would cure her but sexual intercourse and Moody applied the remedy in person and telling her that if he got her pregnant, he would look out for her. [She was] sent to Canada [on] June 24.

Although still a small minority of the cases, more prevalent than the above were cases where children of employers, usually employers of domestics, had sex with those who later came to Tewksbury.

[1893] Ida McGeorge 15 years old admitted from Boston on January 14 she was born in St. John, New Brunswick, Canada, she is single, a cook ... She became pregnant about two weeks after landing by a John Geldert of Islington, he is off for three weeks, she was working in his family ...

[1890] Margaret Feeley admitted February 26, 22 years old, born in Ireland, pregnant, domestic ... The father of her child is John Bourne at #83 Common Street in Lawrence. She has been doing housework for his mother ...

[1880] Salia Cunningham 21 years old admitted from Gloucester on February 4 pregnant, she was born in Cape Sable Island, Nova Scotia and landed in Gloucester on May 1, 1880 ... single, domestic . . . the father of her child is George Lovett of Gloucester. [He is the] son of John H. Lovett in whose family she lived, he has gone west, the family has means. [She will be] sick [e.g., pregnant] in March last, a warrant is out against Lovett ...

[1865] Ellen Morin 20 years old [and] born in Ireland and landed in Boston in 1856 on [the ship] 'Mother of Ireland.' Her parents [are] in Ireland. She came out with her sister, Mary, wife of Charles Vismal who lived in Boston. Single, pregnant, the father of child is John Kelly of Randolph, a married man and in whose family she has been living [for the] past two years ...

As I will return to, the vast majority of women who came into the almshouse were not victims of rape or exploitation, but no doubt stories such as those above confirmed Victorian beliefs and mores, not only among officials, but among the inmates as well.

PUNISHING SEX: THE RISE AND FALL OF IMPRISONING MOTHERS AND PUTATIVE FATHERS

As one would expect of the home of the Puritans, Massachusetts had a fairly strict and stable set of statutes regarding sexuality. However, as we shall see, the law had a lot more "bark than bite" and served as a theoretical model of punishment. Consistency and severity of punishment declined over the years in regards to the treatment of both sexes.

In relation to extramarital sex, men were held to a standard of law that held severe penalties for adultery, bigamy, seduction, and bastardy. While all laws reflect morality, the key focus of male behavior in many ways was property and financially driven; in being adulterous, for example, the male was seizing another's property, and in seduction and producing an illegitimate child, he was, first, violating another male's potential property, and then leaving the Commonwealth with the financial responsibility for another mouth to feed. Women, of course, were held to moral standards of adultery and bigamy, but were also held to much vaguer and more subjective, non-property-based standards of morality—such as "lewd and lascivious conduct," "crimes against chastity," or "promoting prostitution" or "night walking." To be classified as "lewd" was chiefly a determination of local constables, and to dress "provocatively" or talk to a man publicly in a lewd fashion could get a woman a reputation as a "common prostitute." The word "common" in the statute (the same is true for "common" drunkards) meant one displayed attributes typical of a type; it did not require proof that you were indeed a prostitute (or an alcoholic in the case of a common drunkard)!

The dominant powers of the time would have held the laws fair to women, and even more pro-women than men. As noted, women were deemed, at least in the ideal, as asexual and passive, and therefore incapable of initiating sexual acts. Hence, in a case of alleged "seduction," the male was chiefly held responsible. The rub of course, in addition to selective enforcement, was that for those women, particularly lower-class ones, who openly violated Victorian codes, the "protection" of the law disappeared. Having acted as a "loose woman" or being known "commonly" as unchaste turned the tables because the woman alleged to behave in this way was no longer a woman in a moral sense. Men in bastardy and other legal proceedings such as divorce used the allegations of immoral behavior frequently because it was the one type of behavior which could mitigate the usual assumption of the male guilt in sexuality and his patriarchal responsibility for supporting his wife and children.

Table 5.1, showing the number of commitments of women to the workhouse at Bridgewater for having sex out of wedlock and the number of potential warrants for men wanted in bastardy proceedings discussed in the almshouse notes reflects (with some caveats below) the rather meager actual policing of the law. Of 241 cases of women coming to the almshouse with pregnancies out of wedlock, only 24, or slightly under a tenth, were sentenced to Bridgewater. All those sentenced were before 1877 and the most extensive use of the sentencing was in the two sample years of the 1860s when ten of forty-five women, or almost two in nine, were sentenced. Forty-three men who were putative fathers, or a little more than a sixth of these men, had warrants initiated or proposed against them, and again the highest numbers were in the early years, the 1870s, when nearly one in four of those sampled were possibly prosecuted in bastardy proceedings.

There are some caveats to the data above. Regarding the female inmates, I did not include the fairly small number in the sample who

**Table 5.1 Commitments to the Workhouse of Women and Warrants
for Fathers Tewksbury Sample, 1865–1895**

Decade	Number in sample	Mothers sent to workhouse specifically for out-of-wedlock sex*	Warrants for fathers proposed/issued
1890s (1890–95)	55	0	7 (12.7%)
1880s	39	0	4 (10.3%)
1870s	102	14 (13.7%)	25 (24.5%)
1860s (1865–67)	45	10 (22.2%)	7 (15.6%)
Total	N = 241	24 (10%)	43 (17.8%)

*e.g., not committed for prostitution, alcoholism, vagrancy, and other offenses

were specifically labeled as prostitutes. These, approximately two dozen or more inmates, are too small a number to make generalizations about. It may be that some of these women, many of whom were sent to Bridgewater, were innocent of actual prostitution, but I have no way of judging. Secondly, while the archived notes routinely give dates of discharge and destinations of discharged inmates, there is no certainty that more of the women did not go to the Bridgewater workhouse at a later date due to delays in making a criminal case or for other reasons. For the men, the major limitation is indicated in the heading: many times a woman said she was filing a warrant or the state board of charities would do so, but without examining every court record we cannot know if such suits were all filed, much less if a man was convicted. I have, however, included in the cases in Table 5.1 where the notes indicated a financial settlement or that arrest was attempted but the male could not be located.

While unfortunately the archives themselves do not give information on what caused the sharp declines in policing, likely, the reasons were different. There seemed little political or intellectual disagreement at the time about the male responsibility for financial support (if not marriage) of those who were victims of seduction. However, in practice, it was always very difficult to find the actual men, and in most cases, to the dismay of moralists, few had resources to support their children and sexual partners. On the other hand, as the Victorian narrative of seduction and sympathy for the female increased (if in a condescending way), sentiment moved from sending women guilty of out-of-wedlock sex to jail or the workhouse (though this was not the case for those they viewed as "hardened" prostitutes). Instead, by the last decades of the nineteenth century the rise of special homes for unmarried and "fallen" women who might have had some experience with prostitution (such as the Magdalen homes) began replacing the jail term. Some historians have debated how positive such changes were, as they tended to replace the almshouse or workhouse with highly structured levels of social control which entered into all realms of the life of the "client" more intrusively than earlier forms of control. Indeed, while we do not have much information about actual day-to-day life in the Bridgewater workhouse, likely the conditions there were only slightly worse than at Tewksbury. The large number of inmates with relatively few staff made the main dangers of the workhouse disease and squalor rather than the "punishment" of back-breaking work or isolation. Workhouses generally by this time had little or no meaningful work to distribute, and escapes from Bridgewater were also fairly common.

Even in the years when some women were sentenced to the Bridgewater workhouse after coming into Tewksbury, it is difficult from the notes to tell the reasons why one woman was punished and another not. For example, in the 1867 sample, we have the highest rate of commitment in any one year, nine of sixteen pregnant women being sent to Bridgewater. In the abstract, one would think that those admitting to fewer sexual encounters rather than numerous ones, those who had more extenuating circumstances (seduction, claims of possible force or deceit), and those who engaged the officials' favor ("a good girl") would be less likely to be sent to Bridgewater. However, this was not always the case. One factor working *for* a woman was if she came from afar. After all, cost was probably the major factor in the minds of officials. So that year Ellen Jones, a 26-year-old woman from Maine, who admitted contracting syphilis by "going with men," was sent back to Bath, Maine, presumably with the idea that she was now their problem. Another point to keep in mind is that the almshouse was not a prison, and had no, or only token security, so that frequently women (and men) "absconded," or just left. In 1872, a sample year in which nine of the ten women admitted were sentenced to Bridgewater, four women, including two labeled as "bad women" and one as "badly diseased," absconded from the almshouse, likely fearing that once they gave birth they might be sentenced to the workhouse.

When we put individuals side by side, it is difficult to determine why one inmate was sentenced and the other not. For example, in 1867 two women named Mary Welch were admitted to Tewksbury, each of whom was born in Ireland and worked as a domestic. Yet the older Mary, age 25, was sentenced to Bridgewater, while her 20-year-old namesake was not. The first Mary said "the father of her child [was] Pat Herring [who] was working in Worcester three or four months ago ... She stated that she was engaged to him for two years and getting ready to be married when he left her." The notes seem to reveal that almshouse staff believed her, as they stated "[she is a] very nice girl." Still, on June 13, 1867, she was sentenced to Bridgewater. The 20-year-old Mary Welch was pregnant by her husband William through a forced marriage. Not unusually for forced marriages in bastardy proceedings, once the named man married her, he then left her. She was discharged in September 1867. We can only speculate whether the married Welch (though her child was conceived out of wedlock) was perceived more favorably than the engaged Welch, or whether those making the decision to prosecute (probably at the state Board of Charities and Corrections) had different information or considerations. It does seem clear that the note takers did not always have much relation to how the individual inmate's future was determined.

These inconsistent decisions (at least from the modern reader's view) continued over the years. In 1876, the last year any number of pregnant women were sentenced to Bridgewater (at least four of fifteen, although one died and three were discharged to the State Board of Charities, which might suggest some action was taken), we again have puzzling questions. Why was Etta Brown, 23, who admitted she worked at a "house of ill fame," able to escape sentencing? A domestic and "saloon girl," Brown was pregnant by a Frank Lyons, a bartender. This fact pattern would not have impressed the officials of Massachusetts who tended to be not only virulently against brothels, but also advocates for temperance. Many saw saloons as being little different than brothels. In any event, Brown was discharged on June 1. By contrast, 18-year-old Elizabeth Heaney, a recent Scottish immigrant who was impregnated in a Holyoke mill by Homer Herrick, the son of the overseer of the card rooms at the mill, was sentenced to Bridgewater. The younger Herrick had already "disappeared from Holyoke a month ago" and again there is no assessment in the notes that her story was untrue. Perhaps those who decided on prosecution believed the workhouse had a rehabilitative effect, in which case those like Brown who had already "fallen" were less worthy of effort than the younger and perhaps more redeemable Heaney. But this is purely speculative and would be exceptional from what we know of the history of this time.

While the archived notes certainly support post-1960s historians' view of patriarchal social control (and the written comments from

1877 to 1895 continue to reveal stinging words about certain women), the treatment of the women presented here is complex. A small minority of women who were sexually active outside of marriage were ever punished by officials, even in the 1865–1876 period. Later, even when a woman was labeled as a "harlot" or "strumpet," we have no indication that any action was taken (even a referral to a home for unmarried women). While women may have faced later charges, the state ceased to police the women coming into Tewksbury, or so it appears. The decades after the Civil War seem to show that at least in Massachusetts there was a transition from a strong belief in coercive punishment for women who might take the first step in the "slippery slope" toward "falling," to a more rehabilitative focus in which the state supported specialized homes for unmarried women.

In contrast to the women, who, because they entered the almshouse either because of a difficult pregnancy or other need for help, were literally a "captive audience," the fathers of the "illegitimate" children were more distant geographically. The numbers of attempts at arrest were always limited by the fact that some women were made pregnant in Ireland, Canada, and faraway states, and, perhaps as significantly, by the desire of some women to not name the father or even to give misleading information. Early on, the almshouse officials expressed such annoyance that in the case of Ellen Morin (1865) the clerk said he "would suggest that she be retained in the Institution till she tells the truth" about her relationship. Later, however, almshouse officials accepted several women refusing to name their sexual partners. Many times, women did not refuse outright to provide information, but indicated that they did not know the full name of the man or that the man was "off." In the early years, when the notes of state agent Nash were included in the record, we gain more insight into what the officials found when they investigated in the community looking for the men. However, afterwards, we do not have such detailed information. It is clear that in the turbulent depression years of the 1870s there was no way that the vast number of cases could have been investigated, and one gets the sense that by the second half of the 1870s the energy to investigate and prosecute had much diminished. By 1880 and later, the notes themselves seem perfunctory and often report only the name of putative father and his occupation or town of origin.

Moreover, despite the drama of forcible arrest under the bastardy laws and the police search for the male, the main objective was a financial one. That is, while the drama of arrest certainly served as a moral symbol, the key objective for both the local Overseers of the

Poor and the almshouse and other state agents was to have the father support the woman and child. In reviewing the 43 cases in the sample in which warrants were issued or proposed, I found (although not every case provides an occupation) no men listed as unemployed or as laborers (as indicated earlier, the most frequent occupation of poorer men). Rather, the men who were pursued were machinists, plasterers, blacksmiths, shoemakers, fishermen, farmers, or iron workers, not (with a few exceptions) men with great wealth, but those who could afford to provide for their families. Of course, nowhere in the law was the male's ability to pay referenced, but given limited resources, no doubt, both among the women who employed attorneys and the state Board of Charities and Corrections (who for the earlier years of this period would act as their representative in court) strategic decisions were made as to whom to prosecute. Those who had money were not only a more judicious choice, but were easier to find, as they were more settled in a community where they had an address and often property.

Some men did choose to marry their partners upon threat of bastardy proceedings. In the sample notes, eleven men were recorded as having done so. While many, such as George Kingston, who married Ann in 1872 in the Lowell, Massachusetts, central police station, turned around "and refuse[d] to support [his wife] or have anything to do with her," there were those like James Moore, a carpenter, who had been living without the sacrament of marriage, who when forced by her father to marry, according to the notes "provided a good home for her [Mary]." Because of the conflation of all unmarried sex, at least in Massachusetts (including "living in sin," which was the dominant mode of "marrying" in the lower classes), the nature of relationships discussed here are very different. In the follow-up of those admitted for out-of-wedlock sex, we find (see Table 5.2) that many years later at least four women were still married to men who were forced to marry. Two of these women were still married to the same man after more than twenty years.

While many notations of bastardy proceedings leave us ignorant as to the outcome by noting that the woman had obtained a lawyer (or the state provided one) or that the man was now jailed, there are some financial settlements indicated. In 1865, John Florence, a fisherman, settled with Mary Glassed for $65.00; in 1874, Frank Brigel settled with Eliza Killips for $75.00; in 1875, William Grey paid $200.00 in the case of Mary Logan; and in 1895, a Most Kettough settled for $175.00 in the case of a Catherine Burns. These settlements must be considered modest as they probably did not include attorneys' fees and other costs.

Table 5.2 Data from Censuses and Other Sources about Single Pregnant Women Who Were Inmates at Tewksbury

Total = 60

Died within several years (14)

Name	Year of admission	Census or other record
Malvina Ahm	1875	died February 2, 1875 at Tewksbury (no cause of death)
Anna Barker	1875	died Bridgewater workhouse 1876 from phtsis
Eva Bowen	1875	died in 1880 of consumption
Catherine Collins	1876	died 1876 at Tewksbury "pyemia"
Margaret Harrington	1880	died 1880 at Tewksbury (no cause of death)
Elizabeth Heaney	1876	died 1876 at Bridgewater workhouse pneumonia
Winnie Hessian	1872	died 1878 at Bridgewater workhouse phtsis
Ella Johnson	1875	died 1875 Tewksbury phtsis
Hannah McQuade	1873	died 1873 Tewksbury hemmorhage placenta
Sarah Savin	1865	died 1865 Tewksbury (no cause of death)
Julia Seales	1882	died 1882 in Boston consumption
Carrie Stevens	1873	died 1878 Tewksbury syphilis
Clarissa Wheeler	1873	died 1874 in Worcester "inflammation of bowel"
Ellen Whipple	1877	died 1877 at Tewksbury (no cause of death)

Found single some years after (27)

Name	Year of admission	Census or other record
Margaret Beaton	1874	1880 servant
Catherine Belcher	1866	1870 no occupation (with family of origin)
Martha Blunt	1875	1880 servant (died 1900)
Mary Carter	1867	1870 works in a silk mill
Sarah Clark	1866 & 1870	1880 servant
Minnie Cobb	1895	1900 inmate Salvation Army (for fallen women)
Matilda Connors	1874	1880 housekeeping; 1894 directory laundress; 1920 inmate Haverhill almshouse
Mary E. Davis	1882	1900 servant
Catherine DeLory	1875	1880 servant
Mary J. Devine	1885	1893 Lawrence directory cashier
Nellie Haskins	1871	1880 working in a shoe factory 1910 dressmaker

Table 5.2 continues on next page

Table 5.2 continued

Table 5.2 continues on next page

Found single some years after (27)

Name	Year of admission	Census or other record
Mary Holt	1893	1900 servant
Kate Joy	1867	1870 inmate at Bridgewater workhouse
Ana Leonard	1870	1880 servant
Anne Long	1895	1900 laundress 1910 no occupation (family head with children)
Sarah Mann	1870	1880 house girl
Susan McLaughlin	1895	1920 hotel laundry worker
Anne Metcalf	1865	1870 keeping house (with children), 1871 died
Emma Phife	1895	1910 servant 1920 no occupation
Emily Powell (Mary Coran)	1874	1880, 1900 inmate Clinton, Maine, almshouse
Carrie Pumphrey (Oakley)	1875	1890 Washington, DC, directory clerk at the "bur stat"
Elise Ruffley	1885	1900 nurse 1920, 1930 with son lawyer
Maria Sanders	1874	1880 servant
Delia Stafford	1880	1910 no occupation with niece
Anna Suza	1890	1920 spinner 1930 no occupation (with children)
Emily Wardman	1865	1870 servant 1880, 1910, 1920 no occupation (boarder)
Margaret Webster	1871	1880 state almshouse of RI at Cranston

Found married some years after (19)
*married to father of child

Name	Year of admission	Marriage
Mary Alton	1875	1882 to Patrick Meyers, mechanic
Clara Ayers	1865	1866 to Samuel Augustine Cook a mariner 1870 husband works in arms factory
Ruth Bateman	1895	1898 to Louis Dechene, carpenter, 1900–1910 together, carpenter, 1920 divorced, she a stitcher in shoe factory
*Selma Bostrum	1890	1889 to Charles Holden hostler single 1900, 1920 Northampton State Hospital (inmate)
Annette Carlson	1882	1885 married Peter Carlson, 1900 furniture maker, 1920 widow, continues to own home
*Mary Erickson	1885	1900 married 20 years farmer, owned land, Mary 1930 widow lodger

Table 5.2 continues on next page

Table 5.2 continued

Name	Year of Admission	Marriage
Lizzie Fleming	1873	1874 married William Augustus Hunting a farmer 1880 a laborer, 1900 lamplighter
Alice Francis	1895	1896 married Clarence Ringwood a driver. She died 1907
Mary Freeman	1877	1880 married Francis Murphy teamster, 1920 Mary manager of a ranch
Lizzie Garfield	1872	Married in 1890 to L. Bradford Howard, photographer
Jennie Grafton	1876	1878 married William J. Jackson farmer 1900 farmer in Maine 20+ years, owned land, died 1904
Eliza Killips	1874	1878 married David Egan rail brakeman
Clara Norton	1865	1866 married to James Patterson (no occupation available)
Eva Parker	1880	1884 married Andrew J. Smith a coachman 1900, 1910 still together, 4 children he is a teamster, own property
*Mary Perry	1875	1875 Joseph Perry (in Police Court) married 20+ years 1880 laborer, four children 1900 fisherman
Lizzie Pluff	1895	1902 married Albert Frink a laborer, 1920 he is a bleacher in dye shop (at least 18 years married)
Louisa Roberts	1875	1875 married Albert Saunders a machinist 1880 single again, boarder
Elizabeth Sisson	1873	1877 married to Erastus Avery Brown 1880 husband a farmer
*Mary Train	1874	1874 married Edward Train, 1880 married working in a poultry plant

Nevertheless, the prospect of bigger dollars seemed to excite almshouse note takers and lawyers. In 1873, in the case of Margaret Walsh, for example, her attorney, a Mr. Pingrey of Pittsfield (Massachusetts) reported that William Newbolt, the accused, was "worth $2,000 or $3,000 and also has money in the bank." In later years, when the state seemed less involved, private parties pursued the putative fathers in expectation of money and vengeance. In 1893, for example, the brother of Amelia Millios, described as a wealthy cigar manufacturer from Spain, traveled to Massachusetts to obtain an attorney, and according to the notes the brother expected to have the man responsible jailed "in a few days."

Robert Silverman, who studied civil litigation in the Boston courts in the last twenty years of the nineteenth century, suggested that such cases had "disappointing results." He describes them as being a bit of a "paper tiger." The proceedings were quasi-criminal in nature, and guilt beyond a reasonable doubt did not have to be established. "Nonetheless," he notes, "the law in action did not favor the prosecutrix. Adjuctication was slow ... suits usually dragged on four months at least, sometimes for several years. A prosecutrix's reward for her perseverance was disappointing. Only one in four won a favorable decision, and the awards were paltry, based largely on the ability of the father to pay, not on the financial needs of the mother and child. Furthermore, there was little the court could do when a father did not pay. If his whereabouts were known, he could be jailed, but that provided no funds to mother and child." In a study done in 1914 by the Boston Children's Bureau, the figures were even lower, with only 13 percent of illegitimacy cases going to trial and only 7 percent of the total leading to maintenance awards.

No doubt this explains somewhat the move of the almshouse and the State Board of Charities out of the "bastardy" policing business. While in the 1872–1874 sample years we have extremely high rates of at least possible suits (four of ten, nine of eighteen, and three of ten in the three years, respectively), by the 1880s and 1890s we have only one or two a (sample) year, or the totals represented in Table 5.1. Further, the cases after 1877 were almost always of employed private attorneys, not Commonwealth of Massachusetts attorneys.

THE NONDRAMATIC REALITY OF VICTORIAN RELATIONSHIPS

In contrast to what appears to us today as the overheated language of Victorian descriptions of relationships ("criminal intimacies," "bastardy," "harlots," etc.), the almshouse notes provide us with enough information about at least some years (the 1870s in particular) to question (from our own point of view) what all the fuss was about. One of the reasons so many women were classified as having "criminal intimacies" to begin with was the older American law (enforced still in Massachusetts in this period) which deemed couples living together without the benefit of formal marriage as being illegal (in many other states "common law" marriages were recognized). These couples produced a significant number of the cases of "out of wedlock" births in the 1870s. Beyond this, a large number of liaisons described by the notes look like any relationships we would anticipate young people having, mutual relations between coworkers, boarders, and men and women meeting at dances or other amusements. Finally, there are some inmates, in addition to the residents of houses of ill fame, who, contrary to their own interest, did admit to casual sex or what today might be called promiscuous sex, and these cases, while relatively a small minority, certainly must have reinforced the fears of the officials who took down their stories.

The years 1871–77, in particular, provide us with a rich documentary history of these women's lives. Of the less than one hundred cases in 1871–77, at least fifteen involved women who were living with a partner or engaged to be married. For example, in 1873 in the Mary Moore case mentioned earlier, the father of Moore had her paramour prosecuted for bastardy, but the reality was that "her criminal intimacy existed with Moore for six months prior to the marriage and at one time they lived together as man and wife on Avery Place." The comment that Moore "has since lived with and provided a good home for her" afterwards is not so surprising then if we see the two were "trying out" their relationship by living together. In 1875, Anna Barker, a 21-year-old African American woman who was sent to the Bridgewater workhouse (and indeed had previously served a one-year sentence there), was engaged to be married to a Samuel Smith, a waiter at Harvard Dining College. She stated they "had [already] purchased part of the furniture." Often the women cited financial reasons for not marrying. For in addition to the previously cited costs of the marriage ceremony and license itself, the expectation of parents and couples themselves was that the couple would have some sort of financial stability. In 1876, 26-year-old Anna Donnelly was pregnant by a Patrick Curry with whom she had recently entered into a forced marriage at St. Paul's Catholic Church. She had been pressed to have him arrested, but she stated "he would have married her before but [he] had no money and she was obliged to come here [i.e., the almshouse]." Curry still lived with his father, Thomas, in Worcester.

Many parents had rejected their daughters' suitors for economic reasons, and this paradoxically proved to be a legal problem, which fact the immigrant families may not have understood. In 1877, Mary Freeman, the daughter of a recent Austrian immigrant, entered the almshouse pregnant as a result of a "criminal contact" with a man named Thomas Gallagher, whom she had known for five years. According to Freeman, "he [had] offered to marry her in June last, but [her] father would not consent as he was out of work and she was the only support of [her] family." Mary Roach, a 22-year-old inmate in 1882, who had just delivered a child, had recently landed in Boston from Ireland in the summer of 1881. She stated "she was sent by her father who objected to her marrying the father of her child . . . William Ford of County Clare." With almost all the women being from different cultures than the dominant Yankee one, it is difficult to tell if they understood that "living together" was violating the law. For example, Ann Marshall, an 1874 inmate, was 35 and from the Western Islands (now the Azores) and spoke no English. She was described as "single, pregnant by Joaquin Frae of Fayal, [the] child was made in Boston, she [had] cohabited with him as his wife." Yet what she and Frae considered their relationship as opposed to the almshouse we will never know. It is true that with the exception of Barker (who had secondary syphilis) none of these women were sent to the workhouse, and in this sense, we can say living together or being engaged was certainly some defense against the most extreme punishment for sexual relations. However, the fact that they were described as "criminally intimate" suggests how the 1870s morality of Massachusetts law forced both women and men of the lower classes and of immigrant groups into deviant categories that they themselves may not have recognized.

For most of the women admitted to Tewksbury with out-of-wedlock births, the descriptions of how they met their partners were unremarkable. For the entire period studied, coworkers were the most common partners. To take just some examples:

> [1890] Mary Hickerman . . . a Finnish immigrant . . . The father of her child is Arthur Gurthier, he [was] formerly employed in the Old Colony Home [doing] kitchen work [where] she worked there too.

> [1880] Minnie Payne . . . domestic in the family of Mr. John Weston [at] 17 Glenn Street, Somerville in May last and while there became pregnant by one Pierce Kelley also in the employ of Mr. Weston . . .

[1877] Rosa Silva domestic, she is pregnant by a Max Percree a German and a baker, both worked in the family of a Mr. Lepers, he went to her chamber one day in June and persuaded her to have intercourse with him and continued for several weeks ...

[1873] Hannah McQuaid single, operative, [the] father of Ellen is John Goulding of Lowell also is an operative. She first knew him about one year ago while they worked at Hamilton Mill ...

[1867] Mary Carter 20 years old, she was born in Ludlow. single, operative ... she was an attendant in N.L.H. [Northampton Lunatic Hospital] [for] four months.... pregnant. The father of her child [is] John Bracken ... he was a farmer at N.L.H. [Northampton Lunatic Hospital] sick in August ...

The meeting of coworkers does not much surprise us, but at least in the 1860s and 1870s social observers who bemoaned the "decline of the family" disapproved. Such "crowding of the sexes" was seen as pathological and leading to ruination. Citing post–Civil War sources, an early twentieth-century family historian quotes the dismay that traditionalists felt:

Communistic urban habits in work and in dissipation contribute to the swamping of the narrower and simpler family life.... If the morals of a young woman are not destroyed by the associates in the workshop, she stands an excellent chance of becoming stripped of them in the house she has made her temporary home.

According to an 1875 book by Anzel Ames, *Sex in Industry,* there was total "disregard paid for the decencies of life such as the location and condition of toilets, the laxity with which clothing is worn, the positions [that] are assumed in the process of manufacture, and the constant association of both sexes." Of course, men and women had always worked together on farms, but the "simpler life" of the pre–Civil War period often had only family members working together and perhaps a few farm laborers. The crowding together in big cities of large numbers of men and women, and people of different cultures and norms, was shocking to those used to the old ways. To some extent, as with the issue of seduction and prostitution noted above, reformers and labor leaders used this fear as well to try to improve working conditions, and in some cases to later exclude women from some workplaces by protective labor legislation.

However, the panic about women and men working together was overshadowed by a consensus (at least among the more respectable classes) about boarding homes, which were seen by some as virtual dens of iniquity. James Burn worried that "demoralization comes from boarding houses; in consequence of the notions of personal liberty and self-sufficiency entertained by young people of both sexes it is next to impossible to exercise anything like a salutary control over their conduct." He further noted, "I have reason to believe that both these girls were ruined as wives by the habit of living in boarding-houses, when left there without domestic occupation, and like all idle people, exposed to temptations of the worst kind." Here, although the almshouse notes reveal no official opinions, the fact that during the 1870s they pointed out the role of boarding houses in so many sexual encounters was surely not coincidental:

[1876] Mary Ganey She is single, a domestic. She is pregnant by a Francis Donnelly, about 28 years old, an Irishman [she] became acquainted with him in July 1874 in the House where he was a boarder and she a domestic, [the] criminal contact [was] in September 1875 in her chamber in Fay's Boarding House where she was a domestic and he a boarder, she was with him four or five times after, sometimes passing the night until four months ago ...

[1876] Anna Perkins ... 16 years old, she was born in Calais, Maine, and came to Boston from Eastport ... then went to Lowell to work in Merrimac Mill and boarded at Knapps at 135 Merrimac Corporation, there she met Frank Kennett whom she married in Nashua, New Hampshire on October 31, [they] boarded at 139 Merrimac Corporation three months and then went to New Bedford four weeks ago ...

[1873] Mary Owens 24. ... [she was] born in New Orleans. She left there when she was still an infant with her parents. ... single, domestic, the father of her child, John Hanley, is single. She first met him in Dedham in November 1872, he's a plasterer and she is an operative, they both boarded in the family of Patrick Tracey. Their first criminal contact was in her room about 12/15/72 in the evening and again a few evenings after in the parlor, he still boards with Mrs. Tracey ...

[1873] Clarissa Wheeler colored, 22 years old ... she was born in West Rutland, Vermont and was there until 1868, in Worcester off and on since ... single, seamstress ... pregnant by Lewis Brooks, colored of Worcester ... [note on side:] a student at Harvard College, she a domestic in a boarding house in Cambridge...

[1872] Kate Mulligan alias Milligan, 20, from Boston ... She was born in St. John, New Brunswick and landed in Boston in May or June ... single. The father of her child is Michael Cockray a blacksmith in Old Cambridge near Charles River Bridge ... The child [was] made at the house of Mr. James Jenner called the "Avenue House" where she was a domestic. Cockeray boarded there. The child made in August last [she was] outdoors with him twice ...

Placing ourselves back in this time in order not to be anachronistic, we can see how these relationships would be found troublesome by many contemporaries. Women like Perkins were obviously quite young, and particularly at a time when women reached menarche much later than today, they were especially young. No doubt even the older women, particularly those who were regarded (and sometimes labeled by the almshouse clerks) as "greenhorns," such as Irish immigrant Ganey, Canadian immigrant Mulligan, and rural young women such as Perkins and Wheeler, would have certainly been seen as having been taken advantage of. As early as the 1850s, concern about young people in the cities had stimulated the rise of the YMCAs, but these efforts were mostly focused on young men. In the aftermath of the Civil War and the movement of more women to the cities, new protective institutions such as "homes for the friendless" and other religious-sponsored homes were founded. While I found no references to these facilities in the archived notes, a fairly large percentage of the out-of-wedlock pregnancies in the 1870s were (as above) relations between domestics and residents of boarding homes rather than between two actual boarders. Whether this tendency was particular to the clientele at Tewksbury or represented other trends I do not know. The vast majority of unwed mothers at Tewksbury throughout its history were domestics in disproportionate numbers, so that no doubt is a factor in this finding.

Of course, as in any account involving the possibility of negative sanctions, there is the possibility of misrepresentation of facts in any number of these accounts. On a number of occasions, the note takers themselves put in writing their own opinion that something said was "a doubtful story." A woman named Anna Pooler in 1872, for example, claimed to have advertised for a position as housekeeper and a male who "responded to the advertisement" had "during the interview proposed marriage and to make it more binding had criminal contact within the hour, he [then] left her promising to return in a week or so, she has not seen him or heard of him since." One supposes the belief in Pooler's account was not helped by her admission that she had "had criminal contact" with other men in the past. The account of a Mary A. Coran in 1874 was called "very doubtful" when she claimed a policeman in Hallowell, Maine, was the father of her child, though the note takers noted "part of her story" (referring to other events) was "no doubt reliable." However, there is no way of testing the biases of the note takers or finding out what actually occurred in such private matters.

Yet, because of the bias of the Victorian officials, particularly in the early years of the study, I find it more surprising that some women admitted to casual or promiscuous sex when they could be sent to the workhouse or jail. In 1870, for example, Mary Flynn simply said that she did not know the name of the man she slept with. She had "met him on the street in Chelsea and [had] asked him to 'show her the way.'" In 1872, a Mary Leary, who was reported to be "badly diseased" (probably with syphilis), stated "she could not possibly tell who the father of her child was." Ellen Ayer, an 1874 inmate who had already been in reform school, evidently admitted to having sex with a black man whom she met "in a rum shop" and to having sex with him "while intoxicated." Eva Bowen, a 16-year-old 1875 inmate, was an art student in Boston who went to artist "Martin Hearn's studio [on] Hanover Street" to "see his pictures" and "then the intimacy continued all winter [while] she [was] attending [the] Massachusetts Normal Art School ... She then ran away from home" and "went to a house of ill fame where she got syphilis." Some accounts, such as that of Emma Jones, a 17-year-old inmate in 1876, are full of what the authorities would no doubt view as deviancies from the very start. Her mother had run away when she was young with a "handsome mulattoo [*sic*] man." Eventually Emma was placed at the State Industrial School and "put out." She later became a "mistress of Richard Gibbs ... [who] she thinks is the father of her unborn child," but she "ha[d] been with four or five other men," so could not be sure.

About one in five of the total cases of nonmarital sex describe such encounters or series of numerous sexual encounters. Although it is difficult to generalize to the whole population from such a number of cases, in some ways the narratives tend to speak not only against the reformers' tendency to view young women as hopeless victims of seduction, but also more modern notions of a demimonde in which the poorer classes were caught in a world of counternorms. Rather, the post–Civil War period through the end of the 1870s may have been a period analogous to others in American history, most famously the 1920s and 1960s–1970s, in which there was something of a sexual revolution, provoking in turn a corresponding moral panic and a period of sexual repression. The falling off of many of these statements about casual sex in the Tewksbury records after the late 1870s, while certainly in part due to the sparse narrative records overall, may also represent a decline in such "sexual revolution" as the Social Purity and other movements aimed at restricting sexuality began to succeed. This explains, I think, the paradox of such statements declining when the prosecution of sexual activity also declined in the 1880s and 1890s and hence such statements could be made without as much criminal risk.

What Became of the Women?

As noted earlier, the archival data freeze people in time and in the particular view of the note taker or the interaction of the note taker with the inmate when the notes were recorded. Any further information is helpful in providing us with a fuller view of the real people. Although use of census and genealogical records provided some information on about 90 of the 241 women in the sample, regarding what "became of them," I was able to get fuller information on 60 of the women, about one-fourth of the group.

Table 5.2 organizes the information on the sixty women into three categories; those who died relatively shortly after their admission, usually at the almshouse itself or at the Bridgewater workhouse (fourteen); those who were found in censuses or other data subsequent to their admission and were single (twenty-seven); and those who were found through vital statistics to have remarried (nineteen). Although the categorizing is somewhat arbitrary, in general, the deaths represent the extreme negative outcome as these women tended to die young, while the remarriages are at the opposite extreme since, because of the low economic status of most women and the few occupations open to poor women, they tended to do better economically than the single women.

Some facts about women, pregnancy, and the almshouse in the later nineteenth century are fairly clear from the table. The death rate was high for those who entered the almshouse and needed medical attention. Many of the women died in pregnancy, including certainly Malvina Ahm, Catherine Collins, Margaret Harrington, Elizabeth Heaney, Ella Johnson, Hannah McQuaid, and Ellen Whipple. Others besides Carrie Stevens may have died of syphilis, as this was not always entered as a cause of death in the records. For example, the records indicate Anna Barker and Eva Bowen had syphilis. The death rate did decline and there were no deaths in this sample after 1882. Among the women found afterwards who were single, the largest number, thirteen, were employed as servants or laundresses. This is not surprising as the women had entered with such occupations, and, in fact, the various "charitable" institutions such as the workhouse, the houses for fallen women, and others usually placed women out in the community into domestic service. A few, but not a large number were in other institutions. Kate Joy, who we met in Chapter 1, could not be found after 1870 when she was in the Bridgewater workhouse; Margaret Webster, who was in the Rhode Island state almshouse, had been in a mental hospital prior to her Tewksbury admission. Minnie Cobb, who five years after her admission was in a Salvation Army home, had a note in her record that a missionary was interested in her; and Emily Powell (alias Mary Coran) spent many years in the poorhouse in the small town of Clinton, Maine. As noted earlier, only a few women were married to the fathers of their children, who they had prosecuted or married under the threat of prosecution. Still Mary Perry remained married at least twenty-five years, and Mary Erickson at least twenty years.

Among those who did marry, the conventional statuses were higher than the single women, given women's occupations at the time. Ten women married carpenters, farmers (four), furniture makers, machinists, mechanics, photographers, or rail brakemen. In turn, at least four, but probably more, owned property. (Unfortunately, unless they were found through the census which indicates property ownership, we cannot easily determine this. Many women were located through vital statistics documenting their marriages, which in Massachusetts indicated occupations but not property ownership.) A decline in status can be seen when there was a later separation. For example, when Ruth Bateman divorced, at least as of the 1920 census, she was a factory worker, whereas earlier, being married to a carpenter, she did not work. Selma Bostrum, after her marriage broke up, became a patient in the Northampton State Mental Hospital in 1920. Still, among the sample of nineteen women, given that we have such limited information about what became of them long-term, the number of long-term marriages could be seen as reflecting more stability than might be anticipated. In addition to Erickson and Perry, already mentioned, Annette Carlson was married at least fifteen years, Lizzie Fleming at least twenty-six years, Jennie Grafton, twenty-six years (until her death in 1904), Eva Parker at least twenty-six years, and Lizzie Pluff, at least eighteen years. Several women did well from the point of view of upward mobility: Mary Freeman was in 1920 a manager of a stock ranch in Montana; Carrie Pumphrey (alias Oakley), although our information from a directory is abbreviated and therefore ambiguous, seems to have become a clerk at a government office. Elise Ruffley, though we must be cautious in interpreting the occupational label "nurse," which was used in many (nonprofessional) ways even in the early twentieth century, did live with an affluent son, an attorney, in an expensive house in her later years.

What is less evident simply from looking at the table is that (again recognizing our small sample) our modern (parallel to Victorian) instincts about what types of women would do well and what types would not, did not always prove accurate. For example, age of pregnancy is often seen in modern times as critical to the success of the mothers, which has caused a major late-twentieth-century campaign against "teen pregnancy." Yet the fourteen out of sixty inmates sampled who were teens fared no differently on average than their older peers. It is true that Eva Bowen, who was 16 years old on entrance to the almshouse, and Elizabeth Heaney, 18 years old, died young. But this is not true of the other twelve women. Ruth Bateman, 17, Lizzie Fleming, 19, Lizzie Garfield, 19, Eliza Killips, 19, Eva Parker, 19, and Louisa Roberts, 16, for example, did well in terms of the information we have. Nor even does our information about disease and sexuality always mean that the women fared badly. Lizzie Garfield, an 1872 inmate, had first been an inmate at 19 years old when the Commonwealth of Massachusetts prosecuted her first bastardy case. In 1872 she had syphilis and was reported to have lived at several houses of ill fame as well as bearing an out-of-wedlock child. While we have only a tidbit of information, she was alive at 40 in 1890 when she married a photographer after having been granted a divorce from a previous man. Although not in this table, there are three other women found in the overall sample who were reported to be involved in prostitution who later appear to have fared well. One interesting final sidelight is that a fair number of this sample (nine of sixty, or fifteen percent) were African American women. This is probably an artifact of the easier time I had locating those labeled "colored" or "black" in the records of New England where the numbers of nonwhites were low. In any event, African Americans are certainly overrepresented in several deaths (Barker, Johnson, Wheeler), but still a majority fared about as well as the whites (Blunt, Davis, Francis, Haskins, Mann, Roberts). Race and ethnicity in general would obviously be an interesting study as to their impact on how these women fared, although far more information would be needed on many of the women and the impact of other factors such as age, geography, and specific social class status.

Though one could wish for more information, based on what we know from the archives and census and other data, we can again conclude with the thought of the young women being "ordinary people" caught up in the definition of the times of "criminal intimacies." Of course, a few of the women died early due to venereal diseases or poor health care for pregnancies, some of which were likely complex. But, as the table suggests, the majority went on to lead unremarkable lives, as is true today for most women who have children from out-of-wedlock relationships.

SIX

Family Conflict
and Desertion

"[T]he tendency among the poor to wife and family desertion is more
mischievous than the tendency to patriarchal despotism."
Quoted in A. Calhoun, *A Social History of the American Family
from Colonial Times to the Present*

Oh, what was your name in the States?
Was it Thompson or Johnson or Bates?
Did you murder your wife and flee for your life?
Say what was your name in the states?"
Song sung in California (cited by Beverly Schwartzberg)

Although I have suggested that the cry of "a crisis" in the family has
been so common in American history as to be not a very reliable
indicator of much, there were plenty of real tragedies in the families
of the Gilded Age. Everyone from conservatives who wished to push
the clock back to the old agrarian way of life to radicals who criticized
capitalism as undermining family relations saw a negative impact
from the vast changes of the latter nineteenth century on the family.
Urbanization, industrialization, overcrowding, immigration, poverty,
and various forms of exploitation were among the many causes that
politicians, newsmen, and charity officials all identified. For the poorer
classes, not only was their behavior more visible and hence frightening
to the upper classes, but poor people do suffer more from the tragic
circumstances of life that unemployment, low wages, poor health,
overcrowding, and stress bring them. Hence, it is usually the poorest
that experience the most domestic violence and family "breakdown,"
along with social problems such as alcoholism.

This chapter will review first the cases of family abuse and other
severe family problems that came to the almshouse's attention, and

then move to the complex matter of desertion or separation and how we can evaluate it, as well as how it also structured the crimes of bigamy and adultery. Unquestionably, a reading of the almshouse records reveals a rather troubled picture of family life. It is generally the case that the "family," at least as traditionally defined, was hard to maintain under conditions of poverty and transience. When other ills such as domestic violence, alcoholism, or venereal disease are added in as well, it is no surprise that the almshouse was a temporary "home" for many disrupted families. It seems that most of the families so disrupted stayed apart, though not all.

"The Seamier Side" of the Family

From their origin, both the almshouse as an institution, and the Massachusetts State Almshouse at Tewksbury specifically, served a role as shelters for women fleeing abuse; abandoned, abused, and neglected children; and others who were maltreated in their families. It is likely that the functionaries who served in these institutions were among the earliest experts in what we now call domestic violence and abuse and neglect of children as well as exploitation of other types. For example, cases of physical abuse of wives by husbands, although never numerically large at any one time, occurred in almost each sampled year:

[1865] Ellen Hylie, 31 and her children Ellen 9, John 7, Margaret 1 year and four months, she was born in County Clare Ireland [and] married her husband Jereh a laborer over 40. He lives on Williams Street No 10. [She] married him in Roxbury [in a ceremony performed] by father Lynch. He abused her [on] July 4th and kicked her in the eye which is much hurt ...

[1873] Frances Forrest and [her] baby Frank from Boston well, baby is feeble admitted [on] June 23. She was born in Derby, England and landed in New York [on] June 1863 per [the] steamer "City of New York." She went directly to her husband Robert Forrest in Philadelphia ... She married Robert in England. He came over 6 months before she did and landed in NY ... Her daughter, Amelia, is nine and lives at the home at 1 Pine Place, Boston. Their seven other children are dead. Her husband Robert got drunk and came home and broke up housekeeping by throwing the furniture out the windows and beating his wife. He was arrested and sent to the House of Correction for assault and battery for a six month term ...

[1885] Ellen Burns from Boston admitted on January 19, [she is] 25 years old, she was born in Ireland, she is married. She landed in New York in April 1884 aboard the Steamer "Baltic" and went direct to Fall River. She has been there and in Boston since. Her husband Patrick came over with her and [is] now under sentence for assault for beating her. Her parents Michael and Joanna, her father is dead, her mother is living in Ireland ...

Men battered by their wives, and even allegedly poisoned, were present as well:

[1875] Michael Cook 53 years old admitted from Boston on September 10, with his sons James, 10 born in Boston, Herbert 8 also born in Boston, George, 7 [all] born in Boston. He is 53 and born in Ireland, County Cork, he landed in Quebec 1839 and came to Boston in June 1840 ... His wife Catherine is at [the] Deer Island House of Industry [for] three months from August 27 for drunkenness and assault on husband, she struck him over the eye with an iron kettle. She has been there before—also at the House of Correction in South Boston for drunk[eness] ... He is intemperate [too. He was] once arrested five or six years [ago?]....

[1872] Helen Sanborn 19 from Boston admitted on February 14 with her daughter Georgie born [in the almshouse]. Her birthplace is unknown.... In February 1871 she was accused of poisoning her husband and mother-in-law and did poison herself with laudaman [*sic*] ...

Generally speaking, at least for this sample of poor people, Massachusetts authorities appeared to have little hesitation about sending those responsible for spousal abuse to the House of Correction, and the Tewksbury notes usually evinced considerable sympathy for the victims. Though our sample of spousal abuse cases is small (thirty cases), Irish-born men were overrepresented, as they were in arrests for alcoholism and assault in Massachusetts at this time. Many explanations have been offered for this association including Hasia Diner's excellent points about the troubled gender relations in the Irish family. The simplest answer may be, however, that that the Irish were the poorest of the New England lower classes, and as they emerged later from this position, their arrest rates declined.

The number of cases of child abuse seen at the almshouse was also high. For example:

[1875] Augustus Halloran 14 from Boston admitted [on] March 27. He was born in Halifax, Nova Scotia, he first remembers of living with parents John and Mary in West Brookfield. His father died at Fiskedale on October 1872 ... He has lived with uncle Pat Halloran in West Warren and then he died December 1874. Then he went home, but his stepfather is intemperate and abused him. So he left and walked to Woonsocket and other places for work. He was brought up in Newton and arrested by police and sent to the Visiting Agent ...

[1873] Margaret Flynn 4 years old from Haverhill admitted [on] June 16 her parents are Daniel and Margaret, both born in Ireland … The parents of the child were sent to the House of Correction for drunkenness on June 16. The child received the cut upon its head from the hands of its mother. The Overseers [have] asked that the child not be returned to the custody of the parents as they are not fit to take care of her …

In the early- to mid-nineteenth century, physical child punishment was not usually treated as a criminal matter, but was policed as either a matter of civil child custody or the Poor Laws administration of the lives of the poor. Only in the 1870s, when the famous case of "Mary Ellen" in New York City led to the development of the first American wave of awareness of child abuse, did pressure grow for the society to do something more to police the family. The result was the creation of organizations such as the Massachusetts Society for the Prevention of Cruelty to Children (MSPCC), which are referenced a number of times in the later almshouse notes. The SPCCs, by today's standards, were extremely odd organizations. They were privately run, composed of usually affluent citizens who were given the power of marshals. They used their quasi-police powers almost exclusively on the poor, and, not infrequently, exercised power arbitrarily. To the poor and immigrants, the groups became known as "The Cruelty." While no doubt the SPCCs did lead to investigations of abuse which would have gone undetected, the groups also discredited the policing of children and family for many decades, helping at least in part to explain why it took so long for child abuse to return to the radar of American reformers. Complicating the matter was that whether in 1880 or today, child neglect was far more frequently the cause of investigation than physical child abuse. Historically, charges of child neglect have always focused on lifestyle, and have overwhelmingly been made against poor families. In the Gilded Age, immigrant families who sent their children to work, particularly at hawking street wares or other work in the underground economy, or who were seen by Yankee officials (who themselves had fewer children and far more resources) as exercising inadequate supervision were the prime targets.

Elder abuse was not absent in these days either. While much abuse (as with all other types of domestic violence) was psychological, financial, and other nonphysical abuse, the case of Silas Kimball in 1877 below provides a possible example of a case of violence against the elderly:

… 70 years old from Boston admitted [on] January 31 born in Boston always lived there except a short time in New Hampshire forty years ago … widower, shoemaker ... he was stabbed, knocked down, [and] robbed in an alley off Friend Street by his son Henry who was tried and acquitted [for it] . [He?] has been at House of Industry once, years ago, [he] denies drinking ...

But many family problems were not necessarily violent as the two cases below illustrate. Here two women who entered the almshouse had financial grievances with their spouses, in these cases alleged robbery of their savings:

[1880] Josephine Randolph 39 years old admitted on February 5 from Boston, She was born in Baltimore, she came to Boston on February 2, 1880 from New York ... Her husband, Arthur, was born in Virginia. She lived in Baltimore ten years past. She owned a home there on Clavert Street, sold it about three months ago for $5,500, she then gave the money to [her] husband who represented that he was going into business in Wilmington. He eloped with another woman [and] she traced him to Boston. [She] found he had sailed for Europe.... As soon as [she is] able to go her friends will aid her to get to Baltimore.....

[1875] Martha Dimond 33 years old admitted from Waltham on July 12 and Pat H., 2, born in Fall River and James F., six months old and born in Wareham. Martha was born in Ireland, County Antrim, and landed in Boston in March 1871 per the SS "Siberia".... Her husband went to Chicago five weeks ago, taking [the] funds realized from [the] sale of their household goods [and] decamped without them. [She has] no friends or home in Massachusetts ...

Perhaps the most common of the family problems, which I shall return to in discussing the issue of desertion and separation, was sexual infidelity or, in the case of the married individuals or couples below, adultery:

[1895] Mary J. Kelly 23 years old from Boston admitted on May 9 she was born in Ireland single, a domestic, landed in Boston in May 1892 via the S.S. "Prussian" ... pregnant, she will be sick in five or six weeks. The father of her child is John Kane of 29 Norfolk Avenue, a married man with no children. He works in a foundry for $11 or $12 a week. She lived in his house for five months, during the past three months he had intercourse with her twice each week. His wife suspected it, and Mary left the house in November....

[1890] Henrietta Smith 36 years old admitted from Boston on March 25, she was born in Montreal married, [she came] to Massachusetts and Boston in November 1881 there and vicinity since ... she is pregnant, the father of her child is William Hyde of Brookline. Her husband Frank is born in England and they married in Montreal. [They came] to Boston six months before, [and now] his wife is off [from him] for five months ...

[1875] Catherine Cran, 50 and Catherine Jr, 12 years old admitted from Fall River on December 18. Her daughter was born in Biddeford, Maine while she was born in England and landed in New York [in] 1854 with her husband Pat. They went direct to Biddeford until August of 1869, in Fall River since ... [In] February 1873 his wife caught him in bed with a Mrs. Shehan, and he was turned out of the mill. [He?] left Fall River and [she has] not seen [him] ever since, 12 children, all dead but Catherine. [She was] aided by Overseers of Poor of Fall River since 1873....

WERE THEY "OFF," "DESERTED," OR "SEPARATED"?

While middle- and upper-class observers denounced "patriarchal despotism" as we see in the first quote at this chapter's head, they seemed even more concerned at this time about the tendency of men, as well as sometimes women, to simply pick up and leave their families. We find observer after observer making statements that "the American family is like a covey of birds; the young escape as soon as they have wings to fly, and claws for defence. They forget the maternal nest, and often parents themselves no longer recognize them." For Charles Eliot Norton "the rapid spread of the continent and astounding growth of cities" had weakened "the attachment to the native soil, affection for the home of one's youth, the claims of kindred, the bonds of social duty, have not proved strong enough to resist the allurements of hope ... and the love of adventure." And A. Maurice Low opined, "No sacred associations cling to the roof-tree, for the American home is wherever he makes it ... wide scattering of members of a family is regarded as a matter of course."

But though critics acknowledged the key role of western expansion and industrialization in the massive movement of people from their homes, no issue struck them as so malevolent as men leaving their wives. Because of poor records, different laws in each state, and easy ability to change names, bigamy, in their terms, was rampant. French observer Duvergier De Hauranne spoke of the "remarkable facilities" that "legal chaos gives for bigamy, and the great number of double, triple and quadruple marriages discovered each year by female jealousy." The National Divorce Reform League in 1887 cited "instances of persons moving from place to place who are ostensibly married but who are really living in violation of legal marriage ... [they are] numerous—far more so than those of us who have never looked into the subject think." As late as the early twentieth century, a sociologist estimated that the number of illegal desertions and separations among the poor was four times the number of legal divorces.

Not only was divorce expensive, it also required a lengthy court process, and even then it was nearly impossible to achieve in some states. Because of the differences in state law, many partners felt simply separating was a reasonable first step to divorce. In studying the many "widows" who appeared claiming the same men's pensions, Beverly Schwartzberg noted that "many also may have believed that extended separations gave them legal status of divorce, divorce was being made easier and, (and in some states) abandonment was a factor." Yet as we have seen in the last chapter, other states, like those in New England, did not regard marital separation as having any legal meaning and were apt to declare the husband had "deserted." Yet, as Schwartzberg notes about the later nineteenth century, many witnesses in the pension hearings showed a remarkable lack of outrage about bigamy, even third or fourth or more marriages; as her article states, they believed "lots of them did it."

The difficulty of understanding relationships among the poorer classes is complicated still further by other factors. As already alluded to, men often went away to work. For much of the nineteenth (and early twentieth) century, work was either migratory or entailed at least extended stays away from home. Further, as other historians have found, women and children gained more aid when the men were away from the house. Linda Gordon's study of a major Massachusetts charity organization's case records led her to state:

> There was an equally indistinct boundary between deserters and those husbands who were present but nonsupporting. In fact, many separated couples in these case records colluded in presenting their story as one of desertion in the hopes of winning sympathy and material aid for the wife; many husbands dropped in and out of their families, appearing occasionally by the week, the month, or even the year.

Indeed, it is quite difficult to ascertain, being limited to the records only of the officials and what the poor told them, whether the departer (usually male) actually had permanently left or was "off" at work or in fact living in the dwelling on and off. But Gordon points out how Victorian morality also shaped the differential view of men and women's actions. The male *deserted,* he did not separate or divorce or leave.

> [T]he high degree of deserted women in this period, compared with twentieth-century figures, resulted from both different forms of marital separation and from different interpretations of separation. Women's economic dependence,

both their actual helplessness and their sense of helplessness when left without husbands, made some wives call themselves deserted when a modern observer might describe them as separated.

Like other records of the nineteenth century, the archives of the almshouse are both a wonderful place to study the period's family lives, and an extremely difficult arena to develop precise interpretations. What did the note takers mean (or the inmates who spoke to them) that the male was "off"? Was he off at work, away from the house, or gone from the relationship? When the note takers said the woman was "deserted," did this mean "for good" or temporarily? Should desertion imply divorce or separation, or did it mean that at the very moment of difficult times—a pregnancy, a medical problem, a loss of job, a larger family—the male just left? When the almshouse note takers recorded cases of bigamy and adultery, did all parties involved see it this way? Did the participants (and there were obviously men and women who were adulterous and bigamous) see it this way? If they left their spouse ten years ago in a different state, was it logical to believe they would stay chaste or unmarried?

One thing that stands out immediately in the records of the over 170 inmates (this does not include eighteen nonoverlapping case records of bigamy and thirty-eight of adultery in the sample in which the record did not indicate they were separated from their spouses) whose biographies included separation or desertion or "husband [or wife] off" is that there were gender and racial differences in the use of the terms. Indeed, among the at least thirty-two males who reported that they had been married but no longer were, they were usually listed as "separated." They appear mostly to have not even been asked where their wives were or what the cause of the separation was. On the other hand, with the women, the husband was almost always "off" or "deserted." It is true that time did serve as an equalizer: many men, and some women who reported they had not seen their spouses for ten or fifteen years were labeled as "separated." Interestingly too, among African Americans, particularly men, the inmates (or the note takers) reported themselves quite often as "divorced," though there are only five or six mentions of this term among the white inmates in all the years I sampled. It seems unlikely that more formal divorces occurred among African Americans, but rather that the cultural norms of their community regarded the marriage as terminated after some period of time. Further, the fact that the vast majority of poor people were Roman Catholic also obviously limited the number of divorces, even if poor people could go to court.

THE *Inmate Biographies* AND FAMILY SEPARATION

The number of inmates separated or "deserted" was quite high, at least half of the adults who had ever been married. Separation or desertion was sometimes serial, described in at least some of the notes as occurring more than once. The sad case of little 8-year-old William Fahey in 1885 provides an example. "His father married his first wife in Blackstone, she [then] eloped when William was three years old." His father "then divorced and married a second wife in Fall River and he deserted her." After this separation, William was surrendered to the Overseers of the Poor of Fall River. Typically, cases of desertion, even serial ones, went without comment. Annie Long Lawton was left by a husband and, in turn, by a lover who was the father of her latest child:

> [H]er husband Henry Lawton, a shoemaker and taxpayer of Brockton deserted her three years ago. She was aided by the Overseers of the Poor of Brockton and [her] four children are now being aided by Brockton. [She is] pregnant, sick anytime. The father of her child is William Gleason of Fall River. [She has] not seen or heard from him for the past eight months.

Women, of course, did leave men, and the amount of departures of women complicates the Victorian drama of "desertion":

> [1875] Charles Manning 26 years old admitted from Boston on August 10. He was born in England and landed in Boston about 1852 with his mother Sarah ... He married his wife Annie in New York in 1869. She was an actress Annetta Ravel [and she] eloped with a clerk in a leather store in New York and went west. He is a professional gymnast. [He] has been all over the country and in Europe ...

> [1874] Mary Feeley 18 admitted from Fitchburg on March 2. She was born in St. John, New Brunswick, and landed in Portland about 1859 ... She married Timothy Feeley in Upton [on] May 1, 1873, lived with him there and in Boston and left him four months ago because he could not support her ...

When husband and wife both appeared at the almshouse, their views sometimes differed. To take one example from 1867, the almshouse note taker pronounced inmate Catherine Lynch, 26 years old, a "nice girl." Born in County Cork, Ireland, her husband Richard had left her pregnant six months before, and she aroused sympathy from the officials. When her husband appeared, they noted he was gainfully employed by the city, and that he claimed her drinking was so bad "he cannot live with her." He also stated he had not seen her for three years, making his fatherhood a little unlikely. The notes concluded, "He can't do anything for her, all he can do is support [him]self and [his] family." That Catherine was sent to Bridgewater Workhouse suggests that her husband's version of events prevailed.

Despite the difficulties of knowing how to interpret the biographies, some general trends are evident. Those who cited (or who were asked) reasons for their separation most often spoke of infidelity or intemperance, with far lesser numbers reporting issues such as immigration mishaps (see Chapter 3), abuse, the husband being off working, or other reasons such as imprisonment of a partner or problems dealing with children. All of these factors, though, were dwarfed by the finding that much desertion occurred during a woman's pregnancy or while a child was in its infancy, as I will discuss below.

Adultery or infidelity was cited as a cause of separation or desertion in every year of the notes:

[1895] Philomena DeAugustine 40 years old admitted from Boston on April 10 she was born in Italy married, a seamstress, she landed in New York two years ago, and went direct to Boston ... Her husband [is named] Thomasa [*sic?*]. She says [that he] is off with another woman....

[1887] Delia Kilcoyne from Northbridge admitted February 12, 27 years old she was born in Ireland, is single, a domestic ... She is pregnant, the father of her child is one of two brothers named Aldrich of Northbridge. She will be sick in two months ... Henry A. Cook chairman of the Overseers of the Poor of Northbridge, Whitinsville, Massachusetts notes on February 15, 1887 the brother of Delia, Patrick Kilcoyne, 42 Suffolk Street above says Delia has a husband and three children in Ireland. [They] never came to America....

[1880] Hannah Hutchinson 25 years old from Boston. She was born in East Boston and has resided there and vicinity since. Her husband William S. is 53 and was born in Arlington, lived there most part of his life, owned real estate and paid taxes, also has property in Somerville. [He] has eloped with another woman.... she is pregnant ...

[1872] Mary Maginnis, 28 and her three children 9, 5, and 3. She was born in Ireland and landed in New York on February 1, 1867 per the steamer "Edinboro." She was admitted on February 15. [She] came with her husband Frank and her daughter Mary in Boston since ... He left her two months ago and has been told he is living with another woman in Kingston Place, Boston ...

[1866] Anna Florinda 30 years old, she was born in Fayal and landed in Boston April 1866 [aboard] the Bark "Fredonia." Her fare was paid out by Emaneul

Vera with the purpose of marrying her, but finding her with child, he cleared out. The father of the child [is] James Bernard of Fayal where the child was made, it not being known aboard the vessel that she was with child …

"Intemperance" (or "alcoholism" or "drunkenness," the term depending on the specific year or sometimes even the specific note taker) was cited in virtually equal numbers to infidelity as a reason for desertion. In 1895, Jeremiah Sheehan left his wife Margaret, 24, who was in Tewksbury with her four-month-old daughter Mary, after Margaret had completed a ten-month sentence in the Women's Prison in Sherborn (Massachusetts) for drunkenness. One suspects she had many "priors" to receive such a long sentence. Mary Matthews, a 26-year-old inmate in 1880, was left by her husband John in 1877, after she was arrested for adultery and also was sent to the House of Industry for drunkenness and assault. Elbridge Gerry Hardy, an 1877 inmate, was left by his wife seventeen years before on "account of his drunkenness." Jabez Bradbury, an 1874 inmate who had reformed, noted his wife had left him because of "intemperate habits." As with other issues, couples sometimes argued over who was intemperate. In 1875, for example, 25-year-old Patrick Murphy was admitted to the almshouse and reported he was separated from his wife for five months "on account of her intemperate habits." On February 24, a week after Patrick was admitted, his wife Elizabeth arrived and told the officials that *he* was intemperate. She stated that she had "lived with him up [until] to last Monday, [then they] had a quarrel and he kicked her." The note taker, however, remarked "she doesn't deny [that] she is intemperate." Bridget Cahill, who was admitted that same year, and her husband Patrick present a similar complexity in regard to notions of fault. While Bridget stated that her husband was intemperate and arrested for rum selling, under questioning it turned out that she too had been arrested and jailed in western Massachusetts for rum-selling and intemperance.

Despite the no doubt frequent nature of problems such as alcoholism and infidelity and adultery, neither set of reasons were listed for a majority of all of the separations and "desertions." What seems the strongest correlation with desertion or separation is that of the pregnancy of the wife (or in a few cases a long-time lover) or the recent birth of a child.

Table 6.1 below shows the close relation between childbirth and male desertion or separation. Over all the years sampled, nearly half the cases occur at this point in time of a relationship. Unfortunately,

Table 6.1 Relationship Between Male Desertion and Childbirth and Infancy

Decade	Number of cases	Number with infant		Pregnant by husband	Pregnant by partner	Pregnant by other	Total pregnant	
1890s	22	1	4.5%	7	4	2	13	59.1%
1880s	28	10	35.7%	7	–	2	9	32.1%
1870s	80	10	12.5%	12	1	4	17	26.3%
1860s	13	4	30.8%	4	1	1	6	46.2%
Total	143	25	17.5%				45	31.5%

although it appears likely that most of these were first children, there is no way of being sure of this. In any event the percentage of departures during pregnancy or following a recent birth is much higher than half in all decades except the 1870s: in the 1890s, five of eight separations occur at this point, in the 1880s more than two of three, and in the 1860s about five out of six. Why the 1870s, with its still significant nearly two in five, is so much lower is not totally clear. The most likely reason is that during this period of severe economic depression (when the almshouse was the most over its capacity) there was a much wider variety of inmates, including more older women, who were past their child-bearing years.

Some cautions are in order in interpretation. First, as the right-hand column indicates, a not insubstantial number of the sample (nine of the forty-six cases of pregnancy) admitted that the child they were having was not their husband's. This casts Victorian morality in a somewhat different light, as we can't help but suspect that if the man left, it may be because of the wife's infidelity. In many instances the relationship in the true sense of the word may well have ended long before either the pregnancy with another man or the desertion of the husband. A second point is that the second to right-hand column indicates some male partners were not married, and while that distinction in some ways was not major (and among the poor today this can still be said), still the lack of a formal commitment is likely to have had some normative impact on the ease of leaving. Finally, as noted, not all the "deserting" was done by the men. Mary Feeley (1874), noted above, was pregnant when she left her husband who "could not support her." Isabella Catalado in 1895 (who we shall return to) left her husband because of a charge that he had a wife still living in Italy.

Still, while clearly the period of pregnancy and childbirth provoked a crisis in relationships for many reasons, even if we subtract the number of cases in which the woman left rather than the man, and where the father of the child was not the husband, the percentage of departures at this time in the relationship would still dwarf the other reasons that are cited in the almshouse notes. It does seem to reflect the point made by family historian Arthur Calhoun that "abandonment of pregnant wives is especially common."

Of course from the point of view of the "experts" of the times and the manner in which the note takers refer to the men, one would get the impression that pure irresponsibility and wanderlust motivated the male deserter. But likely the situations were more complex, and, interestingly, modern feminist historians such as Linda Gordon present a more nuanced, sympathetic view of the men. Gordon notes the "separate spheres" of men and women, with all its advantages for men, also made women economically dependent. The development of industrialism made it virtually impossible for working-class men to support their families, particularly when the economy failed or they were laid off due to cyclical unemployment:

> Industrial wage-labor conditions as well as the space and mobility of the United States made running away from a wife easier. The same conditions also created a double bind for many poor men: unaccustomed to cyclical, structural unemployment, they often experienced it as personal failure and became depressed; at the same time, they were equally unaccustomed to the contradictory expectation that they were to be the sole support of families ...

For immigrant men, the expectation of solely supporting the family—compounded as this time period went on by the gradual move to outlaw child labor—was made even more difficult by their low status in the economy, and, as Gordon also notes, their separation "from community and kinship networks that enforced marital commitments." Diner adds that for the Irish immigrants, it was often the wife who was disadvantaged by marriage. For her, "marriage was synonymous with economic hardship and duress for unskilled workers." That is, while married women were normatively prohibited from work in the Irish family, as single women they were able to obtain positions that were actually more secure and lucrative as men. Domestic service, for example, provided a more steady and secure wage than most unskilled labor jobs. Later, many Irish single women went into nursing, teaching, and clerical work. Diner notes that the high death rate of men, the large amount of desertion and domestic violence, and other factors, made female-headed households very typical among the Irish, and relatively nonstigmatized. So difficulties in relationships, which perhaps under other circumstances or in other cultures might have been worked out, failed against the centrifugal forces of separation of this time.

No doubt, the birth of a child had serious economic consequences, and, particularly with the birth of the first born, emotional and developmental issues for the man. Economically, for most of those who were ever inmates, the addition of a mouth to feed could provoke a crisis or exasperate an existing one caused by unemployment, low wages, or wage cuts. But life is not purely economic, and having a child would certainly have made the spousal relationship more serious, the pressure for housing accommodations greater, and other elements of the traditional adult role more real and more stressful. As some of the married men entered into these relationships in a forced way, this factor too needs to be kept in mind. A number of the separations followed a woman reporting a man as a father. The man then married to avoid bastardy proceedings, but some time afterwards (such as in the period of the child's infancy) found an opportunity to leave. Unfortunately, the archives themselves are of little help as to the motivations of the departing men nor in answering the question of whether at least some of the men returned to the wives after a period of time or whether they were working and accumulating money or whether they aided their children at all at a later time. The note takers were naturally concerned for the inmate at hand, usually the wife, and were so used to the phenomenon of desertion that they made few inquiries about the husband's psychology or his intentions. Since the almshouse officials, however, did not stay in contact with the families (unless they returned to the almshouse), they could not have known one way or the other how the family made out over time. This leads us again to review what data we have from official records to assist us in seeing whether we can find further answers as to how the families fared.

OFFICIAL RECORDS AND SEPARATION

Unhappily, compared to the issues of downward mobility explored in Chapter 4, and the pregnant women in Chapter 5, a smaller percentage of these cases appear in census records or genealogical sources. Only about 20 percent of the desertion cases could be found, although the addition of some severe family conflicts occurring at the time some families came into the almshouse provides us with more cases to follow up. Generally, the lower numbers are not surprising in that males of some property are easiest to find in official records (as already noted), so that both the females who were left, but also the departing males, for reasons of economy and possible name changes and avoidance of authorities, are not easy to find.

Table 6.2 indicates that among those we can find, the inmates who reported a long separation were providing accurate information, and seemed to have remained apart. However, among those whose conflicts had developed recently (I used a rather arbitrary divide of one year) and led to their separation, there is nearly a fifty-fifty split in the couples found between those who remained together and those who did not. However, adding another eight families who were having family conflicts, but had not separated when they came to the almshouse, only one family of these eight seemed to have remained together. The findings, discussed below, do give one the impression that there was a centrifugal pull among poor families toward separation rather than to somehow "toughen" through the severe problems of their lives.

The first point to make about Table 6.2 is that I have included two of a larger number of inmates who, when their names were found in other official records, created some contradictions with the Tewksbury record. Louisa Arnold, a 35-year-old inmate in 1895, said she was separated from Melzer Arnold for about sixteen years. However, records reveal she married a Harry A. Mason in 1865 and was living with him at the time of the 1870 census. We can only guess if there was a reason not to mention him or to mention that she had married twice. Jennie Baker Canad, a 25-year-old 1877 inmate, stated that her husband had left her in 1875 and the implication of the "inmate biography" was that her 16-month-old child Charles was fathered by her husband. However, the birth records of Boston list Charles as illegitimate, from an unknown father. I note these discrepancies because there were some others, and it is important to keep in mind that we are dealing with personal accountings of difficult situations to authority figures. On the whole, however, at least among the people I was able to locate in other records, there were fairly few obvious discrepancies. The most frequent was for the separated, both male or female, to use the term "widow" or "widower" to describe themselves even if technically still married. In some cases, those women who had never married, but had given birth and then seen a male partner disappear, also listed themselves in censuses as "widows."

A second point is that while a few inmates in each year noted a husband "off" looking for work, and we have two quasi-separations

Table 6.2 Data from Censuses and Other Sources about Separated Families Who Were Inmates at Tewksbury

N = 44

Name	Year of admission	Length of time separated	Later information
Long Term Separated (18, 17 remained, 1 factual issue)			
1. Louisa Arnold	1895	claimed since 19	complex as married a man other than one noted
2. Mary Bennet	1895	separated 25 years	1900 poorhouse (single) in Marlboro
3. Pam Billings	1876	fifteen years	husband remarried before 1870 census
4. Martha Blunt	1875	four years	she is in 1880 census as servant single
5. Jabez Bradbury	1874	nine years	he remarried 1880
6. Willet Brown	1872	twenty years	separated, census has them apart
7. Mary Coran	1874	five or six years	single in poorhouse 1880, 1900 alone
8. Catherine Cran	1875	more than a year	separated 1880 census
9. Frances Day	1880	two years	she died 1880 no sign of husband
10. Elbridge Hardy	1877	seventeen years	he died 1877 without wife
11. Joseph Lakin	1871	fourteen years	separated 1870 different wife
12. George Linney	1895	five years	separated based on 20th-century censuses
13. Anne Long	1895	three years	1900, 1910 alone with children as laundress
14. Ann Metcalf	1865	a year or more	separated, alone in 1870 census
15. William Murray	1880	22 years	prior census separated
16. Ellen Quilty	1880	four or five years	separated 1900 census
17. Elizabeth Sandford	1874	25 years	1850–1870 censuses separated
18. Elizabeth Sisson	1873	one year and a half	she remarried in 1877 to a farmer

Table 6.2 continues on next page

Table 6.2 continued

Name	Year of admission	Length of time separated	Later information
Short term (a year or under)			
(18, 9 together at later time, 8 separated, 1 factual issue)			
1. Selma Bostrum	1890	left one month ago	1900–1920 alone
2. Jennie Baker Canad	1875	few weeks	misrepresented husband as father
3. Raphael Cataldo	1895	recent	together 1900, 1920 censuses
4. Esther Cooger	1880	nine months	separated 1880 census six months after discharge
5. Jane Duxbury	1890	man who was supposed to marry	1891 English census alone
6. Mary Erickson	1885	Husband off looking for work iron works	1900, 1910 census, 1930 together
7. Bridget Ferguson	1873	Weeks	together in 1880 census
8. Augusta Lee	1882	left five months ago	1900–1920 censuses together
9. Elizabeth Martel	1865	not clear	two earlier marriages, anyway she is 1870 census alone
10. Nellie Maxfield	1876, 1880	weeks	she was in and out of Tewksbury for next several years
11. Hannah McCann	1874	several months	together 1880 census
12. Helen Mortimer	1876	recent	stayed together in 1880 census
13. Julia O'Neal	1870	recent	still together 1880 census
14. Mary Perry	1875	weeks	married, together 1880, 1900
15. Sadie Polinsky	1895	three months	1910, 1930 family together married 25+ yrs
16. Josephine Randolph	1865	weeks	he is in 1870 census not her
17. Ellen Rhodes	1885	husband left in August 1900	1920 alone
18. Jane Smith	1870	six months	1870 census four months after discharge alone

Table 6.2 continues on next page

Table 6.2 continued

Name	Year of admission	Length of time separated	Later information
Conflict occurring at time of admission: (8, 1 together at later time, 7 separated)			
1. Matilda Connors	1874	adultery	alone in later censuses
2. Michael Dennison	1876	intemperance/abuse	in 1880 together in census
3. Ellis family	1895	father had deserted	1900 husband remarried
4. Albert F. Fisher	1873	wife suspected of adultery	1880 census by himself
5. Augustine Jacquoit	1893	husband in jail	alone in 1900, 1920, 1930 censuses
6. Alice Kellington	1893	husband in jail	1901 British census alone
7. Margaret Mushet	1874	wife charged with having illegitimate child	husband alone 1880 census
8. Elinora Wallis	1875	domestic violence	1880 Worcester Lunatic Asylum

that turned out to be seemingly work related (Mary Erickson and Sadie Polinsky), unlike in some other studies, this type of absence does not appear to have been a major factor at Tewksbury. Mary Erickson, an 1885 inmate who was pregnant and came into the almshouse with a 3-year-old child, noted that her husband was "off looking for work" and future censuses which show them together for decades would certainly lend credence to this. Sadie Polinsky was a 3-year-old child left at Tewksbury in 1895 for what today might be called "respite care." Her mother was in Boston with her sister after she had suffered a miscarriage. The father, a tailor, was reported in St. Louis. While the wife "had not heard from him for the last three months," the note also said "he is expected home soon." Indeed, the presence of the family in future censuses would support an inference that Hyman, the father, was away for some particular reason, perhaps work. However, on the whole the number of rejoined couples was so small to begin with, and the number of notes that speak of work separations is so few as to make it unlikely that couples were using the almshouse as a strategy to support the family in time of unemployment or a man's sojourn for work. An obvious difference from studies such as Linda Gordon's, which used as their study subjects those who received aid at their homes, is that moving into an almshouse, particularly one that was not local for most inmates, is a more extreme measure. Women whose husbands had left but had the rent paid, for example, might rely on relief to help with food and fuel without mentioning a husband (the form of colluding that Gordon mentions), but it would appear to be quite different to leave a home and go to Tewksbury unless one did not have the rent at all or, as in the case of those fleeing abuse, there was a clear need to get out of the house. Many inmates were homeless, which is worse than being poor but having shelter. Also, it is doubtful that either officials or inmates at most times regarded the almshouse as scarce a resource as "outdoor relief," which was more desirable.

Which couples stayed separated and which did not cannot readily be known. It is no great surprise that those who had reported being separated for years were indeed (among the eighteen I could find) being factually accurate and appear from the information obtained to have stayed apart. But among those who had separated recently, there is considerable movement, with about half being found together in later records. There were few obvious differences between the groups, although those who stayed together included a few women who were considerably older (55 and 46). Additionally, when the families in the third group are added in (those who were mostly in the process of separating) we find far more pregnancy and infant children among those women who separated (nine of thirteen, leaving out the two men in the mix) than among those who stayed together (three out of nine).

One interesting, if unusual, example of a couple staying together was Michael Dennison and his wife Bridget. Michael, 55, was admitted to the almshouse in 1876. Bridget reported that her husband "has been disorderly and drinking quite hard for some ten or twelve weeks past." He had been laid off and "was violent and beats his wife. The night before he left this time he was drunk and so wild and violent that he disturbed the whole neighborhood." Bridget protested "against his being discharged" and even threatened to complain against him so that he "be sent to Bridgewater" saying "she [was] willing to testify before any court." Whether Bridget's intervention helped Michael overcome his alcoholism and violence is not known, but they were together in Cambridge, Massachusetts, in the 1880 census. As before, he was listed as a cooper, they had no children, and he had been unemployed for ten months that year. When Michael died in 1891, Bridget served as the will administrator, confirming their continued relationship. A less dramatic and surprising instance of a couple staying together is that of Ellen and Benjamin Mortimer. Ellen came into the almshouse after having "a quarrel" with her husband. She then left "and wandered about the streets until sent here [Tewksbury]." In 1880, the census recorded them living in Somerville, Massachusetts. Benjamin was a laborer. Like the Dennisons, they were a bit older (Ellen was 50) and had no children at home.

Yet there are examples of couples staying together for whom the text itself would give little hint of such a future. In 1895, Raphael Cataldo, a 30-year-old pregnant woman with a 2-year-old son, Angelo, entered the almshouse and reported that "she heard [her] husband had a wife in Italy" and then had him arrested. He was then "out on bonds" and she did not "know his whereabouts." Nevertheless, this couple appears in the census in 1900 in Boston having been married for eleven years with four daughters, including Catherine who was born at the almshouse in 1895. They were found as well in 1920 living in Chelsea, Massachusetts, with Angelo (the husband) Cataldo aged 65 and Isabelle 59. Did Mrs. Cataldo learn that the bigamy she "heard about" was untrue, or were there other factors which kept the family together in spite of the bigamy? The stories of those who remained separated were naturally as difficult, or worse, than those who seem to have remained together. Margaret Mushet, a 32-year-old inmate in 1874 who had been a former inmate and also committed to the Bridgewater workhouse, quarreled with her husband and while at Bridgewater had an illegitimate child "which was adopted and died soon after." This child "was the cause of the trouble between her and husband." Evidently the husband had decided "unless [she was] sent to Scotland, she will be a subject for Lunatic Hospital." The husband, William, worked in a shoe factory in Haverhill and "would provide for [his] wife if she would stay at home and behave," and even paid $11.50 per week board for [his wife] and four children." In the 1880 census, William listed himself as a widower and a shoe finisher and lived in Philadelphia, while his wife died several years later in England. Elinora Wallis, a 23-year-old inmate admitted in 1875 with an 8-week-old child, William, was married to a rail brakeman named Samuel who was "intemperate and abusive." She came into the almshouse when her husband "was on a spree" (a frequent note in the records). Sadly, in the 1880 census Elinora is a patient at the Worcester Lunatic Hospital. I was unable to locate her afterward. One can only speculate as to whether she was driven there by her husband's actions or was perhaps committed there as William Mushet had threatened to do with his wife. As a final anecdote of those separating, Albert F. Fischer, a 27-year-old inmate admitted in 1873, described himself as "diseased" (syphilis) by his wife. He had left her at his father's house on Cape Cod where she was under the care of a physician. His wife claimed a man came in the "dwelling house in the day time and committed a rape," but although a warrant was issued for the man, the timing of the allegations seemed suspicious, coming well after the syphilis was revealed. Not too surprisingly, the census records Albert F. Fischer as living alone in 1880.

DISCUSSION

The separated or deserted women suffered from severe poverty, often homelessness, and many, as noted above, from domestic violence or other abuse, intemperance or alcoholism, and other difficulties. It is then difficult in this particular instance to know whether a generalization based on the inmates can be made to other populations. Still, the historical record about the period, particularly when referring to poor and working-class families, and to the Irish immigrants, is ripe with stories of desertion, abandonment, family conflict and violence, alcoholism, and other social problems. If some of the particular issues were overrepresented in the almshouse, again for the most part the inmates were "ordinary people" of their social classes.

Charity reformers looked askance at the working-class family. They found it "demoralized" by, as Broder notes, an "alleged unwillingness of working-class men to be manly providers and the lack of clearly defined family and gender roles within the poorest working-class families." Recent historians have looked more sympathetically on poorer families and seen the economic system and countervailing class and ethnic norms as central. Stephanie Coontz argued "that in 1870–1890 the gulf between working-class and middle-class values, behaviors, and everyday life was perhaps greater than at any time before or since," while others such as Mintz and Kellogg in their history of family life explain the differences as a result of the "high degree of transience dilut[ing] the effects of middle-class norms on working-class life." Probably the truth lies somewhere in between. While the economic hardship, transience, and short lives of the poor (and many working-class people) did mitigate against the niceties of formal marriage, and hence make cohabiting, adultery, and bigamy less of a "deviant behavior," few, if any cultures, countenanced domestic violence, desertion of pregnant women, or "intemperance" leading to dysfunction. The conflation of the different behaviors tends to obscure issues, and this was part of the problem with the middle- and upper-class reformers, particularly when they viewed immigrants. Some behaviors, such as lack of formal marital ties, were arguably functional, and indeed became recognized in many states as "common law" marriage. Other behaviors were, as they are today, the result of the particular effects of poverty, stress, alcohol, and the patriarchal social norms of the time.

In sum, it seems that given the high possibilities of severe marital conflict and its impact not only on adults, but on children, many poor and working-class people moved toward separation. This was not just a male action of "desertion" motivated by wanderlust or poverty and failure to face the prospect of nonsupport. It was also an action taken by women against problematic behavior, or its threat, by men. In some cases, too, where women were "intemperate" or having sex with others, men gave up and left their wives. Hence the phenomenon of family "desertion" is far more complicated than moralists believed, because it was so multifaceted and bound in the fabric of the difficult lives these real people confronted.

PART THREE

AGE AND POVERTY: CHILDREN AND THE ELDERLY

At least in modern American history, two age groups among those experiencing poverty tend to evoke sympathy and concern from the American public: children and the elderly. Both populations were well-represented among the poorer populations in the Gilded Age, and specifically among the Tewksbury inmates. Interestingly, however, while reformers, particularly in the Northeast, had begun to recognize childhood as a special period of life which required protection from some of the worst effects of poverty, there was little concern expressed for the elderly. Older people would, in fact, become by the turn of the twentieth century the major proportion of all almshouse inmates nationwide, and they would have to await the 1930s for any major reform efforts to succeed.

In Chapter 7, "Being 'Put Out': Children In and Out of the Almshouse," I begin by noting the campaign of reformers to exclude children from the poorhouse. While Massachusetts was in the forefront of this reform movement, considerable exceptions were always made to the rule excluding children. Hence in the sample drawn of Tewksbury inmates from 1865 to 1895, I found 140 cases of 202 children fifteen or under (many admissions were of multiple children) who entered the almshouse unescorted by adults, and another 138 cases of 259 children who entered the almshouse with one or more parents. If one further includes the fairly large number of sixteen and seventeen year olds who were also inmates of the almshouse, and who today would be considered children, we have far more than the 461 children noted above. It is true that most of the admissions were brief, with children either being discharged to their homes, to orphanages, or, as the chief topic of the chapter will explore, to other families who they were "put out" to (sometimes also called "bound out" or "placed out"). These families, usually within the state or in nearby New England states, kept children on farms as laborers or domestics or sometimes in the cities as workers of various kinds. This "putting out" system, as it was called, had its origin in early Anglo-American apprenticeship law which allowed town Overseers of the Poor to take orphaned and other poor children generally, and put them with farmers or skilled workers for an indentured term to learn a trade. During this period they were, by law, virtually owned by their masters. By the later nineteenth century, apprenticeship indenture was fading out, but reformers developed the "putting out" system as a predecessor of today's foster care system. While certainly in many ways more humane than institutions, not only almshouses, but orphanages or other juvenile homes, no adequate system for selection of families or for monitoring their behavior was developed until the twentieth century. Hence, while some children were taken in by good families, many children were allegedly exploited by those who wanted "strong backs" for farm and other labor, and some children were abused. As is sometimes echoed today in many foster care programs, I will note the bouncing of some children from one home to another. The experience of these Massachusetts children provides us with important information on the experience of children in one of the more progressive states to compare with the well-known and controversial efforts of Charles Loring Brace and his Children's Aid Society, whose "orphan trains" to the West have received more attention.

In Chapter 8, "'We Can Do Nothing for Him': The Fate of the Elderly," I explore the fate of older people in the decades of the late nineteenth century. Unlike the latter twentieth century in which retirement benefits enshrined age 65 as "old," there was little consensus on what constituted "old," and many people, particularly men out of work who were 55 (and sometimes younger) were described as "washed out" or "used up." So, depending on the definition of "elderly," there were approximately 100 cases of people over 65 who entered the almshouse, but closer to 200 if the age 55 is used. As is part of the common historical folklore of the poorhouse, Tewksbury was a place to die for many. At least one-quarter, and very possibly more, died within three years of their admission to Tewksbury. However, for many others who entered, disease or infirmity were not the chief causes of their admission, but rather family estrangement represented by the frequent comment in the *Inmate Biographies* that the family "can do no more for him" (most commonly) or "her." In addition to family estrangement, a significant number of men, particularly in the 1870s depression, found themselves turning to the almshouse because of unemployment and devastating economic conditions. While, of course, none of these issues will be new to experts, they do reflect that being "old" is always socially situated, having to do with work and family constellations, and when these institutions fail, "oldness" comes sooner to many people.

SEVEN

Being "Put Out": Children
in and out of the Almshouse

"There is a great superiority of a Christian home over the mere
mechanism of an Institution."
—John C. Ferris, former judge in an 1883 paper to the National
Conference of Charities and Corrections

"The advocates of this system [placing out] seem to think that almost
any home for a poor child is better than an institution."
—Lyman P. Alden, former superintendent of a Children's Home
in an 1885 paper before the National Conference of Charities and
Corrections

Most historians and sociologists locate the development of a modern
view of "childhood" as a separate time period from adulthood, ensured
by law and social norms, as only emerging gradually in the second half
of the nineteenth century. In early America, and depending on which
state or region studied, even well into the twentieth century, young
children were working long hours at hard labor and young teenagers
were able to consent to marriage. Many of the reform movements of
the late nineteenth century into the Progressive Era involved childhood,
including efforts to raise the age of consent for marriage; to abolish
child labor or to reduce hours, as well as other protective legislation
for older children; and attempts to mandate school attendance and
truancy laws; to prevent child abuse and neglect; and to remove children from institutions such as almshouses where they resided with
adult paupers, and sometimes with criminals.

This chapter will note how the benevolent movement to "save"
children was a complex phenomenon which relied on upper- and
middle-class prejudices against the poor as well as humanitarian motivations. "Saving" children often meant saving them from their *own*

environments, their own parents and extended families. Reformers often saw these families and their urban ethnic enclaves as inherently dangerous, developing patterns of behavior which clashed with dominant values. Given that the "child savers" held these complex motivations, it is not surprising that the fate of children who were gradually moved out of the almshouse was itself quite mixed. By late in the nineteenth century, providing good "Christian homes" came to be a developing consensus among the most advanced child-welfare reformers. Though in some states they faced successful resistance from many entrenched institutional bureaucracies, such as large orphanages, "placing out" came to be a cause championed by reformers. But such "child saving" contained all the contradictions of the reformers themselves. Homes away from the city in families headed by farmers or other respectable people, usually Yankee Protestants, were assumed to be better, based on social class, ethnicity, religion, and, even because of their very geographical distance from children's families of origin. Moreover, since the majority of "orphans" and "half-orphans" (e.g., those with one of their parents still alive) were foreign born or of foreign descent, and the majority of host families were native-born Protestants, it was only a matter of time before ethnic minorities, principally the Irish in the nineteenth century, came to protest the child savers' policies as a form of child removal which targeted their families' and communities' integrity.

CHILDREN AND ALMSHOUSES

Despite the flurry of almshouse building which occurred from the 1820s through the 1870s, it did not take long for scandals and active dissatisfaction with the "poorhouse" to emerge. Many nineteenth-century reforms, starting with the famous campaign of Dorothea Dix to remove the "insane" from poorhouses, can be seen as progressive, "out of the poorhouse" movements: Dix's own efforts for the "insane" were followed by campaigns to remove blind and deaf people; then efforts to segregate the "feeble minded" into their own institutions; movements for orphaned, dependent, and delinquent children; and later the mothers' pension movement whose key argument was that mothers should not be so destitute that they had to go into the almshouse with their children. Though the motives of reformers were humanitarian, they rested their cases on the contrast between a "helpless" or "vulnerable" population and the majority of paupers. In the

1865 Annual Report of Tewksbury, for example, there were calls to protect "the younger inmates, the children, from the contaminating influences of the older in their sin and misery." The report's authors extended their frustrations to mothers "who send their children to [the] almshouse while they continue their licentious indulgences." Such rhetoric continued through late in the century, when C.D. Randall, a Michigan social welfare official, denounced "the county poorhouse" as "yet the home in nearly all the other States for little children, where they associate with the insane, idiotic, and depraved." Well-known social welfare historian Homer Folks waxed on about the awful effects on children of the poorhouse:

> [I]t is a simple statement of fact that the majority of children who grow to adolescence in poorhouses become paupers or criminals. How could it be otherwise? Do we realize even yet to how great an extent every human being is the natural product of his surroundings? ... Protracted residence in a poorhouse produced everywhere a certain type of child—lazy, profane, cunning, immoral, absolutely untruthful, quarrelsome, bold.

Beyond the lack of any proof of this thesis, which seems to be at best greatly overstated, the belief in the depravity of paupers and the foul environment of the poorhouse also made reformers generally disdainful of poor families themselves. They frowned on the continued ability of children to remain with their families both within the almshouses and then upon discharge. William Letchworth, another famous social welfare reformer of the nineteenth century, noted in 1874:

> In some poorhouses I find that the children have one or both parents with them, and the kind heart of the keeper, or mayhap [archaic, "maybe"], of his amiable wife, who is a mother herself, protests against the separation of the child from the parent. But in every case that has come to my notice ... the antecedents of the parent were such as to make it evident that the only hope of rescuing the child from a life of pauperism was to separate it from its parents or parent.

In fact, in his work on the history of "the care of the destitute, neglected, and delinquent children," Homer Folks quoted with approval the attitude of New York almshouse commissioners. Having had trouble controlling the outcome of the lives of children who entered the almshouse, commissioners were more successful when they bound out (sent to apprenticeship) "the [children, the] day they enter the almshouse and the parents lose all control over them." If, on the other hand, the children were not bound out immediately, the parents or guardians could probably demand them and take them out. Reformers' humanitarian prescriptions were always complicated by the deeply felt belief throughout the nineteenth century that poor children were best removed from their home environments, which included, not only their families, but also the urban ethnic non-Protestant enclaves which were associated with crime, intemperance, viciousness, and riot. For some reformers, just as Dix had proposed the mental asylum, various types of new children's institutions were the answer, e.g., large orphanages, juvenile asylums, reform schools, and other homes for dependent children far from the urban areas, preferably in expansive rural settings where the pastoral virtues of rural America would help assuage the harsh upbringing of poor children. Gradually, another camp emerged which criticized the large institutional nature of these new facilities and demanded that poor children be placed in family settings in rural American communities so that their lives more quickly resembled "normal," more middle-class Christian homes.

Interestingly, the theory and practice of officials, and even the law, differed from the complete breakup of families that reformers wished for. The Massachusetts almshouses found it much easier to exclude children in theory than in practice. Some of this was, of course, the implementation of social policy by superintendents and other public officials of reforms. Generally speaking, institutional officials had no self-interest in surrendering inmates, but they did have their own humanitarian experiences of seeing tearful and screaming parents objecting to the removal of their children. Many of these poor parents found their way to local politicians or public officials to complain. Gradually the laws themselves developed many compromises. All states recognized some tender age at which the severance of mother and child was unpalatable, this age tended to be 3 and later 4 years old. Nor could older children (ages 15–17) be forced out if they wished to stay with their parents. Disabled children and others with special needs were always taken into almshouses. It seems that gradually illness of either parent or child became another reason for keeping the family together. Moreover, as the century wore on the ability of the officials to sever the parents and child began to decline, in part due to court interpretations that sometimes frowned on such efforts unless the parents were proved negligent, abusive, or intemperate. A second problem which still plagues modern institutions is that outside placements—to orphanages, juvenile homes, or foster families—could hardly be made overnight. In an era where communication was slower than today and social service procedures were in their infancy, it is not surprising that Tewksbury became a sort of "holding center" even for children who would be severed from their own families. Once they left Tewksbury for the State Primary School (Monson), children also lingered there for long periods of time.

All of these contradictions led, in Massachusetts, to relatively few long-term child inmates or parents with their children (except at the State Primary School in Monson), but still the continued admission of some children for short stays. Children were clearly allowed to accompany parents (usually the mother, though sometimes both parents, and on some occasions just a father) who sought shelter from poverty or domestic violence, or who were facing childbirth or illness. And they clearly entered the almshouse alone or in sibling groups for varying periods and under a number of circumstances.

CHILD ADMISSIONS TO TEWKSBURY, 1865–1895

As noted earlier, despite the creation of the State Primary School at Monson, Massachusetts, which as of 1866 was the state institution for children and families (other than "reform schools"), and the development of numerous institutions such as orphanages and children's homes in the later nineteenth century, over 200 children unaccompanied by adults were in the sample I drew of the inmates. Most commonly, these children were abandoned or deserted children who were sent to the almshouse by local officials, presumably after doing their jobs in determining both their settlements and whether nearby family members could care for the children. Abandoned children appear in each year I sampled. We can give only a few examples.

In 1867, a 10 year old named Thomas Donahue was admitted. His mother had died years before, and his father drank. He then stayed with a Mrs. Mullally in Boston, who, though she was first identified as an aunt, was not a family member. The father could "do no more for the child" and somehow the caretaker was now not available. He was sent from Tewksbury to the State Primary School. In 1872, another 10 year old named Philip E. Snow was admitted from Boston and eventually also sent to Monson. He too was a "half-orphan" as his mother had died. His father, Philip Snow, was a painter who worked "out of town." Philip had been "living with his grandfather Snow in ... Boston, [but now he] says [he is] too poor to keep him so he came here." Phillip appears to have been "put out" from the State Primary School.

Four-year-old Mary Ferrin was left by her mother, Mary, of Lawrence, Massachusetts, with a Mrs. Cross in 1880. The mother agreed to pay Mrs. Cross for her daughter's care while she worked at the mill. The mother evidently left "and her whereabouts [were] unknown." The father was also unknown. Although Mary was discharged in several weeks, it is unclear where the almshouse discharged her to. In 1895, John and Albert Ellis, ages 9 and 13, were brought to the almshouse after their father, Luther, lost his railroad job and deserted them. It is unclear where their mother was or whether they were eventually discharged to the grandparents who were caring for the two other children.

The second largest category of children admitted were those whose parents were jailed, imprisoned, or in mental institutions. Usually these admissions were somewhat longer, as there was some effort to have at least some children remain when the family member's sentence was short or nearing a conclusion. However, for those whose parent, or parents, had longer sentences, they might well be placed out or removed elsewhere. To take three rather random examples:

[1875] Martha McVey, 6 years old, [admitted] from Boston [on] October 25. [Her] alias McVeigh. [She was] born in Londonderry, Ireland. Her father Michael died in Boston. Her mother Isabella is at House of Industry for larceny. Her term expires Feb 24, 1876. [The mother is] intemperate and has been in prison before. Martha was then [placed] with [the] Sisters of Charity. She was sent to the State Primary School on October 29.

[1882] Lucy A. Moore and Sarah E. Moore, 7 years old and 6 years old [were] admitted from Chicopee on March 22. [The] latter [is] listed as born in England, their father Thomas landed in Boston 1878 [doesn't say from where] and [has lived] in Lowell for one year, Chicopee for three months and [his] residence [is] unknown since. Their mother Lucy landed in Boston in 1879 [and] went direct to Chicopee. [She was] committed to NLH [Northampton Lunatic Hospital] on March 22. They were discharged ... to the State Primary School.

[1895] Daniel L. Darwood alias Dorwood 6 years old. [He was] admitted from Fall River and Mary 3 ½ [years old] from Fall River on May 30. They were born in New York and Fall River respectively. Their parents George and Elizabeth nee Sutton were born in Scotland and [illegible] have lived in Fall River the past five years. They were aided by Overseers of Poor in 1893–94. Their parents [are] now in the New Bedford House of Correction awaiting trial for keeping a disorderly home and adultery. [They were] discharged on June 8.

In addition to abandoned children and those whose parent or parents were in institutions, many children admitted having run away, either from home or extended family, or, as we shall see later, from other institutions or from the families they were placed into. For example:

> [1870] Llewellyn Westcott, 13 years old admitted on January 26. He was born in Portsmouth, New Hampshire [and he] thinks his father Charles was born Kennebunkport, Maine. [His father] died in Portland two years ago. His mother Harriet [was] born [in] Freedom, New Hampshire [and] died two weeks ago. He has lived with [his] grandfather in Portsmouth since [his] mother died. [The] permit says he ran away from there. [He] walked from there to Boston....

> [1876] John Kirby 15 years old admitted from Tewksbury on February 10 ... He was born [in] Manchester, New Hampshire. His mother Margaret died when he was 5 years old and he came to [his] uncle Patrick Tracy in Attleboro and [has been] there since except [for] various times when he has run away to Boston and other places ... [He is a] former inmate here and absconded, [he] also absconded from [the] State Primary School and from place[ment]. [He] recently turned up in the police station in Worcester, ragged and filthy, having again runaway from his uncle and [he had] been tramping....

> [1885] Michael Boland admitted from Lawrence on January 20. [He is] well, 12 years old, he was born in Lowell, his parents Patrick and Mary were born in Ireland. His father died in Lowell eight years ago, his mother Marie married an Augustus Johnson in Portland, Maine three years ago. She [has been] there for most of the time since her first husband's death and is now living there. This boy ran away from home and beat his way up to Boston on the cars ...

Finally, there were children admitted, increasingly over the years, whose parents needed some time away because of extreme poverty, loss, illness, or disability. In modern terms, this would be called respite care. In 1877, for example, Margaret Froitingham, a recent Scottish immigrant, had suffered the death of her husband and daughter recently. Mr. Gale, an unidentified man—apparently an agent or Overseer—was quoted as saying "[the] mother has gone out to [domestic] service to maintain herself and wants [her son Arthur, 7] sent to State Primary School until she can take him, as soon as she gets a little something to do so with, she having expended all her means in the burial of her husband and daughter." Arthur was admitted and almost immediately discharged to the State Primary School in Monson. In another example from 1895, Biagio Frezza, a 3-year-old child, was admitted from Boston. His "mother had a shock three years ago and her right side is now paralyzed, but she can do her own work." She had three other children—Theresa, 10, John, 7, and Carmen, 10 months old. The almshouse noted the "family is very poor." Biagio was kept at Tewksbury for nearly eleven months before being discharged.

FROM APPRENTICESHIP TO "PUTTING OUT"

From the very origins of the Anglo-American poor-relief system, Overseers of the Poor had the power to "bind out" children as apprentices to masters, who were to teach the children a trade and, in the interim—usually seven years—care for them. A form of indenture, this practice continued for at least 200 plus years of American history, and its end point is not totally clear. Some Tewksbury records do refer to "indentured children" in the 1860s–1870s. Although undoubtedly some children gained skills and had surrogate families, generally, from a modern perspective, it was a very repressive system. Like the indentured servants who made up a fairly large number of Colonial immigrants, the indentured child was legally the property of the master. One law, for example, enabled the "acquittal of anyone who committed homicide in the process of 'correcting' an apprentice." Although the analogy made by some to slavery is overstated, it is true that, practically speaking, the apprentice rarely had legal recourse against a vicious master and was for the most part a nonperson during the course of his bounding out. Homer Folks stated in his history:

> In its worst forms, and especially in some localities, certain features of the
> indenture system, particularly the recapture of apprentices who ran away,
> painfully reminded one of human slavery ... [I]t has been seriously suggested
> that by the adoption of the constitutional amendment in 1865, forbidding
> "involuntary servitude" the indenture system became unconstitutional.

Folks believed that by 1875 indenture systems were gone. Unfortunately, in part because terms "indenture," "binding out," "placing out," and "putting out" were used somewhat interchangeably, it is not always possible to distinguish when various states and localities or even individual institutions (almshouses, orphanages) moved away from formal apprenticeship. Many later nineteenth-century "placing out" systems, most famously Charles Loring Brace's "orphan trains," which placed thousands of children out in the West, used no legal documentation whatsoever. Children were viewed by townspeople at train stations, and those who liked a child (or believed them to be able to be strong laborers) could select them. In some areas, including Massachusetts's almshouses by the 1870s, a more formal set of agreements began to be made between an institution and a host family. A Visiting Agent was appointed who made certain written requirements of a family. He was to visit the home to make sure it was appropriate, providing adequate conditions, sending the child to school, and not treating the child as chattel labor. In theory, then, children historically moved from being legally bound to the family of a master to being "placed" (as today we do in foster care) with a caring family who provided for their needs for a limited time.

Unfortunately, as noted social welfare figure Grace Abbott argued in the twentieth century, institutions and officials had a vested interest in removing children: "It was a cheap and easy way of providing what passed as care for those children." A scandal developed early in the history of the Massachusetts state almshouse system about what had happened to those placed out. The 1864 annual report noted an investigation had been held into the fate of eighteen boys who were sent to Beverly, Massachusetts, from the almshouse to "learn the shoe making trade." Though they were supposed to be under the supervision of one man, they were not in his care "and not properly treated." Since the state reports are prone to understatement, one can only guess at their conditions and treatment. The boys were brought back to the almshouse. A special report was commissioned after the Civil War in which Visiting Agent George P. Elliot was highly critical of the state almshouse's placing out record. Elliot sought to document hundreds of cases of placing out, but found he could find little good information. He complained:

> Children are charged to families in remote localities, to which your Agent would go to considerable expense of time and money, only to find that years before they had been returned to the almshouse ... A large majority of children have left their original places, and gone from one family, or town, or State, to another, no account of such changes being reported or of record, which often led to a tedious search from place to place, and thousands of miles additional travel.

Elliot did find some "excellent families" in the state and gave some examples of success stories, including a placed-out child who was "now a teacher at a New York university." However, too often he found children lacking education because they were worked so hard at the mills or at the farms; children were denied even religious services so they would not miss work, and were underfed or undernourished. Elliot found it "no uncommon occurrence for persons" wanting children "really ... merely for tending cows on the public highways." Some placed-out children were left suddenly to their own devices once the growing and harvesting season ended. As the opening quotations at the chapter's start indicate, the controversy over "binding out" would continue throughout the nineteenth century, with social welfare experts on each side. Many of the critics could be mistaken for critics of deinstitutionalization of the mentally ill or of the foster care system in the later decades of the twentieth century. The president of Girard College, a special college set up for orphans, complained "Our experience with farmers has not been satisfactory. They are not considerate for the child's welfare, caring only to use them for their profit." Lyman Alden sounded like a critic of modern foster care when he lamented "children ... tossed back and forth like a shuttlecock." Robert W. Hebberd of the State Board of Charities in New York saw states with "miserly constituencies mostly seeking to save money and rid themselves of embarrassing charges." Pressed by financial and political reasons, Superintendents of the Poor or other officials were releasing children to "a class of people who want workers" or just "household drudges."

But just as some critics of deinstitutionalization used horror stories to imply that the old institutional system was better, most reformers argued that children living out their youth in poorhouses or orphanages or asylums was not a better idea. Josephine Shaw Lowell, the famous social welfare reformer, in a study of New York City's massive bureaucracy of children's homes and orphanages denounced the self-interest of these institutions, claiming they had a strong interest in self-perpetuation as they were funded by public money on a per capita basis. Homer Folks remained militant in being anti-institutional: "why have institutions at all? *And why should we* [original emphasis] ... it is a necessary evil, it may be an evil, but it is not a necessity!"

Beyond the heat generated by the conflicts, all parties seem to have agreed that if proper caring families could be found who were not motivated purely by greed but by the real love of a child, and if they were sufficiently monitored by outside parties to ensure school attendance, health, rest, and other good conditions, that family placement could work. Homer Folks in fact was ahead of his time by proposing monetary payments to families, as foster families today receive.

From a more modern standpoint, both sides of the dispute also shared major lacunae. Neither institutionalists nor deinstitutionalists paid much attention to improving the conditions of parents which might militate against the suffering of children, e.g., provision of income or better paying jobs or improved housing and living conditions for the (adult) poorer classes. Such association of economic and social conditions with children's well being would, for the most part, have to await the Progressive Era. Nor did the two sides attend to the psychological and social differences between the types of children. While social welfare institutions and leaders separated "bad" or delinquent children from merely neglected or dependent ones, there was no modern refinement of differences in children such as the trauma of an abused child or the special needs of the disabled child, or consideration of the difficulties inherent in the displacement of a child from one place to another. Hence, no matter the setting of care or the quality of the foster parent, some children would be extremely difficult to care for, while other children would be very resilient. While some, relatively few children always needed specialized settings, most did not.

A Sampling of "Put Out" Children

While there were no doubt thousands of inmates who earlier in their lives were bound or placed out, I have access only to a sampling of adults or children who the *Inmate Biographies* chose to identify as such and/or had returned to Tewksbury as a result of the failure of their placements. Obviously, the sixty-three inmates in the sample serve only as a partial reflection of the little-known experience of being placed out. The experiences conveyed through the *Inmate Biographies* are so mixed that neither a completely negative nor positive view of "placing out" can be supported. On the one hand, a small plurality of those inmates who had been placed out can be judged as having made out reasonably well. Yet the negative stories of placing out were more dramatic, tending to outweigh the more routine notes on the other children.

The Negative Stories of Being "Put Out"

As noted, the failures of indenture and placing out are probably more apparent if one goes by the amount of space devoted by the Tewksbury clerks to this experience. This tendency did not strike me as reflecting a particular bias. Rather, children who did not "work out" in their placements were often viewed (and perhaps were) more complex or difficult "cases" than those who did not come with this past history. Where an inmate had spent a long time with a family, as compared to having run away or frequently moved, this was noted only casually, often without comment.

Most of the negative cases involved issues familiar to us still today in some parts of our foster care system. Some children were "bounced around" from home to home, and some ran away from their host families. Older girls were susceptible to sexual encounters or rape, though most allegations were made against coworkers on farms or other establishments rather than the parents themselves. A small number of children were seen as delinquents who did not work out. One case provides us with an example of how leaving indenture at age 18 led to homelessness, just as today many social workers complain that children "age out" of foster care and other child welfare systems without appropriate assistance or follow-up.

Margaret Lovett, an 1874 inmate, had the kind of story which supports those critics of being "tossed back and forth like a shuttlecock" back then, and many tales of "bouncing around" even today:

> At the age of 12 she was admitted to this institution [on] August 1, 1854 from Boston with her brother Michael. [She was] here until January 23, 1855 when [she was] taken by Plummer Weeks of Lawrence with whom she lived nearly two years. [Then she] ran away and returned here [on] January 29, 1857 from Worcester. [She was then] taken by P. E. Davis of Haverhill [on] February 20, 1857. [She was] with him two weeks and [then] returned March 4, 1857. Then [she was] taken by O. Johnson of North Andover. [She was] with him a short time, [then] ran away to Boston, [and was] committed to Deer Island for disobedience [in] August 1857, there for two years and ten months ...

As the years went by it is not surprising that almshouse clerks expended less energy in listing each and every placement a child had been in:

> [1880] William Livingston, 24 years old ... His own mother died when he was an infant, his father left [his] second wife one year after [their] marriage and she came to America. She placed William in a home in Canada since which time she has had no care of him and he has been moved from place to place. [He] has lived in Harvard, Groton, Pepperell, Barre, Cambridge, Oxford, and Templeton, no other institution ...

> [1895] Ellen Rice, 18 years old ... her father died and her mother deserted her when she was five years old. She was then placed in the Boston Female Asylum. [She was] there until thirteen years of age, then she went to Wadley's Falls, New Hampshire and was there for two and half years. Then [she went] to South Boston for six months. Then [she was] committed to [the] State

Industrial School [for] about three years ago and has been placed in three different families since. [She] knows nothing of her parents....

Of course, for the many children who ran away from placements, such behavior often was consistent with their running away from their own parents, as well as institutions. To take only two examples:

[1876] Mary Burke admitted from Boston on May 20. She is 19 and [was] born in South Boston ... [She] ... went to the Sisters of Charity [on?] Camden Street, [then to the] St. Vincent Orphans Home at 11 years of age. [She was] there for one year and [then] returned to [her] parents, [but she] soon ran away and returned to the Home. She has run away from home two or three times..... [She was] put out by visiting agent in the family of Mr. Gleason Lexington, [and was] there for three years and [then] ran away. Then to BB Johnson's [placement?] and [then] sent to State Primary School, then [she was sent] to a place in Norwich, Connecticut for eleven months, then [sent] to Wilbraham and Ware until she was sent here ...

[1895] Harold Wilson from Boston admitted [on] March 12. He is 14 and his birthplace [is] unknown. He was here before four years ago and he was sent to the State Primary School. He was there for two years [and then he was] placed out with Mr. Grisley [of] Brattleboro, Vermont. He was there for two days and returned to [the] State Primary School, then [he went] to Mr. Shelly of Holyoke, he was there until three weeks ago when he ran away and was sent here by Mr. Emery ...

We should keep in mind that many of these children would have been considered more "grown up" than their chronological counterparts today. Clearly, as a sample drawn from an almshouse population, most grew up in poverty, and in adverse circumstances which might have included abuse, neglect, alcoholism, or other difficulties. Moreover, in several cases where we have follow-up data, the history of running or multiple placements did not mean the subjects did not go on to live "normal" lives. Margaret Lovett, for example, married a soldier in 1878, and Lizzie Fleming, an 1873 inmate with a history of multiple placements as a "put out" child, married a farmer.

Quite a few of the females who were placed out returned to the Tewksbury Almshouse pregnant. The women who returned included those who had been recently placed, those long-term placed, some who were as far as we can tell accepted into their placements, and those who perhaps were not. Most cases of "criminal intimacies" developed out of relationships with coworkers. Most placed-out females were employed as servants or laundresses or cooks. In the following sample cases, coworkers were blamed for the "intimacies":

[1874] Ann Ilsley 20 admitted from Boston on April 23. She was born in Salem ... [She was] sent to the [State] Industrial School [in] Lancaster. She was there [for] one year, because she kept company with lewd girls. [Then?] there placed out by visiting agent in the family of James Howard of West Bridgewater and there until removed by Visiting Agent to a Boarding House on Ferdinand Street, Boston as she was pregnant by Maynard W. Ilsley a farm hand of Mr. Howard's. Criminal intimacy commenced over one year ago one evening in a ploughed field while out for a walk, frequently after in the barn and other places....

[1880] Minnie A. Payne 15 years old admitted from Boston [on] November 20. [She is] pregnant [and was] born [in] Nova Scotia, came to Boston in 1875 with [her] grandmother Martha Payne. She died last winter. Minnie has been in the Little Wanderers Home for the greater portion of the last four years. [She] was [then] placed in the family of Mr. John Werton [of] 17 Glenn Street, Somerville in May last and while there became pregnant by one Pierce Kelley [who was] also in the employ of Mr. Werton, was returned to the home in August last and as soon as they found out her condition they sent her to her uncle Joseph? Payne in Arlington ...

In some cases, the host or foster family defended the woman against charges of impropriety. For example, in 1876, Kate Jackson, a 17-year-old woman, was admitted pregnant. She had been placed out of the State Primary School at Monson at about age 8 or 9 to the family of David Harrington in Paxton, Massachusetts, a rural town near Worcester. The Harringtons brought Ms. Jackson first to the Visiting Agent and in turn to the almshouse, "saying she is a good girl and her present trouble is not her own fault." Her pregnancy resulted from the actions of one William McCarty, a farmhand of Mr. Harrington's.

In October last Mr. Harrington's family being away, McCarty came to the kitchen where she was working and commenced taking liberties with her finally resulting in sexual intercourse. He had previously had intercourse with her in the barn several months before this. A few days after this affair she told Mrs. Harrington about the affair. McCarty was still living at Mr. Harrington's [when] she came to Boston ...

At the other end of the spectrum, there were some cases (and likely others not reported) where the host family itself was directly responsible for the sexual encounter. In the 1865 case of an Isabella Gillespie, 15, who had been placed out directly from Tewksbury, the host father, Edmund Davis of Portsmouth, New Hampshire, blamed the son of a neighbor for Ms. Gillespie's pregnancy. The almshouse ascertained, however, that the father of the child was Charles H. Davis, 17, Edmund's son. In 1895, Mary L. Ryder, a 17 year old who was orphaned very young and had been at an orphanage, had come to Tewksbury from the family of Dr. William Peterson of Waltham, Massachusetts. She was pregnant by Dr. Peterson, described as a "veterinary surgeon of Waltham and her former employer."

Some children were identified by host families or other institutions as being young criminals or delinquents. It is, of course, not possible to unearth all the actual facts, but no doubt there were children for whom families either were inappropriate or who would have been troubling wherever they were. John Mann, an 18-year-old man admitted to Tewksbury in 1875, was an orphan who was placed out at the age of 12 to a Joseph Morgan, a painter. Morgan charged that Mann was a young thief who stole from him, but John denied "ever stealing anything but once when he took three cents from a draw[er] in Mr. Morgan's house." Interestingly, the almshouse did not always take the side of those who reported misbehavior. For example, Alice Chase was an 11-year-old girl admitted to Tewksbury in 1876 from the Convent of the Sisters of Mercy in Worcester. The Convent had "turned her over to the City Marshal because she was a *thief* [their emphasis] and altogether too *vile* [their emphasis] to be retained in the convent and she was sent here." The almshouse clerk opined "she appears [to be an] unusually bright and interesting girl. She admits she used to take the pencils and paper of the other girls because she had none of her own." Alice was sent to the State Primary School and likely placed out, and it is hard to know which description, if any, stuck with her. Meanwhile, in the same year, Agnes Goddard, an orphan girl "put out" to a home in New Hampshire, was charged with attempting to poison her host family, "and was discovered shortly after she set fire to [a] barn which was entirely consumed with its contents of eight oxen, five cows, and two horses, sheep, calves, hay and utensils." The clerks judged that she "doesn't appear to be insane, [but] can give no reason for her conduct." She was taken to Boston and committed to the State Industrial School (Reform School) in Lancaster.

Finally, the case of a John Bridge, a 20-year-old man admitted in 1876 with frozen hands and feet, reveals that whatever his placement was like he was not prepared to weather the aftermath. He was an orphan placed out from the State Primary School. Since his "indenture ended" in the rural town of Goshen, Massachusetts, he had "been drifting about the country [for the] past three years ... he has worked for awhile and then tramped and bummed." Of course, these were depression years, so he had much in common with non-bound-out people, but social service professionals would surely make the connection of the frequent problems even today of what happens to children following their years of foster care placement.

Some Positive Outcomes of the "Putting Out" System

As noted, the examples of "putting out" are drawn from notes that are not specifically on the topic, so we are making inferences in judging how these children fared. Several pieces of information indicate that while stories of multiple placements, runaways, sexual contacts, and other issues were certainly common to the "putting out" system, some inmate biographies indicate some children may have done well.

First, among those descriptions of "put out" children that provide specific information on how many years a child spent with a host family, the majority were not "bounced around" but in fact fairly stable. In thirteen cases, one or more children stayed with one host family for five or more years, and a total of nineteen stayed for three or more years, while only nine stayed for less than three years. Second, some anecdotal information might support a more positive view. This includes a number of children who asked to be put out, a number of inmates who had been placed out and were complimented by the clerks' notes, and a few who seem to have fared well occupationally.

As Table 7.1 indicates, there were those "put out" (among those "inmate biographies" for whom specific information could be obtained) who spent a fair amount of time with one family. These cases contradict the image of "bouncing around." To take several examples:

[1867] Ellen McCarty 20 years old, she was born in Boston. Her father [illegible] died in Tewksbury Almshouse. Her mother Mary died in Boston. Ellen was placed out on April 18, 1859 to Edward Short of Lowell. [She] has lived with him ever since except for two or three months....

[1871] John Higgs admitted from Boston on March 11. He is 21 years old and he was born in Boston. His parents died when he was small, their names [are] unknown. He [was] sent to Deer Island and from there he went to Monson almshouse and was there until he was ten years old. Then he was indentured to a William McCarty of Barre. He was with him for nine years, in Barre and vicinity until April 1870 ...

[1882] Jane Richardson, 25, from Boston admitted on June 2. Her birthplace is unknown, [she was] born on January 7, 1857. Her parents [are] unknown. They died when she was a school girl. She went from Goffstown, New Hampshire to Milton, New Hampshire poorhouses. For the past one year and a half, she

Table 7.1 Length of Longest Stay of "Put-Out" Children with One Host Family*

Name	Year admitted	Approximate length
Isabella Gillespie	1865	Just short of four years
Ellen McCarty	1867	Eight years
Mary Carter	1867	Three years
John Higgs	1871	Nine years
Catherine Heiser	1872	Six years
Lizzie Fleming	1873	No stretches longer than 2–3 years
John Barry	1873	Three years
Maria Sanders	1874	Seven years
Edward Jelly	1874	Nine years
Ann Ilsley	1874	Three years
Margaret Lovett	1874	Two years (maximum)
James O'Neil	1875	Three years
Louisa Roberts	1875	One and a half years
John Mann	1875	Two years
Caroline Tolladay	1875	Six years
Mary Burke	1876	Three years
Emma Jones	1876	Five months
Betsy Kelty	1876	Three years
Kate Jackson	1876	Seven to eight years
James Woodbury	1876	Eighteen years
Jacob Jackson	1876	Five years
James H Smith	1877	Ten years
Minnie Payne	1880	Six months
John Thorton	1882	Seven years
Jane Richardson	1882	Ten years
George E. White	1893	One and a half years
Frank McNamara	1893	Seven years
Martin Green	1895	Six years
Ellen Rice	1895	Two and a half years longest
Mary Ryder	1895	Two years

*Many of the sixty-three placed out children's *Inmate Biographies* were either not specific enough on the length of placements or the children were just about to be "put out" to a family.

has lived with Dr. Marshall S. Brown of Brighton, and previously ten years with Mrs. Brown's sister, Mrs. Ball, of South Boston ...

Of course, length of time in a family does not equate with quality of life, and, conversely, youth who were only placed out at fifteen would only have a few years left of "their minority," while those put out when very young would naturally have more years to spend with families. Still, those who stayed with families for many years contradict the stereotypes of repeated placements. Some "inmate biographies" also provide a sense of how placement developed into more of an adoptive relationship. James H. Woodbury, a 26-year-old seaman with epilepsy admitted to the almshouse in 1876, had lived for eighteen years in the family of Richard S. Roberts of East Boston. The Robertses were not relatives, but the 1860 census shows both James and his father living with that family. His father died of small-pox, and whether this relationship evolved into a formal adoption or a continued residence, we cannot be sure. He was in fact sent to Tewksbury "at their [the Roberts'] request." Solomon Conway, an 1880 inmate who was labeled "simple minded," was an illegitimate child bound out as a boy. Although he left an indentured relationship with "one Tufts of North Brookfield" at age 21, he lived most of his life under the guardianship of William P. Stone of North Brookfield. Stone was a fairly affluent farmer, and census data confirm the "In-mate Biography" that Solomon "has earned a little money from time to time and has been taxed for it." He was listed as having $600 in personal property in the 1860 census. It is hard to know the extent of Conway's disability, but clearly he spent much of his life living with Stone and his family.

Some children expressed their desire to go to the State Primary School and be placed out. Catherine Sweeney, a 13-year-old girl admit-ted in 1870, expressed this desire. Her father was in prison and her mother had deserted her. Similarly James Johnson, a 15-year-old boy admitted in 1880, specifically asked to be "placed out on a farm." He too had a father in and out of the House of Industry and his mother was dead. He had been living with an aunt, but had left her and ran off to Boston. For children with few options and no family to care for them, being put out provided a new start. Some children hoped that the new families would provide them with skills or economic security. For the boys especially, the hope of learning a trade or farming must have been appealing.

Charles Thayer, a 24 year old admitted in 1876, was bound out in 1858 when his mother died and his "father put him in a place in Ohio." We are told little about this except he was there until 1870. He was an engineer and a fireman, and also a "musician [who] gets a portion of his living in the exercise of this latent [talent] on several different instruments." The note takers tell us he was "a fine appearing young man, apparently entirely out of place in an almshouse." Jacob Jack-son, a 28 year old admitted the same year, was a furniture polisher who upon the death of his uncle "was taken from there by a farmer with whom he lived for five years." He was described positively as "appear[ing] well disposed" and "a temperate man."

For a variety of reasons, it is not possible to make strong statements about the fate of either the "put out" children themselves, or the children who were admitted to the Tewksbury Almshouse, as a whole. We can tell that generally those bound out did not differ greatly demographically from the rest of the children in nativity, gender, or any other clear way. A higher number of those bound out were illegitimate children. Also among the bound-out children disabled children were slightly more numerous. Occupationally, a large number of the children became domestic servants in the case of girls, and laborers, and later factory workers, in the case of the placed-out boys. From one point of view, the effort to continue the farm tradition by placing boys into "good respectable farms" did not work in an era and region witnessing the decline of farming as a main occupation.

Still, there are sufficient examples of "put out" children gaining decent jobs that we can say the system worked for at least some children. As we have noted above, even in their twenties, Charles Thayer and Jacob Jackson appeared to have skilled trades. Alfred Williams, whom we met in Chapter 4, was a bound-out child who became an oiler; Edward Jelly, an 1874 inmate who was bound out when ten years old, was a machinist in the 1880 census; and at least three of the four Briggs children who were placed out after they entered the almshouse in 1895 (see Chapter 4) did well, with Frederick ultimately becoming a mechanic at the successor to the almshouse itself and owning a home, Frank becoming a restaurant cook and having a servant of his own, and Robert working as a civilian employee in a police department.

THE FAILURE OF SIMPLE SOLUTIONS TO CHILDREN'S PROBLEMS

In retrospect, we can, on the one hand, see Massachusetts officials as being relatively reformist in their being in the forefront of efforts for children, while on the other hand, we can see, as was evident to reformers themselves after the turn of the century, the failure of simple solutions to succeed very well.

Certainly, in comparison with the early nineteenth century, and with other states in the Union even at the time, Northeastern reformers saw the need to remove children from squalor and poor circumstances relatively early. Hence they became among the first to experiment both with specialized institutions (orphanages, juvenile homes, children's homes) and with the equivalent of modern foster care and adoption.

The public reaction, as early as during the Civil War, to the failure of state officials to account for children placed out was certainly a good sign of concern for the state's children. And, unlike Charles Loring Brace and his Children's Aid Society, there is no evidence that New England public or charitable officials massively moved children out of the states to get rid of undesirables or, as the Catholic Church charged, convert them to Protestantism.

Still, the reforms of one era often seem inadequate or even naive to later generations. Because the overall situation of those living in poor conditions did not change, but in many ways worsened during the Gilded Age, as the factory system grew willy-nilly, and urban slum overcrowding continued, the severity of social problems that families encountered continued to grow. Only in the Progressive Era, when some reformers supported "mothers' pensions" to provide cash assistance to poor mothers, did the idea of income support gain acceptance. Of course, by this time, populist and more radical movements were far ahead of the reformers in their diagnosis of the problems of capitalism. Later reformers and child welfare experts recognized simply moving children from almshouses to orphanages, asylums, or reform schools was no solution, nor was placing them out with farmers and others who needed labor. This is not to deny that some children, such as the severely disabled or disturbed, might not always need facilities. Nor is it to deny a role for foster care with supervision and support for qualified caregivers. But these issues are marginal to those experts and reformers of a hundred years or more later who recognize that the overall fate of children is bound up with the quality of adult lives and with the low social welfare support given in the United States. Ironically, the gains in social welfare made in the twentieth century would benefit the elderly more than children, leaving even twenty-first-century America with one of the highest rates of child poverty in the world.

EIGHT

"We Can Do Nothing for Him": The Fate of the Elderly

> "[His] brother Eugene ... can do no more for Cornelius, he is an old man himself and has a family to support ... "
>
> "Inmate Biography," Cornelius McCuddy, 70, 1865

> "His daughter ... is intemperate and will do nothing for him, [he] has slept in the station house [the] past few nights, [and has] been aided by the Overseers of the Poor occasionally, [he is] infirm ... "
>
> "Inmate Biography," James Fitzpatrick, 78, 1876

No group became more associated historically with the "poorhouse" than the aged. Even when life spans were far shorter in earlier American history than they would become in the twentieth century, elderly people must have been common sights at poorhouses, particularly when the cold winters ended, and those able to leave their town poorhouses did so. By the late nineteenth century, the elderly would become overwhelmingly the most dominant population in the poorhouses. Yet even earlier than this, American culture captured the harshness of the poorhouse system by associating it with aging and the rejection of parents and grandparents by their youngers, most famously in Will Carleton's 1870s poem (later a popular song) "Over the Hill to the Poorhouse":

Over the hill to the poor-house I'm trudgin' my weary way—
I a woman of 70 and only a trifle gray—
I, who am smart an' chipper, for all the years I've told,
As many another woman that's only half as old ...
What is the use of heapin' on me a pauper's shame?
Am I lazy or crazy? Am I blind or lame?
True, I am not so supple, nor yet so awful stout:
But charity ain't no favor, If one can live without

Over the hill to the poorhouse—my child'rn dear, goodbye!
Many a night I've watched you when only God was nigh:
And God'll judge between us; but I will always pray
That you shall never suffer the half I do today.

Although the verse above is the most famous part of the song, the original Carleton poem spoke of the rejection by one member of the family after another of this "woman of 70":

So 'twas only a few days before the thing was done—
They were a family of themselves and I another one;
And a very little cottage one family will do,
But I never have seen a house that was big enough for two.
I went to live with Susan, but Susan's house was small,
And she was always a-hintin' how snug it was for us all;
And what with her husband's sisters, and what with chil'rn three,
'Twas easy to discover that there wasn't room for me,
An' then I went to Thomas, the oldest son I've got,
For Thomas' building'd cover the half an acre lot;
But all the chil'rn was on me—I couldn't stand their sauce—
And Thomas said I needn't think I was comin' there to boss.
An' then I wrote to Rebecca, my girl who lives out West,
And to Isaac, not far from her—some twenty miles at best;
and one of 'em said 'twas too warm there for any one so old,
And t'other had an opinion the climate was too cold.
So they have shirked and slighted me, an' shifted me about—
So they have well-nigh soured me, an' wore my old heart out;
But still I've borne up pretty well, an' wasn't much put down,
Till Charley went to the poor-master, an' put me on the town.

Interestingly, the typicality of Carleton's story about the rejection of elderly people in this time period has been the subject of some revisionist history. Early work on the history of aging in America contrasted the great respect afforded elders in the seventeenth and eighteenth centuries with the decline in status and value placed on old people as industrialization occurred. More recent work has questioned this, painting the status of the old as remaining relatively the same until reform movements pushed the elderly out of the workforce in the 1930s. Noting that workplace participation remained high for the elderly and that most remained in their own family constellations until the 1930s, Carole Haber and Brian Gratton argue it was policymakers and professional advocates who constructed a sympathetic portrait of the old that provoked pathos and anger, eventually leading to the passage of pensions and a set retirement age. While well meaning, those who told the story of almshouses, outdoor relief, poverty, and despair among the elderly did not provide a true picture. For our purposes, it is important to acknowledge that relatively few of the elderly as a percentage of the population ever went to the poorhouse, just as today the vast majority of elderly people live in their own homes, not in nursing homes or other institutions.

This chapter dealing with a sample of poorhouse inmates cannot resolve the broader debates as to when and how conditions for the aged changed or whether there was exaggeration in the portraits of the treatment of the elderly. On the one hand, observers such as Haber and Gratton may miss the point that social significance does not reside in only numbers, but in the powerful fear that the poorhouse established for generations of elderly people of the possibility of ending one's days there (as the saying went, you had "a reverence for God, the hope of heaven, and the fear of the poorhouse"). On the other hand, this chapter, in exploring the elderly inmates at Tewksbury, does find their presence part of a multifaceted issue, hardly reducible only to unkind families or societal hostility. Without what at the time would have been an extremely unusual amount of money saved (since there was no health insurance at the time and few public hospitals), many ill and infirm people entered the almshouse, many dying there. Naturally the aged were the primary population at risk of illness, death, and disability. In some cases, family estrangement played an important role in their placement into the almshouse. But in many cases family problems went both ways. Some inmates were always single and lost touch with their families of origin; others suffered from alcoholism or other problems and had alienated their families. Some families had maintained their relatives at home only to find they could no longer do so, or an elderly person himself or herself left home stating that he or she "did not want to burden" their families. Some inmates stated a distaste for various relatives and came to the almshouse to find shelter. Finally, many elderly people did well until their source of employment ended. Hence, while the "Over the Hill to the Poorhouse" lyrics are a critically important part of American history, they do not provide a complete or balanced picture of the complexity of the treatment of the aged.

A PLACE TO DIE

The number of elderly people in this sample is deceptively low. As noted in the introduction to this Part, I found only between 100 and 200 inmates in the sample dependent on the age cutoff used (55 or 65).

However, this is misleading in the sense that at any one time, a large number of the inmates were elderly. For example, a review of 1880 census enumeration sheets for the Tewksbury almshouse shows that about forty percent of the inmates were over 55 on the date the census was taken. Annie Sullivan, who was an inmate at Tewksbury from 1876 to 1880 (see Chapter 1), told a biographer of "[t]he ward ... filled with old women, grotesque, misshapen, diseased and dying." Even her close friend there, inmate Maggie Carroll, "was a cripple whose poor body was so warped and twisted that she had to be strapped to a wooden frame." Clearly, although, as we have seen, admissions to the almshouse included all ages and all types of people, since most admissions were short, particularly for children and healthy adults, the almshouse population was overly composed *at any one time* of old and disabled people who were not able to leave. Later in the history of the poorhouse—by the turn of the twentieth century, or earlier in some facilities—the dominant population at almost all times, and even for cumulative admissions, came to be the elderly. In part, this was a function of reform: the removal of children and of populations of the disabled such as the mentally ill and the blind and deaf, and the ability of adults of working age to leave the almshouse and take jobs when the economy was better.

It is important to remember that for most of this time—there were some changes which were occurring at least in New England in the last decade of our study—there was not much of a medical safety net for the poor or working people. Generally only paying customers were served by the private hospitals such as Massachusetts General Hospital. While Boston City Hospital originated in 1864, it was small relative to the large demand, and other cities in the state (and elsewhere) did not have free hospitals, though some church-related hospitals did serve poor Irish and other immigrants. Some Tewksbury inmates who were veterans awaited admissions to veterans' hospitals. Even where a public or charity hospital existed, care was restricted, and often totally unavailable for stigmatized diseases such as venereal diseases and tuberculosis. No system of nursing homes, old age homes, rehabilitation facilities, or what we would today call "long-term care" existed. Once an acute phase of disease or recovery from an accident was over, patients were discharged to fall upon their own devices. Individuals and families were forced to live with many diseases for which no treatments existed. If inmates had families, they were often crammed into crowded quarters. The disabled, ill, and infirm came to impose a financial, emotional, and spatial burden even on the most loving families. Most families attempted to keep their elders at home, but for various reasons some could not or would not. Table 8.1 shows what happened over the thirty-year period to the elderly people who were admitted to Tewksbury. While our records are probably incomplete, at least forty-eight (or a fourth) of the 192 people over 55 years old admitted to Tewksbury died within three years of admission. The figure may be an underestimate because I am dependent on either the *Inmate Biographies* noting the person died or on the state Vital Statistics indicating death. Neither source is entirely reliable. An inmate may have left and then had a further admission later upon which a note of death was attached. In instances where a name was extremely common, it may not have been possible to match an inmate with his or her death.

Still the rate is high enough to note that the facility did serve as a "place to die," a stereotype about the poorhouse. Causes of death were extremely variable, and because the nineteenth-century taxonomy of death mixed the symptoms with the diseases, any list of causes of death is somewhat of a "hodgepodge." For example, in the twenty-two out of forty-eight cases where cause of death could be identified, four inmates died of paralysis; three of heart disease; three of phthisis (tuberculosis); two each of rheumatism, "old age," and "debility"; and one each from gangrene, an accident, diabetes, chronic diarrhea, cancer, and nephritis. Unfortunately, because the notes are nowhere as detailed as today's hospital charts, it is impossible to judge the inmates' specific medical conditions and whether they could have been cared for at home, nor can we assess the medical care they received at Tewksbury.

Table 8.1 Disposition and Deaths of Elderly Inmates at Tewksbury, 1865–1895

	65 or older	Age 55–64	Total
Died at Tewksbury Almshouse in year of admission	21 (20.6 %)	10 (11.1%)	31 (16.1%)
Discharged/Absconded	55	62	117
Stayed (Likely Low)*	15	7	22
Sent to Bridgewater Workhouse	4	5	9
Not clear*	7	6	13
Total	102	90	192
Died at Tewksbury Almshouse within three years	33 (32.3%)	15 (16.6%)	48 (25%)

*Unfortunately a number of inmate biographies do not include discharge or disposition information. I believe those who were never discharged (e.g., "Stayed") are probably higher, likely including the "not clear" ones.

We can certainly at times have a peek into the tragic circumstances of the care of the elderly during these times. In 1871, for example, James McIntire, 74 years old, apparently "got up in the night, raised a window in the attic, sat on the sill, lost his balance and fell to the ground. He died from the injuries received." Many elderly people wandered away, suggesting they had little supervision. Sometimes, though, they did fare alright, as when Mary A. Kearns, 65, of Fall River "strayed away in the woods in Fall River and fell in the snow. [She was] there from Thursday PM until Saturday PM, [and was] found by a man hunt." Kearns was discharged and went back to England where other family members lived. In 1882, despite advanced age several inmates left the almshouse to work, could not manage it, and then returned to the almshouse. Evart A. Van Gogh, a 62 year old, despite having "throat disease," "went to work in Neponset, Massachusetts, house painting. He then broke down and [was] obliged to return [to Tewksbury]." He died shortly thereafter of "debility." To take another frequent example, many inmates were described as "demented." Paul Gruzot, a 75-year-old man born in France and a widower, was admitted in 1885. While he seemed to have no relatives, he "has been provided for by the French Catholic priest at the Freeman Place Chapel ... [who] wants to be notified in case of Gruzot's death." Gruzot died two years later.

FAMILY AND WORK SITUATIONS OF THE ELDERLY

Clearly chronological age offers little clue to the well-being of the elderly, whether in 1865 or 2007, and even the health status, where available, is limited in identifying the issues the elderly faced. As is true today, supportive families with resources allow older people in a wide variety of health statuses to live in the community, and often to maintain their functioning until life's end. In an era long before the concept of "retirement" existed, the presence and availability of work was also key to the well-being of the elderly, and its withdrawal was also a major factor in the admissions to the almshouse.

Without or in Conflict with Families

Although there were certainly some elderly inmates who had supportive families, generally speaking most of the elderly admitted to Tewksbury were alone, either because they had outlived members of their family, were estranged from their family, or had found that care at home had become problematic. By "problematic," this is not to indicate fault necessarily belonged with either the inmate or their family. As often as not, the "can do nothing for him (or her)" comment made by the clerks of Tewksbury, may have represented a limit imposed by the poverty of the families. Or, to put it another way, the conflicts between family members derived from crowding and competing obligations. It is also likely that clerks writing these notes—who after all were charged with enforcing the old Poor Laws which held families chiefly responsible for aiding paupers—were acutely sensitive to this issue and may have been insistent on asking why the elderly person was not at home or could not be cared for at home. Interestingly, as the "inmate biographies" shortened in length in the 1880s, we get far fewer clues to family situation except for bare facts such as whether the inmate lived alone, was married, or, occasionally, whether they were in touch with their families. Family strain over age and health no doubt did not disappear in the later years of the Biographies, though these issues became less a topic to record. Hence, our best examples are from the first half of the *Inmate Biographies*. Additionally, an interesting finding is that while, as anticipated, men were dominant among those admitted to the almshouse who had outlived their partners (or occasionally other family members they had lived with) and those who appeared to be totally estranged from their families, among those who had problematic or conflictual issues with family members (hence provoking the "they can do nothing for him/her any longer") women were as well represented as men.

It was, of course, not unusual to find elderly people in the almshouse who had never married or who had outlived their spouses or other family members. Frederick Merritt, who was 64 and single, was admitted in 1866. He had been a farmer who lived with a William Bartlett in West Newbury, Massachusetts. He had "no relatives in America" (he was born in England), but he stated that Bartlett had "given him a bond for his land, and someone had then stole[n] the bond." Upon the death of William Bartlett, this put Merritt in dispute with Bartlett's son, William H. After the lengthy "Inmate Biography," the agent, Mr. Nash, stated that "(I) am satisfied [Frederick has] no claim good for [the] 5 acres." Bartlett was now alone and without funds and was not discharged for a number of years, but in the 1870 census he was listed as an inmate of the West Newbury poorhouse. John Lyons, another single inmate, 72, was admitted in 1875 and appeared to have managed well throughout his life until a recent illness. He was a cabinet maker and a carver who had owned property in Columbus, Ohio. He had been blind for twenty-five years, but was able to support himself until eight years before when he started being "supported by friends." His brother, Henry, had meanwhile recently committed suicide by taking poison. John was now blind and infirm, and in the in last few months he had taken sick in Rutland, Vermont. The note taker complimented him as "an inveterate talker and will tell his story his own way." Still another single man whose age "was nearer ninety than eighty" was African-born Dennis Brooks, admitted in 1876 and also infirm.

> He was brought to New York when he was quite young, [he stayed] in New York [for] a few years and [then went to] Washington DC for many years. [He was] in the war of 1812 [and] was a servant to General Stansberry [and] lived in Washington and vicinity until 1865. [He] then came to Boston and [has] since [lived] in various places about Boston [including] at City Hotel [in] Taunton [for] a few months as a waiter.

Brooks had "no relatives or friends in the world" and already been an inmate for several months at Tewksbury in 1874 and at Deer Island House of Industry for vagrancy for four months in 1872. He does not seem to have been discharged, but to have died at the almshouse.

Among the many widowed and separated elderly inmates at Tewksbury was Fanny Austin, aged 70 in 1866. Fanny had been married to Edward Whiting in Pittsfield, Massachusetts, for eleven years. Whiting died in 1864 in the Great Barrington, Massachusetts, poorhouse, and this apparently led to Fanny's admission to Tewksbury. She would remain at the Tewksbury Almshouse until she died on August 9, 1871. Felix Neptune was a "colored" man said to be 71 years old, who was admitted in 1870. After his first wife died, he remarried but she then left him in 1861. Neptune had "always followed the sea," and left no children or friends in state. His status was marked simply as "old age." He was not ready at this point to stay at the almshouse, and "absconded" in 1871, but records indicate he did die in 1874 at Tewksbury. Clerks felt bad for John Gale, a 75 year old also admitted in 1870. A landowner and carpenter from New Hampshire, he was said to be "troubled in mind since his family died … including [his] wife [who] died within a few days of his daughter." He came "in very lousy and feeble and lame," but he was discharged. In 1887, Lucy Mason, a 70-year-old widow, was admitted to Tewksbury. She and her husband, Charles A. Mason, were living in Rhode Island when her husband became ill and they both were taken to the Rhode Island State Almshouse. He died there of paralysis in 1881, and she was now on her own and had been sent by Rhode Island to Massachusetts in a settlement dispute.

Many inmates, almost all of them men, came to the almshouse estranged from their families. Often we do not know why, as in the following somewhat random cases:

[1866] Dennis O'Neil 80 years old. He was born in Ireland, County Cork [and was] married. His wife died in Ireland. He landed in New York 16 or 17 years ago. [He spent] two days there, then [he lived] in Fall River for six years, then to Providence, Rhode Island [for] ten years. [He] came to Boston the day before yesterday to Charlestown and [was] sent here … [He is] not naturalized. He has two sons in Army, [but he] do[es]n't know what regiment … He "has no friends but [his] wife and she died twenty years ago." He was sent to Providence July 27.

[1866] Thomas Fallon 76 years old, he was born in Ireland, County Roscommon, single, laborer. He landed in Quebec 26 years ago. [He spent] three weeks there, then [he went] to Boston. [He has lived] in Roxbury since, he is not naturalized. His sister's children James, Ellen, and Margaret live in Roxbury, Thomas in Woburn. [He has] plenty of relatives, but no friends. [No one] will do anything for him.… He was never in an institution before …

[1890] Philip B. Cook 57 years old from Boston admitted January 2. He was born in Ireland, a widower, a barber. [He] came to America when he was five years old with [his] parents[,] Thomas and Catherine née Smith. First [he went] to Providence[,] Rhode Island and was there for about fifteen years when he married to Anastasia Thompson. He continued to live in Providence until [the] breaking out of the war, then [he went] to Lynn, Massachusetts and was there for eight years in Boston since, except occasionally out of the city. He kept a barber shop at 1416 Tremont Street for five years from 1880 to 1885.… His father owned real estate in Providence … [He has] children Henry P., Joseph, Rebecca, Johnson and Maud Peterson all somewhere in Lynn …

On examination, many who were estranged from their families appear to have had alcohol problems. Willett G. Brown, 59, admitted in 1872, came from a fairly affluent background, his grandfather being a large landowner. His father, Stephen, carried on a weaving business in Pawtucket, Rhode Island. Willett had been separated for over twenty years from his wife and also had two children about whom he knew nothing. He was in the Providence, Rhode Island, jail two or three times for drunkenness, and then housed in various town almshouses and station houses. He was described as "intemperate" and sent to Bridgewater Workhouse. Honora Murphy, 56, was one of the few females who fit a similar description. Admitted in 1873, she had "gotten on a [drinking] spree" and had delirium tremens (DTs) as a result. She had been married but her husband Dennis had left ten years before. They had seven children—two now were dead, and the others were in Canada. According to the notes "she has been a drunkard for years. She was at Deer Island [House of Industry] twice [and] she has been in a number of almshouses." Timothy Kenney, 56, admitted the same year, was a laborer who had owned property. His wife, Mary, died in 1872. While he had daughters—Mary, wife of Richard Reeves, and Margaret, wife of John Simmons—who lived nearby, "his people will do nothing for him" commented the almshouse officials. He had been in Deer Island's House of Industry five or six times for drunkenness and was labeled "a common drunk."

Not surprisingly, it was not only the inmates, but sometimes their families whose drinking caused problems. The quote at the start of this chapter about inmate James Fitzpatrick in 1876 notes that his only daughter, Annie, who lived in Boston, was intemperate and "will do nothing for him." As another example, an 1866 inmate, Catherine Quinn, 60, was a widow who had a daughter with whom she landed in Boston years earlier from Ireland. The notes at first indicated that her son-in-law owned two houses and was able to care for her. In an added note from August 4, 1866, Mr. Nash, apparently after visiting them, described the son-in-law as "a hard and ugly man." He further noted that her daughter had a drinking problem and that "she [now] denied [that they] were able to care for Catherine." In this case, another daughter, who lived in New Orleans, was able to care for her and arrangements were made to send Ms. Quinn on the next steamer.

Most families of the elderly though, even ones who ended up in the Tewksbury Almshouse, did attempt to care for their relatives, at least until some straining point occurred. In the 1867 case of a James Farrell, 73, he was recorded as feeble and infirm. He had two daughters with whom he had lived, but "both have large families and [they] can do nothing for the old man [any longer]." Poverty was sometimes cited directly as a reason. In 1876, 86-year-old Morris O'Connell was admitted and was "well" except for old age. He was a widower who had been living with his daughter Mary O'Leary in Boston. O'Connell "came here without her knowledge because O'Leary was working on half pay and he did not want to burden them." Less than four months later he was discharged again at the request of Mrs. O'Leary, indicating either their economic situation had changed or they had decided to carry on the living arrangement. In the same year Thomas Pratt, 76, was admitted with a cough. Also a widower, his wife had died recently, and he was living with his daughter. The notes indicate "she has five children to support on what she can earn as a rag sorter and could keep him no longer." He did have another daughter, but that family was described as "poor." Pratt eventually died at the Tewksbury Almshouse. In some cases, as elsewhere in the book, we can glean information from the census and other data which show change from the *Inmate Biographies*. In 1877, for example, Michael Murray, 83, was admitted from Lawrence, Massachusetts, and had a rupture and a cough. He was described as having a wife and daughters in Lawrence, "all three [were] at work in mill and won't provide for him." However, I was able to find the family in the 1880 census present still in Lawrence. Murray was listed as 80 (these age discrepancies among the elderly were very common) and retired, while his wife, Katherine, 52, and four children worked at the mill. Another daughter, Ellen, 27, was listed as "keeping house." Of course, we again only speculate on the cause of the change, including possible pressure placed on the family by the Poor Law system, either through the almshouse or the Overseers of the Poor.

Given the job market, young children and women who were hired in factories were more valuable to families than those, like the elderly, who could not support themselves. While such calculations may seem inhumane to us, they were built into the worldview at the time, particularly among immigrants. Today we no doubt make such calculations too, and the sentimentalization of both childhood and, more recently, the elderly, may only have come about after these groups lost their labor value as a result of the reforms abolishing child labor and promoting retirement and pensions.

Besides alcoholism and the general degree of poverty and unemployment which burdened families, both elderly people and younger generations rubbed against one another in interpersonal conflicts. No doubt the overcrowding and inadequate housing of multiple generations strained relationships. Some families who, had they lived in later decades, may well have had resources to live apart, could not in these years. In this situation, the almshouse seems to have been used as a resource by elders when conflicts occurred. In 1870, for example, James Mellen, 79, came to the almshouse. A widower, he had lived in Boston with his daughter Mary E. for some time but at some point, her husband brought home his aged mother. She (evidently the mother-in-law) "didn't like to have the old man there." His voluntary departure to Tewksbury was not disapproved of by the note takers, who called him "a nice smart old man." In-laws were a particular source of problems and were cited again and again:

[1873] Mary Wilkenson 68 from Fall River ... She was born in England and landed in New York in July or August 1871 per the SS "Inca" ... She went directly to Fall River via the Fall River Lines and went to her son James' home there. She has resided in Fall River since, her husband James died in England. Her son James has since married. She did not want to live with her daughter-in-law, so she came here to be sent back to England where she says she has a good home ...

[1875] Amelia Mellett 75 years old she was admitted from Springfield on July 1. She was born in Canada [and lived] there [and] in New York and Vermont until March 1873. [Then] she came to Springfield. Her husband Clement deserted her on March 30, 1875. Her son Clement [is] in Springfield with whom she has been living. [She] quarreled with his wife and he turned her out doors. [She says that] no one [will] do anything for her....

[1877] John Coffin 76 years old, he was born in Ireland, Kings County admitted on February 14 from Boston. He landed in Boston in 1823, [he has been] at sea for thirty years, on shore fifteen years [and he] made Boston his home ... widower. [He] has been living with his sons William and James in Milford for the past three or four months. [He] came to Boston two weeks ago and has been knocking around since ... [He] says [his] son's [sic] wives were cross to him....

Of course, these short notes in many ways tell us too little of what we might like to know of family dynamics. The elders had been married and had lost spouses, now they were crowded into newly formed households with relatives; both sides may well have resented the intrusion into their privacy that crowding entails. It is not to minimize the harshness of the almshouse to note that, for some elderly people, being separate from their families but with age peers may have helped constitute a supportive community. It also may be true in American culture that in-laws are easier to blame than blood relatives. There were other problematic issues with closer family members which are often not explored fully enough in the notes other than to record:

[1870] Hugh Lohan admitted on February 11. He is 70 years old and was born in Ireland [and] landed [in] New York in 1848. Came into this institution on February 29, 1856 and been here all the time until January 12, 1870 when his son came after him and took him to Salem. In Salem until February 11 when he came back here saying his son had done nothing for him ...

[1873] Hannah Granger 82 from Newburyport admitted on June 13. She was born in Ireland, County Cork, and landed in Boston in 1854 on the ship "Mary Balch." She went directly to Newburyport, then to Lawrence and to Lowell

since. Her husband William died forty years ago. Her daughter Hannah, the widow of Joseph Patch, resides on Merrimac Street in Newburyport. She says her daughter did not treat her well, so she came here....

[1895] James Kalugher admitted January 10, 70 years old, he was born in Ireland and he landed in 1893. He was a corn miller, a widower. He landed in Boston and went direct to Salem to son-in-law and daughter. The old man became discontented and strayed away and was sent here. The daughter is able and willing to care for him and wants him ...

In all these cases, it would be too easy to ascribe inhumanity to the younger generations. Many notes do not detail medical conditions, and that so many inmates died shortly after admission, such as Lohan and Granger above, indicates the inmates may have had serious medical problems. Moreover, without more information and the views of the family members, we cannot tell what combination of issues existed, including problematic behavior on the part of the aged family members, stresses of poverty and overcrowding and long hours of work on families, and finally to what extent some elderly may have preferred the almshouse for the medical attention, camaraderie, and community it provided. It appears too simple to ascribe all difficulties to what David Hackett Fischer called the "gerontophobia" of the times when more complex patterns were at work.

The Depression of the 1870s and Unemployment among the Elderly

It has become a truism in our contemporary times that work and other productive roles are critical to keeping people engaged in life and society. In the days before there was retirement, much less any culture of "leisure" among the mass of people, the loss of work for male breadwinners was not only devastating (as it is today) but potentially deadly, as the loss of income and status also led to a total loss of role, and hence a place in family and the community. Further, until seniority rights were established in many workplaces in the twentieth century, older workers who could not keep up with the press of work were often let go, and the last to be hired. Labor historians also note that the high rate of industrial accidents and harsh working conditions made factory and other workers appear far older than their ages because of disabilities and infirmities. Alexander Keyssar cites this to note that "working-class old age had emphatically different tones than did old age among ... middle-class residents."

Although there were some aged men at Tewksbury who were unemployed or recently let go from work during the entire period I studied, the largest number arrived during the depression years of the 1870s. The watershed depression likely increased the number of older men out of work dramatically. Prior to 1873, the large pool of poor and unemployed immigrant workers available for jobs was numerous as the economy grew, but certainly less so than in later years. The difficult depression years, of course, led to a large shedding of workers, but given the continued immigration from overseas and migration from rural areas (as discussed in Chapter 3) it may be that the number of available jobs for the older worker never returned to the previous levels. As industrial development continued in the late nineteenth century and thereafter fewer "old" men would be hired (or rehired) as laborers, factory workers, or rail workers.

Older men out of work during the 1873–77 depression came from all occupations, including rail workers, mill workers, laborers, and farmers:

[1873] James Stevenson 81 from Worcester ... he was born in Scotland and landed in New York on October 22, 1867 and went directly to Hyde Park for three years, then he moved to Worcester.... His wife June died eight years ago, his daughter the wife of James Boag resides at 455 Southbridge Street, Worcester. He says he came here because the mill broke down and he was out of work ...

[1875] Thomas Gallagher 60 years old ... He was born in Ireland, County Tyrone, and landed in Boston in June 1863. He went direct to Lowell. His family has lived there since except in 1873 in Wilton, New Hampshire, he has been away from Lowell most of time working on railroads.... He lost his earnings by failure of contract and returned to Lowell [on] August 6 [and] has been in search of work, finding none, his wife upbraided him. He [then?] attempted to cut his throat with a razor. [He] says he has not eaten for three days ...

[1876] William Curtis 69 years old admitted January 14 from Taunton ... He was born April 6, 1806 in Leeds, Maine.... and lived in various places until about 1842 and [he] has been employed by O.C. Iron Company until two or three months ago ... He owned a house and land a short time in Gardner, Maine ... has been aided by the Overseers of the Poor for the past four or five years and in city almshouse three months last winter ... [He has] been idle the past two or three months about East Taunton says [he] could get no work. [He has a] bad cold.

[1877] James Mount 68 years old admitted from Boston ... He was born in New York City and first came to Massachusetts in 1845 and about Boston most of the time since. [He is] single, a carpenter ... [He] has done but little work in the past year and has nearly starved himself, no relatives, friends or home, [he is] infirm. [Has] cash $7.75....

As is the case with Mount and Gallagher above, many inmates died within a relatively short time after their admissions. It is tempting to draw the conclusion that the loss of work and income was so upsetting and uprooting that it led to death. But many men may have been unable to find work in part because they had ailments, and so entered the almshouse after failed job searches. For example:

[1873] Henry L. Joy, 70 years old admitted from Boston ... He is formerly a bartender and hotel keeper in Quincy [Massachusetts] and kept a restaurant [at the] corner of Chatham and Commercial Streets in Boston ... a widower ... [He has now become] idle most of the time unable to work on account of his rheumatism ...

[1875] Charles B. Allen, 69 years old, he was admitted on January 16 from Boston, lame. He was born in Brimfield on September 3, 1805.... He was a clerk on railroads and steamboats. Pennsylvania Central, Baltimore and Ohio, Metropolitan SS Company [in] Boston ... His wife is Mary Ann nee McCormick is now with her sister Delia, widow of Frank Vincent at 58 East Broadway, New York. [He has] no [other] family ... [He has] never [been] aided. [He] has not been able to work much for the past two years on account of rheumatism and catarrah [*sic*]....

[1877] Patrick Conley, 65 years old from Boston, [he was] born in Ireland, County Galway, admitted February 6, he landed in St. John, New Brunswick and came to Boston in 1847 ... [He lived] there and other places until 186? [and] in Boston steadily since ... single, hostler ... [He is] out of employment and not earned $20 the past three years on account of sore feet. [He has] no[t been in an] institution [before], [he is] temperate ...

As we can see from the above examples, there is, first of all, not surprisingly a strong overlap between old age and disability. Secondly, in an age in which physical labor was still dominant, it is not a great surprise that those cast out from work with some disability did not easily find jobs. Thirdly, since so many men came into the almshouse "lame," "feeble," "with a cough," and so on, it is very difficult to disentangle what symptoms were a result of being out on the streets, which were a result of starving or deprivation, and which were results of long-term illnesses which may have affected the men even when they were employed. Hence it seems appropriate to put the elderly and disabled on the same continuum of those both at risk of unemployment and those who, even if able to work, were unlikely to be reemployed.

Although a certain link between the end of employment and disability and death cannot be made on such a small amount of information, it does seem clear that the almshouse admissions among the elderly were provoked as much by lack of work and the suffering that followed as well as the lack of family support and care in some instances, and, of course, underlying medical conditions and health problems generally. Hence the "we can do no more" comment must be read broadly to include all the complex attributes of aging, which include health, family, and work life.

NINE

From History's Shadows: Partial Views of the Poor

"We're working class ... well that is if we had jobs."
From the 1991 movie *The Commitments*

This book, using archival data from one of America's largest almshouses combined with official census and other data, has shown the great heterogeneity and diversity of the poor in the Gilded Age. Poverty itself has been shown as a fluid monster affecting many "average" people. The book has addressed many of the key issues of the Gilded Age including geographic and economic mobility, family conflict and unwed motherhood, and the care of children and of the elderly. While some of this material is known to experts, many of the areas of interest such as the family life of the poor, how people moved upward and downward in the class system, the fate of bound-out children, and the care of the elderly poor have been understudied. Cast into the shadowlands of history, those who fell into poverty emerge at least partially through the notes of the almshouse. In turn, of course, those who wrote the notes about the poor, and made the decisions as to which inmates went to the workhouse, which children would be bound out and to whom, and who should be aided at all, also partially emerge.

This chapter will briefly return to the theme of our "ordinary people" and how the stigma of poverty obscures much about the life of the poor. Secondly, we will touch on areas of this book that contribute to the study of the Gilded Age, particularly the understudied areas of institutions of social welfare at that time.

To return to the first broad theme, the following six cases of "ordinary people" show how inmates at various life stages—a child of 10, a teen woman admitted for pregnancy, an elderly woman, and three people, two men and one woman, of adult age—moved back and forth from poverty to working-class status. After noting how these cases illustrate the diversity and fluidity of poverty, the chapter discusses what weaknesses and strengths this research has in shedding light on what have been hidden historical shadows occupied by ordinary people for whom little direct evidence is available.

MORE ORDINARY PEOPLE

Ruth (née Bateman) Dechene

Ruth E. Bateman was born in Moncton, New Brunswick, in 1878. When she was 12 years old, her mother, Josephine, took her on what must have been a very long train ride to emigrate into Boston. They then lived in nearby Dorchester, where Ruth started working as a domestic. Her mother tired of Boston and went back home to Moncton, although Ruth's four sisters and two brothers stayed in Massachusetts. Ruth was admitted to Tewksbury from Boston in 1895 as a 17-year-old single pregnant woman. She stated that she "got sick" the previous April and the father of her child was a Charles S. Barnes who was also from Moncton. He was "now off" and she had not heard from him since the previous November. Ruth was discharged on April 3 with no record of a baby having been born. We do not know if she miscarried or the almshouse arranged for an adoption.

Ruth married Louis Dechene, a carpenter, in 1898. He was fourteen years her senior and from Quebec. It was a first marriage for both. They appear together in two censuses, first renting in Everett, a suburb of Boston, and then in Boston. They had a lodger living with them in the 1910 census. By 1920, however, when Ruth was 42, the couple had divorced. Ruth worked as a label stitcher in a shoe factory and lived with Grace, 13, her youngest daughter at the last date she could be found.

Frank Edwin Cole

Frank E. Cole was born in the small town of Dover in western Maine in 1853. His father Henry was an overseer in a woolen factory there, but such a title did not reflect high pay as he was worth only a modest amount in real estate. Frank's mother, Gracie, née Smith, was a native of nearby Foxcroft, and died when Frank was just 2 years old.

His father remarried, to Mary from Lewiston, Maine, and Frank and his sister Ida were joined by three half-siblings. In April 1873, he left Maine and came to Boston on a steamer called the *Katahdin*. Identifying as a moulder by trade, he settled in Lawrence, Massachusetts, from where he was admitted to the almshouse in October. Cole had caught typhoid fever, a common disease at this time.

Although he could not be found in records for awhile, he was married in 1888 to Jennie, also born in Maine, and they gave birth in 1892 to a son, Allen. In 1900 Cole worked as a teamster and the family lived in Cambridge, Massachusetts. In 1910 the three are found in Bourne, Massachusetts, at the base of Cape Cod with a boarder, and Frank working as a watchman in a car works.

Patrick Jennings

Patrick Jennings was born in 1868, the youngest of four children, to an Irish family in Gloucester, Massachusetts. Like others in the famous fishing town, his father was a fisherman. Patrick was admitted at 11 years old to Tewksbury in 1880. Patrick's mother had died in East Boston in June 1875, and he was sent to live with his cousin Michael Clancy in Boston, while his father continued fishing. But after several years, he was brought to the almshouse when the cousin concluded he "cannot care for him." He was kept for only a short time at the almshouse and discharged in one month (likely to the State Primary School in Monson).

Patrick was married sometime between then and 1900 to Margaret, six years his junior. They lived in Boston and Patrick became a fireman. They stayed there for at least most of the rest of their lives, until Patrick was in his 60s, when the available censuses ended. They had at least seven children together—Mary, John, Henry, Stephen, Francis, William, and Catherine. They continued to rent in Boston with Patrick remaining in the fire department. His daughter Mary was listed in the 1930 census as a clerk for the state government, his son John a police officer, and Henry a planner for industry.

Ellen (née Kelly) Quilty

Ellen Kelly was born in Ireland in 1852 and landed with her family in Boston when she was 2 years old. Her parents were John and Julia, Irish immigrants who stayed in the Boston area, her father working as a junk dealer.

Ellen worked as a domestic and married Joseph Quilty on February 25, 1868, when she was 16. Joseph was also a first-generation Irish American. He was three years her senior and worked as a trunkmaker. Their marriage failed, and when she arrived at the almshouse in 1880 she had "not lived with him for the past four or five years." Her husband had been "at Deer Island," the Boston workhouse, "many times since 1873" and, in fact, "was there the last she knew." Her father had died in 1874 and her mother in 1877.

After the period in the almshouse, Ellen lived in Lawrence, Massachusetts, much of her remaining life with her sister-in-law Mary Quilty. Both were single, and Ellen worked as a nurse for a while. In later censuses, the two elderly women were listed as single and without occupations.

Joseph Rice

Joseph Rice was born in the Polish part of Russia in 1876. His parents were Adam and Orsu. He was born in Virevia, which is 68 miles from Tilset. He stated he would never return because he had "deserted from the army and he would be sent to the mines." He had three brothers and two sisters still in Russia, and no family other than cousins in America. He came to the United States by Berlin, Hamburg, and Liverpool, and landed in Philadelphia in 1893. He then went to New York City for two months, and worked his way up to Hardwick, a rural Massachusetts community where his cousin Andres Erausch lived.

He was admitted to Tewksbury in 1895 at 19 years old. He was single and a farm laborer. He had been sick for four months. Evidently it was not too serious or was treated successfully as he was discharged in about a month.

Rice moved to Pennsylvania where he worked as a laborer in Shenandoah. Later he married Margie, ten years his junior, and became a coal miner in Schuykill County, Pennsylvania. They had at least two children together, Adella and Annie. He was listed in the last available census as a miner with his two children, but his wife had died. He owned a house worth $5,000 in 1930.

Elizabeth (née New) Sandford

Elizabeth (née New) Sandford was born in 1799 in Grafton, Massachusetts, a small town about forty miles west of Boston. Both her parents hailed from Attleboro, Massachusetts, her father James New a property owner who died in Holliston, Massachusetts, in 1825, and her mother Annie Perry. When she was 4 the family moved to Bellingham, and later to Medway and Holliston, all in Middlesex County, Massachusetts. Elizabeth married quite late for the time at age 39 to Giles Sandford, a farmer who owned property. They settled also in Holliston. He was eight years her junior. They had at least two children together, though subsequent censuses do not reveal their whereabouts.

According to Elizabeth's recollection, when at 74 she was admitted to Tewksbury, she had not lived with her husband since 1849. Indeed in the 1850 census they lived apart. Giles owned $1,000 worth of real estate while living with his father and several other families, while Elizabeth cannot be found. The almshouse notes do say that "for the past 25 years [Elizabeth] has supported herself by nursing and as a seamstress." In 1860, while Giles was in nearby Milford, Massachusetts, and was listed as a farm laborer, Elizabeth was a domestic in Bellingham living with the family of farmer Seneca Adams, who had a fair amount of property. Giles owned no property and lived in the family of a George F. Bailey, a boot click who had $1,000 in real estate property. In 1870, Giles was still in Milford and back as family head and a landowner with $3,000 in real estate and $150 in personal property, living now with Nancy Wood, 65, and Frank E. Bailey, 8. Meanwhile Elizabeth was in nearby Hopkinton living with an Isaac Temple, a 72-year-old farmer with $800 real estate value. She was then 71 and "keeping house." Giles died in 1872 and Elizabeth was admitted to Tewksbury in February 1874, where she died on May 16 that year.

Heterogeneity and Fluidity of Poverty

These six people, like the hundreds profiled elsewhere in this book suggest the diversity and heterogeneity of poverty. In the Gilded Age, poverty was socially constructed by the media and culture as male in the tough, wizened face of the tramp. He was young to perhaps prematurely middle aged, white, and perhaps distinctly Irish. Yet, as we have seen, many women were poor, such as Ruth Bateman, Ellen Quilty, and Elizabeth Sandford above. There were millions of children like Patrick Jennings who were poor, and also millions of elderly people like Elizabeth Sandford. Poverty in these and other instances throughout the period combined persistent economic features that denied working people adequate living standards, and this problem was compounded by the cyclical economic downturns of depressions.

Additionally, situational and developmental factors always affect poverty and employment. The situational, of course, include illness, as in the case of Edwin Cole above, or desertion and separation, as was the case of Ellen Quilty. The risk of poverty with developmental issues ranges from the problems of children such as Patrick Jennings to those of the elderly such as Elizabeth Sandford. Poverty and other problems among the many immigrants such as Ruth Bateman from Canada and Joseph Rice from Russia have also been well documented.

Whether poverty is looked at as the legal status of pauperism in the nineteenth century, as a more absolute measure of deprivation, or as a relative measure (as discussed in Chapter 1), those who fell into poverty were a heterogenous group, and so diverse as to make it difficult to find common bonds. Beyond age and situation, race and ethnicity, culture, gender, specific occupations, and region separated the poor sharply, as well as, no doubt, their different beliefs about being able to eventually obtain the "American Dream." The economic change and fluidity that marked many of the lives we have discussed no doubt added a level of hope and uncertainty to the despair many may have felt.

For example, four of the six people above were from immigrant families (Bateman, Jennings, Quilty, and Rice). We do not know what expectations these families actually had of America. In some ways, they could have concluded they did well in a conventional sense—Bateman married a carpenter; Patrick Jennings became a fireman, and his children appear to have succeeded perhaps even more; Quilty and Rice escaped impoverished Ireland and repressive Russia and seem to have done adequately. It is harder perhaps to surmise how rural migrant Cole or Massachusetts-born Sandford saw their own lives. Their gains from their parents' lives are more ambiguous, but Cole may have felt good about leaving the isolated rural town of Maine for Massachusetts, and Sandford about eking out a living for herself for twenty-five years after her husband and she had separated. It is important to note that most people compare themselves to their own reference group, not to millionaires or the famous people of their times. On the other hand, all at least for a time experienced poverty, and Bateman, divorced, was at work as a stitcher when we last have information about her, while Sandford died in the poorhouse. Nor does it appear that by most conventional measures any of the subjects escaped from working-class jobs. As noted, Stephen Thernstrom would no doubt count them as having moved from "rags to respectability," particularly the immigrants who came from impoverished conditions. But we must caution that much is not known and hence is open to interpretation: Did Elizabeth Sandford's children do well? How and where did Ruth Bateman, a stitcher in 1920, live, retire, and die? A similar question can be asked about the Quilty sisters. Nor can we interpret Edwin Cole's job as a watchman, Ellen Quilty's job as a nurse (most likely akin to a nonprofessional caretaker rather than a licensed nurse), or Joseph Rice's job as a coal miner as any buttress against poverty. Without more details of their lives, we can confidently say that while poverty is fluid and diverse, we cannot say for sure these families had escaped it, as the twentieth century in turn brought plenty of poverty, economic downturn, and insecurity as well.

HISTORY AS A "SHADOWLAND," AND THE PROS AND CONS OF INVISIBILITY

To some extent, constructing the history of poor and other ordinary people from over a century or so ago is as difficult as the task of an archeologist using traces of evidence to plot events thousands of years ago. In either case, what is left to us are shadows of beings who lived and are no more. We have no sight or pictures of them, no voices or sounds, no smells, not even a writing sample. The official record in a census, even added to our admission biographies of the almshouse, is only a slight trace of a human life filled with tragedy, but also joy and other human feelings. Of course, even the bloodless records are not existent for many, forcing us to speculate about what happened before or after the admission to the almshouse or before a recorded death in a city record. We gain something, of course, from the work of others who have studied the shadows and from various means of collecting quantitative and qualitative data on the period, but overall we are still wandering in the darkness. Throughout this venture, I often felt that researchers needed closer ties and more of a strategy to gain data, to link people across regions and time. Perhaps with hundreds of researchers employed all over the country, the same name would appear here and there. Perhaps some information has been lost in histories where people's names have been kept confidential (as in certain case record studies) and perhaps there are ways to declassify such documents to find the real names of such people. But for all the ideas I came up with, I realized that a massive historical dragnet to search for the poor or others was no more realistic nor necessarily desirable than the tendency to overextend personal surveillance in our own time.

After all, for many reasons cited, part of being "ordinary" has historically been anonymity. Without social security numbers and computer
programs, the poor could pass at will through different regions and
areas, could change their names (as well as have the experience of
having officials change their name) at will, and could hide from officials if they were in trouble, or not be caught when they sought work
or poor relief. Record keepers are just as much a part of the problem
since they did not have the sophistication nor could they even spell
correctly or understand the languages of the immigrants, much less
the mores and habits of immigrants and poor natives. Hence census
takers and town and city record keepers made careless errors themselves, and did not understand what they were told. To reconstruct
life in any exact fashion, then, except for the most respectable and
literate people of the past, is impossible.

Despite the obvious deficiencies in seeing shadows for real people,
there is at least one strong advantage that over time began to dawn
on me as writer. The poor and near poor have historically been hurt,
not just by their awful circumstances, but by the stigma their appearance and habits evoke in others. It is a historical consistency at least
from this period to our own that "tramps" were sometimes stoned and
otherwise attacked, while today homeless people have been subject
to hate crimes and even murder. In less extreme ways, to be poor is
to be an outcast and held in contempt. Over the years, the almshouse
staff, generally more liberal than many citizens of their time, themselves
stigmatized the poor by their close "gaze" at the appearance, both facial
and that of their general body, their health, their clothes and dress,
as well as occasionally the sounds and smells of their charges. Three
sets of examples are provided below: some are simple statements as to
condition; others are personal assessments of the writers often related
to possible insanity or drunkenness of an inmate; and the rest are
more broad statements about inmates based on appearance or feeling.
It is my suggestion that for a variety of reasons many of the issues in
this book and surrounding the life in the working classes benefit from
moving away from the physical and other observational "data" made
by people at the time to a more "objective" (e.g., with the benefit of
seeing only shadows) view that time forces us into.

Some sets of observations were relatively factual. Many inmates
came in "ragged," "filthy," or "lousy." Some years this was spelled out
in more detail in the *Inmate Biographies*. For example, an inmate
"came in swarming with vermin" or had a "sore head from vermin."
Comments on clothing sometimes were made such as "he was clad

in two or three coats and as many vests." On the other hand, women were labeled "looks like a strumpet" on occasions where the justification for such a label was unclear. Sometimes the physical observation led immediately to a negative general observation such as "she has sore eyes and [a] humor on face, [she is] not over bright," or, he has "an eruption on [his] face and [he] looks pitiful." An 1876 inmate was noted to have "claim[ed] to have a disease of the nose which is very [offensive]," and the note taker went on to label him "a professional and constitutional bummer." This does not mean, as we have seen, that observations yielded only negative judgments. We have seen that inmates were labeled "well disposed," "appears respectable," "appears bright," or, in cases like Charles Thayer, "a fine appearing young man, apparently entirely out of place in an almshouse."

Many negative characterizations were made based on observations that suggested insanity or alcoholism. Many inmates were labeled "flighty," "looney," "insane," or "slightly insane." How these assessments would fit with modern diagnoses is anyone's guess.

At times, the qualified assessments of insanity sound odder than the simpler ones. These include "she appeared troubled in mind when she came [but is] better now," "he is unsettled in mind," and "[she is] a trifle flighty now but one should not call her insane." One man "appears excited but not violent," another woman "appears a little looney and very much 'browned' [tanned] as if she had been tramping and very much exposed to the sun." A female inmate was described as "her mind seems affected and broken down," a man "appears a little demented," and a 13-year-old child is "deformed and demented." The possibility of alcoholism was generally judged more harshly than insanity or feeblemindedness, and other explanations were often not accepted if the examiner felt the cause of a person's problems were drink. So in addition to the many notes of "hard drinker," "used up," or "on a spree," there are many examples of evaluative statements like:

> He has a variety of other complaints and troubles, but from his appearance, the chief [one] of these is rum.

> He claims he hadn't drank for quite awhile, but [his] looks may contradict his statement.

It is, of course, not the point that alcoholism or insanity were not valid conditions to comment on, but rather that both the reliability of the clerks and the use of such statements as an explanatory cause for poverty are not very strong. Like many officials and service workers even today, it was too easy to assume that the person being viewed at their worst represents the whole person, and that, even if the observation is correct, these issues (insanity and alcoholism) are primary causes of poverty rather than its effects.

Finally, we have examples of summary statements which are puzzling at times, and offensive to modern sensibilities at others. Among the puzzling is a description of Catherine Cunningham, an 1870 inmate who "appears strangely. [We think] she has been drugged and may be encumbered. She either can't or won't tell what ails her." We have no idea what evidence the almshouse clerk or others had of either her "strangeness" or why they thought she might be drugged. In 1872, 38-year-old blind musician William Fallowfield was summed up as "he appears to have seen better days." Perhaps a truism tossed in or perhaps this is a more specific comment on his disability or some other aspect of his appearance. An 1874 inmate was both "offensive" and "used up," but what gave offense was unclear, whether it was her language, her drink, her poverty, her looks in general, we do not know. An 1876 inmate, Delia Turner was married to an African American man who was characterized as "a miserable deformed Negro [and] crippled." What led to this unusual exclamation of both racial and physical disgust is not clear. An 1877 inmate, Jennie Baker Canad had been ill with "neuralgia in [the] head [which was] very bad" and "had small pox." The note takers saw fit to add that "she looks as if she had a combination of cussedness, both moral and physical."

The point here is not to point out the obvious failings of the nineteenth-century recorders, but quite the opposite, to show how similar the physical and moral descriptions of the poor were then and now. For the "objective" comments on the poor even today overlap with a moral order of appearance, deportment, temperance, and respectability, which are often seen as violated by the poor. No doubt just as many inmates lacked the virtues sought by the almshouse note takers, today's case records complain of poor appearance and hygiene, substance abuse, prostitution, unsafe sex, and other health/moral issues.

The question is how much does the constant labeling and describing of people who come into our institutions or social welfare systems actually help us understand the poor or those who pass through a period of poverty. I would suggest that the factual elements in our data are more reliable than such descriptors. We know that poverty brings with it all sorts of diseases, weaknesses, decaying appearance, and poor general health. It does not look very good! Indeed some of the poor will fall to alcohol (or drugs) or to psychiatric problems or to prostitution and all sorts of vices, today as in 1870. But since all of this is known and obvious, it actually disguises in many ways the more interesting stories of the journey of people into and out of poverty. Hence the shadows may tell us more, by keeping some of the constant focus on appearance and behavior away from view, and making prominent the family and work backgrounds of subjects, their migration patterns, family life, homeownership, and other facets of life that we have focused on. In this sense, there may be a positive gain for lack of knowledge in that the well-known sight, sound, and smell of poverty are much less of a mystery to either historians or society as other elements in the lives of ordinary people.

THE GILDED AGE, THE POOR LAWS, AND THE ALMSHOUSE

The period between the Civil War and the twentieth century is often seen as one of massive change, of industrialization and urbanization, in which the great fortunes of industry were made at the expense of the vast numbers of immigrants and native-born migrants whose working conditions and wages were quite poor. Certainly, this research supports the overall view, at least in its look at those who were poor and/or from the lower half of the population. By necessity, we have had to generalize over the thirty-year period studied, and, of course, historians are well aware that the America (and New England) of 1895 was in many ways quite different than that of 1865. The rhetorical flourishes against foreigners that marked the Know-Nothing days and the rhetoric which justified the state almshouses were long gone by a couple of decades after the start of this period, at least in New England. While no doubt great prejudice against foreigners and the poor remained, reformers in the East were moving gradually to an outlook that presaged the Progressive Era. For example, child labor laws were put on the books in New England states, protective legislation on hours of work was proposed, the 1893 depression led to public works projects, and the beginning of discussions of the idea of mothers' pensions and unemployment insurance began in the 1890s.

The notes of the almshouse show on a micro-level how the period began to shift. The notes change markedly after 1880 into a "just the facts" approach in which many of the negative characterizations quoted above were no longer used. In this specific case, there is little doubt that the scandals at Tewksbury, including the campaign led by General Benjamin Butler (see Figure 2.1), had a major effect on the documentation of the state almshouse. But likely these changes were not merely local. The idea of the almshouse had begun to fall out of fashion in expert opinion by the late nineteenth century, at least for groups other than the miscreants (to be placed in a workhouse) and the residual groups of elderly and disabled. Such views were voiced nationally, as well as locally. By the 1890s, reforms were moving Tewksbury toward an "Infirmary" for the ill and aged, while Monson's State Primary School had already been closed. Of the three state institutions founded in 1854, only Bridgewater continued on, as a work farm primarily for alcoholics, prostitutes, and vagrants. While towns and cities continued to have almshouses, and the giving of outdoor relief remained stingy and controlled by the poor laws, opposition by increasingly powerful immigrant groups and nascent trade unions exerted a counter-pressure which led to the provision of mass public works during the depression of 1893.

It is difficult to disentangle—and this is an important area for research—how much of the changing sentiment of elites toward the poor and working class was due to militant pressure and protest among those at the bottom of society as opposed to other influences on them. In the initial stages of national unrest during the depression of the 1870s, including the great railroad strike, and later the agitation of the Knights of Labor and the famous Haymarket "riot" of 1886, if anything, social unrest among the poor appeared to further polarize the nation and move elites further away from any sympathy with the lower classes. New England, however, with only minor exceptions, did not see the rise of militant unionism, anarchism, or socialism in these years compared to other areas, so its more "radical" models of reform ended at Henry George (*Poverty and Progress*) and Massachusetts-born Edward Bellamy (*Looking Backward*). Whether then the more-collaborative nature of the political and economic conflict was a factor in the spread of reform in New England may be an interesting question for research.

The other obvious change in Massachusetts and southern New England, at least, was the rise to power of immigrant politicians, particularly the Irish beginning in the 1880s. No doubt the Brahmins were greatly chagrined, and the pessimism felt by the likes of Henry James captured the literary and philosophical leaders of New England who saw the end of their power. But on a more pragmatic level, it became clear to politicians, government officials, and experts that the immigrants, even the least "couth" and "respectable," needed to be accommodated in many ways. As city halls and police departments, and even some Overseers of the Poor became immigrants themselves, the strong line of ethnic prejudice which had melded with class prejudice throughout the earlier nineteenth century started to change. Later ethnic politicians, most famously, James Michael Curley of Boston, made giving out of alms and city jobs to the poor a mainstay of their political appeal. It was only a matter of time before almshouses and workhouses receded into history, and a somewhat more generous social welfare system would emerge (although not until the 1930s).

These broader changes are difficult to see in the individual case write-ups at Tewksbury, except in the decreasingly stigmatizing and negative characterizations of the "inmates." Still the institutions of the poor-relief system were changing as well. It would be too easy to label these social institutions as totally negative and repressive. The Poor Law system, with all its flaws to a modern viewer, held many objectives, and one was to maintain the poor, if not comfortably, then presumably at least on a subsistence level, for both humanitarian reasons, but, as importantly, to retain a labor force when conditions improved enough for work to be available. Further, at a time when New England was struggling with the role of women and children in the workplace, expert opinion on the different groups covered by the Poor Laws was also mixed, and many were unhappy with the treatment of more "vulnerable" groups. Throughout the nation, the trend throughout the nineteenth century and into the twentieth century would be the adoption of a more specialized system, in which each group had its own place—the home for fallen women, the maternity home, the juvenile home, the old age home, the asylum for the insane, and so on. The differentiation of the poor had its humanitarian elements, but also was not free of fear of contamination of the young and old, and the "virtuous" (as they were called) being infected by the "vicious." Such separation then also had social-control motives including limiting crime, alcohol, malingering, and possibly also political contamination among the large army of paupers and near paupers. I have explored in this book a period in which there were the very beginnings of this differentiation, starting with a time when pregnant women, old men, young children, and adult drunks and ill patients occupied the same space in a Massachusetts facility. Gradually the populations were separated physically at the institution, and in the longer term, as noted, some groups, such as children, prostitutes, criminals, and others, were removed from Tewksbury. "Each to their own place" was the expert motto. Again, as the with the role of social unrest and other pressure by the poor, working-class, and ethnic minorities and its impact on elites, the expert move toward the specialization of social welfare has been underexplored and certainly rarely truly scrutinized. Was the separation of poverty and unemployment and other social ills into "mental illness," "criminality," "child welfare," "elderly," "women," and "adult men," with their own subcategories, a tactic that helped the broader class of poor people lose any vision of commonality with their less fortunate comrades, or were these splits already so defined among the poor that their further separation did not matter? Clearly the strategies of the states and local governments through the Poor Laws, almshouses, and other policies has been an area quite understudied in relation to the broad issue of working-class and ethnic history.

Appendix:
Statistical Profile of Tewksbury
Inmates, 1865–1895

The following tables are demographic statistics developed by inspecting each admission entry for inmates at the Tewksbury almshouse for sample months of thirteen years of the thirty-year period studied. Some entries are not included—for example, foundlings left at the almshouse for which no information other than sex was provided, and transfers or "nominal admissions" of inmates to and from asylums or other institutions for which little or no demographic data was given. Other entries at times were incomplete, but in those cases the material available is entered.

After each variable—sex, age, marital status, nativity, occupation, and color—an average is noted for the thirteen years. Additionally, two state censuses from Massachusetts, 1875 and 1895, are provided for comparison. See notes for Chapter 2 as well as this appendix.

Table A.1A. Sex of Adult Inmates of Tewksbury State Almshouse, 1865–1895

Sample Years	Male	Females
1865	30.7%	69.3%
1867	39.2%	60.8%
1870	67.1%	33.0%
1872	62.4%	37.6%
1875	71.7%	28.3%
1877	82.0%	18.0%
1880	70.9%	29.1%
1882	64.0%	36.0%
1885	63.7%	36.3%
1887	66.3%	33.7%
1890	62.8%	37.2%
1893	68.4%	31.6%
1895	79.9%	20.1%

average: 63.8% men (adults only)

**Table A.1B. Comparison of Tewksbury Inmates
with State of Massachusetts Population (includes children)**

1875 TAH	Male	67.4%	Female	33.6%
1875 State of Mass.	Male	48.1%	Female	51.9%
1895 TAH	Male	78.6%	Female	21.4%
1895 State of Mass.	Male	48.6%	Female	51.4%

**Table A.2A. Age of Inmates of Tewksbury State Almshouse in 1865–1895
2A. Children (under 15 years old)**

Sample Years	Percent of Admissions
1865	32.2%
1867	22.2%
1870	12.2%
1872	16.4%
1875	14.6%
1877	16.0%
1880	13.9%
1882	14.7%
1885	13.1%
1887	10.9%
1890	14.8%
1893	9.9%
1895	6.7%

average: 15.2%

Table A.2B. Adult Inmates by Age

Sample Years	% age 15–30	% age 31–49	% age over 50
1865	36.6%	46.9%	16.6%
1867	49.1%	32.2%	18.8%
1870	51.1%	19.8%	19.0%
1872	48.6%	28.9%	22.5%
1875	57.2%	26.3%	13.8%
1877	53.8%	30.0%	14.8%
1880	45.7%	35.0%	19.3%
1882	45.8%	31.9%	22.3%
1885	53.5%	30.9%	15.8%
1887	37.8%	43.6%	18.6%
1890	42.3%	39.2%	13.9%
1893	40.8%	39.6%	19.6%
1895	39.7%	43.9%	16.7%
average	46.3%	34.5%	17.8%
Male	38%	38.6%	23.4%
Female	60%	28.2%	11.9%

Table A.2C. Comparison of Tewksbury Inmates with Massachusetts Population

	15–30	31–49	50 over
1875 TAH	57.6%	26.3%	16.1%
1875 Massachusetts	44.8%	33.1%	22.1%
1895 TAH	39.7%	43.9%	16.7%
1895 Massachusetts	39.7%	36.6%	23.7%

Table A.3A. Marital Status of Inmates of Tewksbury State Almshouse, 1865–1895

Sample Years	Single	Married	Widowed	Divorced
1865	35.6 %	32.1%	31.0 %	1.1%
1867	51.8%	24.3%	23.9%	0
1870	58.8%	23.8%	17.6%	0
1872	51.5%	26.5%	22.1%	0
1875	63.2%	24.3%	11.9%	0.3%
1877	55.8%	27.1%	16.6%	0.3%
1880	54.6%	22.1%	22.7%	0.3%
1882	52.3%	28.4%	18.3%	0.9%
1885	63.3%	20.9%	15.3%	0.3%
1887	60.4%	19.3%	19.8%	0.3%
1890	57.1%	24.7%	18.1%	0
1893	65.6%	22.5%	11.9%	0
1895	69.8%	16.5%	13.7%	0
average	57%	24%	18.7%	
Male average	61.4%	18.6%	19.3%	
Female average	47.5%	33.3%	18.9%	

Table A.3B. Comparison of Tewksbury Inmates Marital Status with State Population

Sample Years	Single	Married	Widowed	Divorced
1875 TAH	63.2%	24.3%	11.9%	0.05%
1875 Mass.	54.9%	39.1%	5.7%	0.002%
1895 TAH	71.9%	15.3%	12.8%	0%
1895 Mass.	55.4%	37.7%	6.6%	0.2%
Males				
1875 TAH	72.0%	16.8%	11.2%	
1875 Mass.	56.7%	40.6%	2.6%	
1895 TAH	73.9%	12.9%	13.2%	
1895 Mass.	64.9%	31.8%	3.0%	
Females				
1875 TAH	45.0%	40.0%	13.3%	1.7%
1875 Mass.	53.5%	37.7%	8.6%	0.2%
1895 TAH	54.2%	30.1%	15.7%	0%
1895 Mass.	61.3%	30.6%	7.8%	0.2%

Table A.4A. Nativity of Tewksbury State Almshouse Inmates, 1865–1895 (Place of Birth)

	USA	Foreign Born	Ireland	Canada	British Isles
Average	25.7%	74.3%	43.9%	11.5%	11.5%
1865	19.2%	80.7%	58.2%	11.3%	7.3%
1867	26.5%	73.5%	53.3%	9.8%	7.3%
1870	26.0%	74.0%	45.7%	12.4%	10.5%
1872	24.8%	75.2%	44.8%	11.5%	14.5%
1875	34.2%	65.8%	39.1%	6.6%	12.4%
1877	34.2%	65.8%	39.4%	9.2%	11.9%
1880	33.1%	66.9%	38.7%	12.2%	9.7%
1882	26.7%	73.3%	37.6%	13.8%	13.0%
1885	21.5%	78.5%	43.5%	12.1%	13.6%
1887	19.4%	80.6%	47.8%	14.0%	12.4%
1890	22.1%	77.9%	37.4%	11.1%	14.7%
1893	24.0%	76.0%	44.0%	12.0%	8.9%
1895	23.0%	77.0%	41.6%	13.1%	12.9%

	Scandinavia	Germany	Italy	Russia	Other
Average	1.6%	2.3%	3.5%		
1865	1.7%	2.3%			
1867	2.1%	0.7%	0.3%		
1870	1.2%	2.3%	1.9%		
1872	1.8%	1.2%	1.2%		
1875	1.0%	3.1%	2.7%		
1877	2.5%	0.3%	2.8%		
1880	2.0%	1.0%	0.5%	2.6%	
1882	2.0%	4.5%	0.4%	2.0%	
1885	1.4%	3.3%	1.4%	2.8%	
1887	2.2%	2.2%	1.1%	0.5%	0.5%
1890	4.2%	2.1%	1.6%	6.8%	
1893	3.5%	1.9%	0.8%	2.7%	2.3%
1895	1.7%	1.5%	1.7%	2.0%	2.5%

Table A.4B. Comparison of Nativity of Tewksbury Inmates with State Population

Sample:Years	Native Born	Foreign Born
1875 TAH	34.2%	65.8%
1875 Massachusetts	74.2%	25.8%
1895 TAH	23.0%	77.0%
1895 Massachusetts	69.4%	30.6%

Table A.4C. Ireland (Birth)

Sample Years	
1875 TAH	39.1%
1875 Massachusetts	14.2%
1895 TAH	41.6%
1895 Massachusetts	10.3%

Table A.4D. Britain (Birth)

Sample Years	
1875 TAH	12.4%
1875 Massachusetts	3.9%
1895 TAH	12.9%
1895 Massachusetts	4.3%

Table A.4E. Canada (Birth)

Sample Years	
1875 TAH	6.6%
1875 Massachusetts	5.2%
1895 TAH	13.1%
1895 Massachusetts	10.0%

Table A.4F. Scandinavia (Birth)

Sample Years	
1875 TAH	1.0%
1875 Massachusetts	0.3%
1895 TAH	1.7%
1895 Mass.	No separate listing (5.1% all Europe outside Britain and Ireland)

Table A.4G. Germany (Birth)

Sample Years	
1875 TAH	3.1%
1875 Massachusetts	1.1%
1895 TAH	1.5%
1895 Massachusetts	No separate listing (5.1% all Europe outside Britain and Ireland)

Table A.4H. Others (Born Outside of U.S. and Above Countries)

Sample Years	
1875 TAH	3.4%
1875 Massachusetts	0.7% (excludes unknown)
1895 TAH	6.2% 9.4% Scandinavia + Germany + Others
1895 Massachusetts	5.1%

Table A.5A. Occupations of Tewksbury State Almshouse Inmates, 1865–1895
(Selected occupations and categories only; figures do not add to 100%)

Sample Years	Laborers	Domestics	Operatives & Other Textile	Shoemakers	Seaman/ Sailor	Skilled Craftsmen	Farmer
1865	19.6%	26.1%	8.7%	4.3%	6.5%	6.5%	0
1867	19.0%	32.5%	14.1%	4.3%	5.5%	11.0%	0
1870	23.3%	17.2%	14.7%	0	9.8%	16.6%	4.9%
1872	26.8%	16.5%	7.2%	0	10.3%	14.4%	3.1%
1875	13.1%	6.5%	19.6%	0.9%	9.3%	21.5%	6.5%
1877	23.5%	5.4%	8.1%	3.3%	10.7%	16.1%	7.4%
1880	33.1%	11.3%	9.0%	0.8%	6.8%	17.3%	2.3%
1882	27.0%	14.8%	8.2%	5.7%	7.4%	21.3%	0.8%
1885	31.7%	22.5%	7.0%	2.8%	4.2%	14.8%	1.4%
1887	32.2%	25.8%	6.5%	3.2%	2.6%	18.1%	2.6%
1890	31.3%	20.4%	9.5%	2.0%	2.0%	17.0%	2.7%
1893	36.5%	12.3%	9.1%	1.8%	1.8%	20.1%	4.1%
1895	39.1%	11.9%	9.8%	1.6%	3.1%	17.4%	1.8%
average	27.4%	17.2%	10.1%	2.4%	6.2%	16.3%	2.9%

Table A.5B. Comparison of Occupations of Inmates with State Population

Sample Years

Domestics. Average 17.2%

1875 TAH	6.5%
1875 Massachusetts	10.4%
1895 TAH	11.9%
1895 Massachusetts	14.2%

Laborers. Average 27.4%

1875 TAH	13.1%
1875 Massachusetts	8.3%
1895 TAH	39.1%
1895 Massachusetts	8.6%

Textile Workers. Average 10.1%

1875 TAH	19.6%
1875 Massachusetts	18.6%
1895 TAH	9.8%
1895 Massachusetts	12.8%

Shoeworkers. Average 2.4%

1875 TAH	0.9%
1875 Massachusetts	7.8%
1895 TAH	1.6%
1895 Massachusetts	5.9%

Seamen. Average 6.2%

1875 TAH	9.3%
1875 Massachusetts	2.4%
1895 TAH	3.2%
1895 Massachusetts	1.0%

Farmers. Average 2.9%

1875 TAH	6.5%
1875 Massachusetts	7.6%
1895 TAH	1.8%
1895 Massachusetts	3.0%

Skilled Crafts. Average 16.3%

1875 TAH	21.5%
1875 Massachusetts	24.2%
1895 TAH	17.4%
1895 Massachusetts	14.7%

Table A.6A. Inmates Labeled "Colored" at Tewksbury, 1865–1895 ("colored" includes all labeled as such, including African American, mulatto, some Hispanic and Portuguese people, Asian and African, but usually not Native American)

Sample Years	
1865	0.4%
1867	5.8%
1870	6.8%
1872	7.2%
1875	2.6%
1877	1.7%
1880	3.0%
1882	2.0%
1885	1.4%
1887	0.5%
1890	0
1893	1.0%
1895	1.6%
average	2.6%

Table A.6B. "Colored" Inmates Compared with State Census

Sample Years	
1875 TAH	2.6%
1875 Massachusetts	1.3% (includes black, mulatto, Chinese, Japanese, Indian)
1895 TAH	1.6%
1895 Massachusetts	1.2%

Notes

In order not to disturb the flow of the text, in-text citations were not used. Source notes and explanatory notes appear here by page number with a reference phrase to the text.

ABBREVIATIONS USED FOR SOURCES:

FS: Familysearch.org, an Internet site of the Church of Jesus Christ of Latter-Day Saints.

IBAMPHM: Inmate Biographies at the Massachusetts Public Health Museum in Tewksbury, Massachusetts (see Chapter 2). These were used when additional data was entered for an inmate in addition to the TAIB below.

MVS: Massachusetts Vital Statistics 1840–1910, available through the New England Historic Genealogical Society (NEHGS).

OWT: "One World Tree" a feature of Ancestry.com website.

TAIB: Tewksbury Almshouse Inmate Biography, 1860–1896. Available at the Massachusetts State Archive, Boston, Massachusetts, and the Center for Lowell History, Lowell, Massachusetts (see Chapter 2).

USC: United States Census, enumeration sheets, downloaded from Ancestry.com.

CHAPTER I *Ordinary People*

p. 1 William Sylvis quote: Cited in Sherri Broder, *Tramps, Unfit Mothers, and Neglected Children: Negotiating the Family in Nineteenth Century Philadelphia.* Philadelphia: University of Pennsylvania Press, 2002, p. 21.

p. 1 *"Defective, dependent, and delinquent classes"*: The U.S. Census grouped paupers both in almshouses and on "outdoor relief" (aid from towns) with "insane," "feebleminded," "prisoners," "homeless children," and "orphans" in a mix that typified the nineteenth-century merging of poverty and deviance.

p. 2 *Frank Cross:* TAIB #59089, 1880. Other information from USC 1880 (Lewiston, Me), 1900 (Medford, Ma), 1910 (Malden, Ma), and 1920 (Wakefield, Ma).

p. 2 *nine month sentence:* Unfortunately no further information is available as to his infraction, but a nine-month sentence was considerable for the house of correction. Usually children were removed from their parents upon imprisonment, often even if another parent was alive.

p. 2 *sometimes exploitative:* Hundreds of thousands, perhaps even millions of children were taken from their families in the nineteenth and early twentieth century and placed out before any organized system of foster care or adoption was developed. Perhaps most famous and organized of these was the "orphan trains" of Charles Loring Brace's Children's Aid Society. These wholesale transfers of children stopped after protests about mistreatment, the breaking up of families, and allegations from the Catholic Church that the children were being converted. For a good general summary of the care or neglect of children see Homer Folks, *The Care of Destitute, Neglected, and Delinquent Children.* New York: Arno Press, 1971 [original 1900]. On Charles Loring Brace's efforts see Marilyn Holt, *The Orphan Trains: Placing out in America.* Lincoln: University of Nebraska Press, 1992. See Chapter 7.

p. 2 *Robert Delaney:* IBAMPHM, 1875, #45416. Marriage information and information on his wife and mother, IGI Individual Record, FS. Also USC, 1900 (Atlantic City, NJ) and 1910 (Paterson, NJ).

p. 2 *employed many African Americans:* Although generally only a small percentage of the population of New England was African American (about 1%), in the years between the Civil War and the late 1870s they ranged as high as 7% of Tewksbury's inmates. Quite a number of the "inmate biographies" of African Americans mentioned their employment at the Harvard Dining Saloon.

p. 3 *Bridget Hennessey Ferguson:* IBAMPHM, 1873, #342072. Information on marriage from IGI Individual Record, FS. Information on children of Ferguson from OWT. Also information from USC, 1880 (Boston, Ma) and 1900 (Boston, Ma, for son).

p. 3 *according to her interview:* As will be explained in further detail in Chapter 2, all inmates were given a permit after answering interview questions and were then further written up upon arrival at Tewksbury.

p. 3 *Augustine Jacquoit:* TAIB, 1893, #95285–8, 1893. USC 1900 (Great Barrington, Ma), 1920 (Albany, NY), 1930 (Albany, NY).

p. 4 *what became of Julius Senior:* A sample of inmates was researched through genealogical methods. However, there is considerable art in this process, including deciding when names were spelled slightly differently (such as foreign names) as well as detecting errors, misrepresentations, or other reasons for changing ages of people with different censuses.

p. 4 *Kate Joy:* TAIB, 1867, #28532, USC 1850 (Newburyport, Ma), 1860 (Newburyport, Ma), and 1870 (Bridgewater, Ma).

p. 4 *owned their home for awhile:* Most working-class people were not homeowners throughout the nineteenth century, though, of course, this differed widely depending on whether the area was urban or rural.

p. 4 *than an almshouse:* The institution of the workhouse goes back to Europe and in the American Colonies seems to have preceded almshouses, for example, the 1660 founding of the Boston workhouse. The workhouses were initially used for both poor people generally and those who disobeyed the law; most, including Bridgewater State Workhouse became Houses of Correction beginning in the Post–Civil War period. See Chapter 2 for further information on Bridgewater, Massachusetts's state workhouse where Joy was sent.

p. 4 *unusual length:* Generally houses of correction were used for misdemeanor crimes punishable by a year or less. Since the state and the laws governing the poor were somewhat in transition, it is possible she was held there for other reasons than another criminal conviction. There were no state institutions for the "feeble minded" (e.g., mentally retarded) at this time, for example.

p. 5 *David Ring:* IBAMPHM, 1873, #41164, USC, 1860 (Salem, Ma), and 1870 (Salem, Ma). For information on date of marriage and death of wife, see MVS, NEGHS.

p. 5 *Unfortunately the growth of railroads:* See Oscar Handlin, *Boston's Immigrants 1790–1880.* New York: Atheneum, 1977, pp. 71–73, for one of the more poignant descriptions of rail work.

p. 5 *Overseers of the Poor:* The Anglo American Poor Laws (see Chapter 2) rested on the appointment of local officials by each town and city who judged applicants for relief as to their worthiness and settlement in the town. They could grant "outdoor aid" such as food and fuel, later monetary relief, no aid at all, or provide aid in a poorhouse.

p. 5 *68 years old at the time:* I was unable to find any record of Ring's death. He was discharged on August 27, 1873.

p. 5 *John Wyman:* TAIB, 1874, #43242. Wyman's birth, marriage, and death, as well as some information on his parents and siblings were obtained from OWT. Also USC, 1850 (Grand Rapids, MI), 1860 (Ronald, MI), and 1880 (Tewksbury, Ma).

p. 6 *Temperance and Phrenology:* Though these causes, or at least the combination, may seem odd to the modern reader, both were reform movements in this general period which appealed to Yankee Protestants. Phrenology, while clearly now regarded as a pseudoscience, seemed to many intelligent Americans a part of a new rationalist system of analyzing people.

p. 6 *according to his interview:* The figure of $40,000 noted above would be many times that in current dollars.

p. 7 *more reported domestic violence:* The major forms of domestic violence such as wife beating and child abuse have always been mostly heavily reported among the poor both historically and currently. While some advocates and scholars accurately criticize certain biases in official reporting, extreme cases of abuse, which can be well measured, would seem to support this. The increased stress, poor living conditions, poor education, and many other factors associated with poverty and economic hardship (such as unemployment) do likely support higher rates of domestic violence among the poor. See Linda Gordon, *Heroes of Their Own Lives: The Politics and History of Domestic Violence.* New York: Penguin Books, 1988, for one of the best historical analyses.

p. 7 *absolute monetary amount necessary:* See Sar Levitan, *Programs in Aid of the Poor. Sixth Edition,* Baltimore: Johns Hopkins Press, 1990, pp. 1–5, for a good description of the measures of poverty.

p. 8 *to be a pauper:* This issue has received surprising little study in modern times. An excellent book which describes the legal status of the poor for hundreds of years as contrasted with the nonpoor is Jacobus ten Broek, *Family Law and the Poor.* Westport, Ct: Greenwood Publishers, 1971.

p. 8 *also from the seventeenth century:* Though property qualifications for voting were gradually removed in most states for white males during the first half of the nineteenth century, this did not include paupers. The legal theory viewed paupers as state clients who were seen as analogous to slaves in that they could not represent themselves but only their patrons. Poll taxes imposed in the late nineteenth century further depressed voting even among those who were not paupers (see Frances Fox Piven and Richard Cloward, *Why Americans Do Not Vote*. New York: Pantheon, 1989*)*. Of course both the law and the poll taxes were not always enforced, and, in fact, some inmate descriptions note that their "poll taxes were paid for by politicians."

p. 8 *laws of settlement:* As will be described further in Chapter 2, all American Poor Laws came directly from the English Poor Laws initially promulgated in the sixteenth century and revised periodically. Most importantly, the responsibility for the poor was placed with the village or town (originally, in English law, "the parish") and hence battles over whether a poor person was settled in one town or another preoccupied local officials in the U.S. for the first 300 years of our history.

p. 9 *before the 1930s:* The passage of the Social Security Act of 1935 did much to lift some populations out of the local poor-relief system, but by no means did it lift all; see discussion in David Wagner, *The Poorhouse: America's Forgotten Institution*. Lanham, Md: Rowman & Littlefield, 2005, pp. 132–34.

p. 9 *Tewksbury's Most Famous Inmate:* TAIB #48457–8, 1876. This inmate write-up was given to me by staff of the Massachusetts Public Health Museum which now occupies the oldest building of the former Tewksbury almshouse.

p. 10 *biography of Anne Sullivan:* Helen Keller, *Teacher: Anne Sullivan Macy*. Garden City, NY: Doubleday and Company, 1955, p. 9.

p. 10 quotation from Keller: *ibid.,* p. 10.

p. 10 *Gilded Age:* The term "Gilded Age" was coined by Mark Twain in a book with Charles Dudley Warner, *The Gilded Age* (Hartford: American Publishing Company, 1873).

p. 11 *Ellis Island:* My analogy refers not to the point of embarkation, but to the scale of the number of immigrants at Tewksbury.

p. 11 *"Uprooted":* Oscar Handlin's famous book by this title (Boston: Little, Brown and Company, 1952) won a Pulitzer Prize but has received some criticism over the years for painting with a broad stroke the amount of social disorganization among immigrants.

p. 12 *low wage workforce:* Stephen Thernstrom's classic works (*Poverty and Progress: Social Mobility in a Nineteenth Century City*. Cambridge: Harvard University Press, 1964; and *The Other Bostonians: Poverty and Progress in the American Metropolis 1880–1970*. Cambridge, Harvard University Press, 1973) were among the first to make the point that without the rural migrants who joined the vast labor pool, the rapid industrialization of the Northern states would not have occurred.

p. 12 *domestic work:* See, for example, Hasia Diner, *Erin's Daughters in America* (Baltimore: Johns Hopkins University Press, 1983) on ethnic dimensions in the preferences or rejection of domestic work.

p. 14 *ethnic history:* Academic treatments such as Diner's (above) present an almost glorified account of Irish women with little recognition of the large amount of social problems that the Irish lower classes of both sexes faced. Another book, Mintz and Kellogg's *Domestic Revolutions: A Social History of Family Life* (New York: Simon and Schuster, 1989) strains so hard to portray ethnic, immigrant, and African American families as "just like us" that it also tends to minimize how much poverty and discrimination, as well as different norms and customs, made these groups' family lives quite different from the middle-class Protestant norm.

p. 14 *dramatic events:* An example of the exceptional event focus is Jeremy Brecher's *Strike!* (Boston: South End Press, 1972), an interesting and dramatic book, but one which uses extremely exceptional times in American history to portray a militant working class.

p. 14 *work of Stephen Thernstrom:* as above.

CHAPTER 2 *The Context: The Massachusetts State Almshouse at Tewksbury, Immigration, and Industrialization*

p. 19 Trachtenberg quote: From *The Incorporation of America: Culture and Society in the Gilded Age,* New York: Hill and Wang, 1982, p. 5.

p. 20 *As New York social welfare historian David Schneider: The History of Public Welfare in New York.* New York: New York State, 1939, p. 46.

p. 20 *As early as 1636:* Trattner, W., *From Poor Law to Welfare State: A History of Social Welfare in America.* New York: The Free Press, 1989, Fourth Edition, p. 20.

p. 20 *anecdotes of dumping the poor:* See especially Albert Deutsch, *The Mentally Ill in America,* Chapter III (pp. 39–54), New York: Columbia University Press, 1949.

p. 21 *one inmate of Tewksbury:* Charles Kemp, an inmate admitted to the almshouse in 1871, was forced by the selectman of Mason, New Hampshire, to give up his father's home to finance the latter's care in old age. Of course, this does not differ so much from the modern American social welfare system, as thousands of elderly and disabled citizens find they must deplete their assets, including houses or cars, for Medicaid financing, particularly for long-term care.

p. 21 *all rogues, vagabonds and idle persons:* This was fairly standard language for some of the "unworthy poor" to be sent to workhouses or houses of correction; see Deutsch (above, p. 52) for Connecticut's language. The same language appears in the Maine state laws which came in turn from Massachusetts state law *(Powers and Duties of the Town Officers,* Hallowell, Me: Glazier, Masters and Company, 1833, pp. 237–8).

p. 22 *relatively few institutions of any kind:* David Rothman's *The Discovery of the Asylum,* Boston: Little, Brown and Company, 1971, is still the best source of the "utopian optimism" which led to institution building in America during the Jacksonian period.

p. 22 *Famous investigations of poverty:* The most famous are the New York Yates Report and the Quincy Report in Massachusetts.

p. 22 quote on Yates report: Cited in David Rothman, *The Discovery of the Asylum.* Boston: Little, Brown and Company, 1971, pp. 166–67.

p. 22 *Nostalgic for an earlier time:* This is Rothman's thesis. His reliance on a kind of status threat or utopian optimism was not always borne out in my own research; see Wagner, *The Poorhouse,* Chapter 3. Many localities stressed only the efficiency and fiscal relief and seemed to have no great ideals attached to the building of these institutions.

p. 23 *the poor were not prisoners:* This is actually a complex issue and ultimately what divided the workhouse and poorhouse. Only with the 14th amendment after the Civil War did the forcible placing of paupers in workhouses or poorhouses generally cease as a violation of involuntary servitude. Hence, at the point of our study, to be sent to the workhouse or house of correction, one had to be convicted of a crime, although many crimes such as loitering and tramping were synonymous with poverty.

p. 24 *"Almshouses are their inns:"* Quote from Robert Kelso, *Public Poor Relief in Massachusetts 1620–1920.* Boston: Houghton-Mifflin, 1922, pp. 118–19

p. 24 *"Common domestic animals:"* Quoted in Michael Katz, *In the Shadow of the Poorhouse: A Social History of Welfare in America.* New York: Basic Books, originally published in 1986, second edition 1996, p. 33.

p. 24 *Sarah Orne Jewett:* Quote from the short story "The Flight of Betsey Lane," in *Betsey's Flight: The Country of Pointed Firs and Other Stories.* Garden City, NY: Doubleday, 1956, p. 172.

p. 25 *Boston was the second largest port of embarkation:* Information on Boston in the paragraph from Handlin, 1977; Albert B. Hart, ed., *Commonwealth History of Massachusetts,* Volume IV. New York: The States History Company, 1930; and Thomas O'Connor, *The Boston Irish: A Political History.* Boston: Little, Brown and Company, 1995.

p. 26 *The nativist Vox Populi in Lowell:* Cited in Brian Mitchell, *The Paddy Camps: The Irish of Lowell 1821–61.* Urbana: University of Illinois Press, 1988, p. 99.

p. 26 *"The evil (of foreign paupers) is a not a temporary one:"* Report cited in Massachusetts Public Document, No. 19, 1864, Board of State Charities, pp. 243–44.

p. 28 *And so in their first report in 1864:* Massachusetts Public Document 19, p. 235–56.

p. 28 *According to historian Alexander Keyssar: Out of Work: The First Century of Unemployment in Massachusetts.* Cambridge, Ma: Cambridge University Press, 1986, p. 14.

p. 29 *Economists see the American contribution to industry:* see Peter Temin, ed., *Engines of Enterprise: An Economic History of New England.* Cambridge, Ma: Harvard University Press, 2000, Chapter 3. Several other good sources of Massachusetts's economic dominance in this period, in addition to Keyssar above, are Hart, 1930, and Jack Tager & John Ifkovic, eds., *Massachusetts in the Gilded Age.* Amherst: University of Massachusetts Press, 1985.

p. 29 *By 1880, 80% of the national textile industry:* Temin, p. 121.

p. 29 *As Massachusetts urbanized:* Figures from Temin, p. 131.

p. 30 *Massachusetts embraced the inevitable:* Because of the more distant locations of Bridgewater and Monson from both Boston and other industrial centers of the state, they never served the number of inmates that Tewksbury did. Monson, in fact, would last only sixteen years as the "State Primary School."

p. 30 *children who as of 1866:* See Chapter 7 for the reasons why some children continued to be admitted to the Tewksbury almshouse after the development of the State Primary School in Monson.

p. 31 *Upon completion of a book on the almshouses/poorhouses of New England: The Poorhouse: America's Forgotten Institution* (2005). I had initially planned and was able to obtain a University of Southern Maine Creativity Grant to study Tewksbury and the large Long Island (Boston) almshouse. I also explored briefly the large New York City almshouse at Blackwell's Island.

p. 31 *Neither the Archives:* Neither the Center for Lowell History nor the Museum of Public Health staff were able to account for the differences in the descriptions of the same inmates, particularly in the 1870s.

p. 33 *who were most likely the clerks of the state almshouse:* This is my educated opinion based on perusal of the staff lists at the almshouse in this period and is concurred with by Martha Mayo, director of the Center for Lowell History. The clerks from 1865 to 1890 were sons of the Superintendent Thomas Marsh: Thomas J. Marsh Jr. and then another son, Charles. In the 1890s a man named Hiram J. Dinsmore, not evidently related to the other officials, became the clerk.

p. 33 *the impact . . . investigations:* See Box 2.2. The 1883 scandal dominated state news during the one-year governorship of Benjamin Butler, a bombastic populist who moved from Democrat to Republican to the Greenback Party. Some of the more severe charges, such as making products with dead inmates' skin, have not held up well to historical light. The Republican Legislature rejected all the charges, though no doubt some had truth to them.

p. 34 *Tewksbury's Biggest Scandal:* The case of Governor Butler is summarized in pamphlet form including graphic images of tanned human skin and other images in "Argument before the Tewksbury Investigation Committee" (originally in the *Sunday Globe,* July 15, 1883). To see the opposing side, I read several months of the Lowell, Massachusetts, *American Citizen,* a Republican paper (the *Globe* was Democratic) which heaped scorn for months on Butler and proclaimed Tewksbury the best, most-progressive facility in the nation. The majority and minority reports are summarized in the July 27, 1883, *American Citizen,* p. 1. The quote about "paupers' skins" is on page 38 of Butler's "Argument before the Tewksbury Investigation Committee."

p. 34 *The most dramatic charges:* See, for example, the discussion in Michael Sappol, *A Traffic of Dead Bodies: Anatomy and Embodied Social Identity in Nineteenth-Century America.* Princeton: Princeton University Press, 2002, p. 318. The author notes "the affair did little to rouse the working-class and rural electorate against the Republican Party, despite ample press coverage. The old general lost his reelection bid by a wide margin, putting an end to his colorful political career." See also Dale Baum, "The Massachusetts Voter: Party Loyalty in the Gilded Age 1872–1896," in Tager & Ifkovic, p. 49, on the "failure of Butlerism."

p. 35 *one fifth of the inmates:* There were not actually 85,000 discrete individuals as there were return visits, which I estimate at between 15 and 20% of the population. Also some entries noting deceased foundlings or nominal transfers to institutions such as asylums reveal little or no information.

p. 36 *identified as deviants:* With a few exceptions, notations that the inmate was labeled "insane," "drunk," or otherwise precluded much detail and, in all probability, much of an interview with the inmate.

p. 36 *about one in six:* Any age for a cut-off between children and adults is difficult in an era where norms were constantly in flux, and child labor regulation was just beginning. In the early part of the era, many children as young as 10 or 11 were working, but by 1895 considerable progress was made in New England in eliminating youngsters 14 and under from the workplace. Generally though, even a 15 year old was considered an adult during this era.

p. 36 *The numbers of African Americans:* See, however, the caveat on page 43 on the use of the term "colored" to represent various groups.

p. 37 *I am in debt:* "Early American Microhistories," National Endowment for the Humanities Seminar, June 2005, at the University of Connecticut—Storrs.

p. 38 *In some cases, it seemed lazy census:* This appears particularly true in the censuses of institutions such as asylums, orphanages, almshouses, jails, etc., in which census takers may not have wanted or lacked time to talk with each inmate, and simply wrote down places of birth and occupations willy-nilly.

p. 39 *As advocates and fundraisers:* I have taken this issue up elsewhere; see, for example, David Wagner, "The Universalization of Social Problems: Some Radical Explanations." *Critical Sociology,* 23:1, 1997, pp. 3–24.

p. 39 *U.S. census conclusions about almshouses:* Between 1880 and 1925, the United States Census Bureau did a series entitled "Paupers in Almshouses." While I have argued in Wagner, 2005, that the census vastly undercounted inmates, the characteristics they showed (male, foreign born, more single and widowed, occupations led by laborers and domestics) have been upheld in most academic studies; see, for example, Katz, 1996, and in *Poverty and Policy in American History.* New York: Academic Press, 1983. The one exception for the Tewksbury facility which may have been due in part to the almshouse being a state facility for the "unsettled" is the age structure. Many town and city almshouses were known—and increasingly by the twentieth century were dominated—by the elderly. Perhaps because many elder residents of the state qualified for local assistance, they were not as numerous at Tewksbury. Further, as noted, populations such as men looking for work, and women with out-of-wedlock births were young.

p. 39 *Tables A1–A6:* It should be noted that I have focused on admission data rather than express occupancy over time such as for a whole year, information which is unavailable except at the time of the U.S. census each ten years. In other words, while the data are broadly reflective, they may over- or understate what the almshouse population might have been like at any point in time. For example, the number of male admissions may overstate the composition as in some years women may have stayed longer, and so on. Unfortunately, while the Archive is now indexed by name, there are no corresponding dates of stay with the name. Even if one went to each microfiche entry it would not necessarily tell you discharge dates (some years note discharge, while some do not).

p. 39 *a comparison of the inmates:* I found the best two censuses taken of the state that provide good detail to be those of 1875 and 1895. Also since annual data of one entity such as Tewksbury are highly variable as compared with the trends of a state, it was not felt as necessary to sample other censuses for each year.

p. 39 *Few women were ever labeled:* Anti-tramping legislation increased everywhere with the depression of the 1870s and the unrest of this time such as the mass rail strike of 1877, which scared the upper and middle classes. Massachusetts's 1880 statute defined all men who were not residents and apparently not working as "tramps," but excluded women, the blind and lame, children, and the town poor. In 1896, the law was amended to be even tougher (see Keyssar, 1986, pp. 135–37). Another excellent discussion of this period's anti-tramp laws is Amy Dru Stanley, "Beggars Can't be Choosers: Compulsion and Contract in Postbellum America" *Journal of American History* 78 (March 1992), pp. 1265–93.

p. 39 *As some historians have pointed out:* see particularly Katz, 1983, 1996. In this study, many elderly men and women (see Chapter 8) were recorded in the *Inmate Biographies* as having families that "would do nothing for them." Often issues of drunkenness or unruliness were cited, though there may also have been issues of aging, such as cognitive deterioration, at work. Of course, for very poor people, the ability to support any family member, parent or child, was difficult when the average male wage worker made only two-thirds of the money necessary to support a family.

p. 40 *though the findings support:* see Katz, 1983, 1996, US Census 1880–1925; Estelle Stewart, *The Cost of American Almshouses.* Washington, D.C.: Government Printing Office, 1925.

p. 40 *many people remained legally married:* See the excellent study by Beverly Schwartzberg, "'Lots of them Did That': Desertion, Bigamy, and Marital Fluidity in Late-Nineteenth-Century America," *Journal of Social History* 2004 (4), pp. 573–600. So many women were deserted despite formal marriage ties that the term "grass widows" was coined for them—i.e., the husband had gone off for greener grasses. Of course, complete data are impossible to find, but certainly far more men abandoned their wives than vice versa.

p. 41 *dramatic difference between the percentage:* Of course the state of Massachusetts was still rural in many parts, and is today, like most states, greatly suburban. The percentage of Irish at the almshouse was only somewhat higher than among its urban populations of Boston, Lowell, Lawrence, and Worcester, for example, but far lower than the statewide totals.

p. 41 *Hence a comparison with contemporary:* To remedy these problems would take vast work. On the issue of current work, it is difficult sometimes to determine from the inmate biographies. Often a man labeled "laborer" was out of the almshouse in a week or two, so would clearly be a laborer. But the laborer might have been ill or unemployed for a year. As Keyssar points out, there was no clear modern definition of unemployment as a concept at this time, particularly before the 1880s and 1890s. On the vast number of occupations, a chart reflecting the complete list would be unwieldy and find many occupational names with very few occupants. For grouping of occupational titles of skilled craftsman I have used Stephen Thernstrom's groupings of the mid- to late nineteenth century.

p. 42 *the complexity of this relation:* The relations between domestics and their employers ran the gamut of positives and negatives. Some inmate biographies suggest great fondness for a particular worker and even cases where employers offered to keep jobs open after they gave birth. Other domestic servants, on the other hand, had been raped by employers or had "criminal contact," whether consensual or forced, with the sons of the employers.

p. 42 *skilled craftsman:* This measure is admittedly rough. First it is not clear that every self-identified carpenter or baker should be judged as skilled, but I did not have enough information to develop criteria to separate them. Second, the census made no effort to separate the trades by category. I took the state census and added up the industries that had a heavy concentration of skilled workers such as the building trades, printing, rail, machine production, etc., so this comparison is extremely rough.

p. 43 *shoe makers:* For some discussion of the shoe workers as opposed to textile workers in Massachusetts, see Keyssar, 1986; David Montgomery, *Citizen Worker: The Experience of Workers in the United States with Democracy and the Free Market during the Nineteenth-Century.* New York: Cambridge University Press, 1993; and Tager & Ifkovic, 1985.

p. 43 *farm comparisons:* Most farmers who were admitted to the almshouse were elderly men or disabled. The census of Massachusetts has some good data on certain aspects of land ownership, but the number of people who owned farms from which they derived all of their living (as opposed to some) is not clear.

p. 44 *have come in for some criticism:* Although not by name, the concept of "uprooted" has drawn some criticism in Walter Nugent, *Crossings: The Great Transatlantic Migrations 1870–1914*. Bloomington: Indiana University Press, 1992; see also, for example, Roger Daniels, "The Immigrant Experience" in Charles Calhoun, ed., *The Gilded Age: Essays on the Origins of Modern America*. Wilmington, De: Scholarly Resources, 1996, and "The Challenges of Economic Maturity: New England 1880–1940" in Temin, 2000. Of course, much of this difference may be semantic as Handlin spoke at a high level of generality, and almost exclusively used as an example the Irish experience. The "revisionist" authors are correct in noting that many immigrants and immigrant groups did not suffer as much as the Irish and that it is possible to exaggerate the experience of immigration.

Part I Mobility: Geographic and Economic

p. 47 Thernstrom quote from Melvyn Dubofksy, *Industrialism and the American Worker*, 1865–1920, AHM Publishing, 1975, p. 12.

p. 47 Dawley quote, *Class and Community in Lynn*. Cambridge, Ma: Harvard University Press, 1976, p. 139

p. 47 *Very much a liberal historian.* A very good essay on Handlin's work is Reed Ueda, "Immigration and the Moral Criticism of American History: The Vision of Oscar Handlin." *Canadian Review of American Studies* 21 (2) (Fall 1990), 183–202.

p. 48 *"rags to respectability"*: Thernstrom, *The Other Bostonians,* p. 73.

p. 48 *Handlin's work in particular was criticized as overstating:* The best source for a discussion of the "new immigration historians" and critiques of the "uprooted" are Virginia Yans-McLaughlin, ed., *Immigration Reconsidered: History, Sociology, and Politics*. New York: Oxford University Press, 1990. See also Rudolph J. Vecoli, "The Resurgence of American Immigration History." *American Studies International* 12 (Winter 1979) 46–71; John Bodnar, *The Transplanted: A History of Immigrants in Urban America*. Bloomfield: Indiana University Press, 1985; and Walter Nugent, *Crossings: The Great Transatlantic Migrations 1870–1914* (above).

p. 49 *"oversocialized" conception of people:* I am using a phrase associated with a famous article by Dennis Wrong, "The Oversocialized Conception of Man." *American Sociological Review* 26 (1961), pp. 183–93. Wrong's critique of much of sociology of the 1950s was that it reduced humans to fixed categories who demonstrated theory, particularly within Parsonian structural-functionalism. I am using this term slightly differently to critique modern social science and history's tendency to perhaps overstress association, for example voluntary associations, which in today's world particularly has become a middle-class sign of approval, but does not necessarily fit the lives of all people.

p. 49 *Several authors now criticize:* See articles in the special issue "Comment and Debate: Thernstrom's Poverty and Progress." *Social Science History* 10:1 (Spring 1986). The "dead end" phrase comes from Michael Frisch, *"Poverty and Progress:* A Paradoxical Legacy," p. 19.

p. 49 *Other critics remark:* Hartmut Kaeble, quoted in David Grusky & Ivan K. Fukumoto, "Social History Update: A Sociological Approach to Historical Social Mobility." *Journal of Social History,* 23:1 (Fall 1989), pp. 221–232.

CHAPTER 3 *The "Uprooted": Immigrants and Migrants*

p. 51 *James Jasper has remarked:* See above, 2000, p. 53.

p. 52 *Patrick Forbes:* TAIB #41636, 1873.

p. 52 *Patrick Sweeney,* TAIB #41137, 1873.

p. 53 *"coffin ships":* See Handlin, *The Uprooted;* Mintz & Kellogg, *Domestic Revolutions,* p. 86; and Nugent, *Crossings,* pp. 29–33.

p. 53 *Herbert Gutman notes:* See "Class, Status, and the Gilded-Age Radical: A Reconsideration of the Case of a New Jersey Socialist," in Herbert Gutman & Gregory Kealey, *Many Pasts: Readings in American Social History 1865–The present.* Englewood Cliffs, NJ: Prentice-Hall, 1973, p. 129.

p. 54 *Hannah Donahoe: TAIB* #25373, 1866.

p. 54 *Julia Ryan:* TAIB, #36594, 1871.

p. 54 John Day: TAIB #47855, 1875.

p. 54 *William Wilson:* TAIB, #59077, 1880.

p. 54 *Johanna O'Connor:* TAIB, #95303, 1893.

p. 54 *Anne Lee:* TAIB, #103283, 1895.

p. 54 *As noted by Handlin: The Uprooted,* p. 50.

p. 54 *Annie White:* TAIB #45681, 1875.

p. 55 *Eva Dorr:* TAIB, #59155, 1880.

p. 55 *Sarah Boyle:* TAIB, #102605, 1895.

p. 55 *Mary Butler,* TAIB, #34244, 1870.

p. 55 *Michael Murray:* TAIB, #45948, 1875.

p. 55 *Mary Peterson:* TAIB, #59191–2, 1880.

p. 55 *Jane Duxbury:* TAIB, #87250–3, 1890.

p. 55 *For while Charlotte Erickson: Invisible Immigrants: The Adaptation of English and Scottish Immigrants in Nineteenth-Century America.* Coral Gables, FL: University of Miami Press, 1972, p. 241.

p. 55 *Hasia Diner makes the important point:* Diner, *Erin's Daughters in America,* Chapter 3.

p. 56 *as charged by the founder of modern social work, Mary Richmond:* Cited in Broder, *Tramps, Unfit Mothers, and Neglected Children,* pp. 16–17.

p. 56 *Walter Nugent, for example: Crossings,* p. 35.

p. 56 *Ellen Whittaker:* TAIB, #46272–73, 1875.

p. 56 *John DeGraaf:* TAIB, #56335, 1877.

p. 56 *Rose Harpp:* TAIB, #102334–5, 1895.

p. 57 *Victor Swinson:* TAIB #48266, 1876.

p. 57 *Ida Johnson:* IBAMPHM #74273–75, 1885.

p. 57 *Joseph Rynkella:* TAIB #86976, 1890.

p. 57 *Victoria Voski:* TAIB #87040, 1890.

p. 57 *Johanna McCarty:* IBAMPHM #41099, 1873.

p. 58 *Anna and Charles Razoux:* TAIB #38105–6, 1872.

p. 58 *Ellen Doherty:* TAIB, #46152–155, 1875.

p. 58 *Michael Collins:* TAIB, #47844, 1875.

p. 58 *Michael McGuire:* TAIB, #74411, 1885.

p. 58 *James Kelley:* TAIB, #40221, 1872.

p. 59 *Thomas McCalliacut:* TAIB, #51184, 1877

p. 59 *Gicinto [or Giacinto] Tocchio:* TAIB #102483, 1895.

p. 60 *migration to and from Canada was sieve-like*": Nugent, *Crossings,* p. 138.

p. 60 *ship masters were trying:* N. Thayer, "The Immigrants" in Hart, 1930, p. 144.

p. 61 *As Handlin and others have noted: The Uprooted,* pp. 59–60. See Arthur L. Eno, ed., *Cotton Was King: A History of Lowell, Massachusetts.* Lowell, Ma: Lowell Historical Society, 1976, p. 193 about immigrants walking from Quebec.

p. 61 *John Bohen:* TAIB, #36668, 1871.

p. 61 *Shaw family:* TAIB, #23368–73, 1865.

p. 61 *Edward Poor:* TAIB #22522, 1865.

p. 61 *Arthur Archibald:* TAIB, #86979, 1890.

p. 62 *A.L. Eno's history of Lowell:* Eno, *Cotton Was King: A History of Lowell, Massachusetts,* pp. 191–2.

p. 62 *Rachel Stannes:* TAIB #24882–3, 1865.

p. 62: *Josephine Austin:* TAIB #28377, 1867.

p. 62 *Louisa Sweeney:* TAIB, #27979, 1867.

p. 63 *Ann Scott:* TAIB, #34323, 1870

p. 63 *Mary Green:* TAIB, #48248, 1876.

p. 63 *Rebecca Barker:* TAIB #79175, 1887.

p. 64 *Celia Brown:* IBAMPHM #74315, 1885.

p. 64 *Ada Sanborn:* TAIB #27818, 1867.

p. 64 *Mary A. Boyce:* IBAMPHM #46054, 1875. This entry was heavily edited as the first paragraph was filled with material later judged to be "lies" by the alms-house staff.

p. 65 *Marie Duroche:* TAIB, #45616–18, 1875.

p. 65 *Jenny Smith:* TAIB #87030, 1890.

p. 65 *Elizabeth Green:* TAIB #59495, 1880.

p. 65 *Thomas Maxim:* IBAMPHM, #41256, 1873.

p. 65 *Daniel Lewis:* TAIB #38264, 1872.

p. 66 *historians note that:* See Tim Cresswell, *The Tramp in America.* London: Reaktion Books, 2001, pp. 37–39, for example. See also Eric Monkkonen, ed., *Walking to Work: Tramps in America 1790–1935,* Lincoln: University of Nebraska Press, 1984; and Kenneth Kusmer, *Down and Out, On the Road: Homelessness in American History.* New York: Oxford University Press, 2002.

p. 66 Walt Whitman (1879) quoted in Trachtenberg, *Incorporation,* p. 70.

p. 66 *As noted by Raymond Mohl:* Quoted in Charles Calhoun, *The Gilded Age,* p. 96.

p. 66 *point was made as well by Thernstrom:* See "Urbanization, Migration and Social Mobility in Late Nineteenth Century America" in Gutman & Kealey, *Many Pasts,* p. 112.

p. 66 *The movement away from rural areas:* see Harold Wilson, *The Hill Country of Northern New England: Its Social and Economic History 1790–1930.* New York: AMS Press, 1967, original 1936. See also Hal Barron, *Those Who Stayed Behind: Rural Society in Nineteenth-Century New England.* Cambridge, UK: Cambridge University Press, 1984, for a needed corrective that argues that out-migration did not destroy rural life, and that discusses who left and who stayed.

p. 67 *Harold Wilson is likely right:* Wilson, *ibid.*

p. 67 *Historian Peter Knights well locates the migrants:* Peter Knights, *Yankee Destinies: The Lives of Ordinary Nineteenth-Century Bostonians.* Chapel Hill: University of North Carolina Press, 1991, p. 15.

p. 67 *Generally inheritance was not necessarily by primogeniture:* Barron's study (above) of Vermont suggests that there it was often the youngest son who got the farm.

p. 67 *Knights notes that many:* Knights, *Yankee Destinies,* pp. 26–33.

p. 67 *Webster Powers:* TAIB, #40441, 1873. USC, 1860 (Orfand, NH), 1880 (Boston, Ma), 1900 (Stratford, Vt).

p. 68 *Meanwhile, his oldest brother:* Information on Chandler Powers from USC, 1860 (Orfand, NH), 1880 (Ely, Vt), 1900 (Veshire, Vt), and 1910 (Veshire, Vt); in addition Ancestry.com shows he married and gave birth to his first daughter in 1869 and served in the military as a seaman 1862–65. On Jacob Powers, other than the USC 1860 (Orfand, NH), I could only find him in the 1920 Census (Skagit, Wa).

p. 68 *William S. Pennock:* TAIB, #45380, 1875. He was born August 22, 1832, in Windsor to Cyril and Sarah (née Weatherbee) (FS). William, married in Boston on January 25, 1857, to Sarah D. Smith (FS). In 1850 his family of origin is in the census in Windsor, Vermont. Cyril is a mason with $500 real estate property, there is a Sarah Bownel, 24 (unexplained), as well as mother Sarah and seven Pennock children and a Charles Bownel, 2 months. William L., at 18, seems to be a mason as well; he is second oldest of the children (USC, 1850). In 1880, William has passed from the scene (I suspect he died, though I could find no evidence); his wife Sarah and youngest daughter Adeline are in the 1880 census in Provincetown, Massachusetts, as boarders with no occupations given (USC, 1880).

Cyril and Mary Pennock remained in Norwich in the 1860 and 1870 census with daughters Cynthia and Ada. He remained a mason and in 1870 had $500 real estate (as above) but also $480 in personal property. In 1880, the family had moved to St. Paul, Minnesota. Interestingly, Cyril is indicated as an 80-year-old school teacher but his line is then crossed out, perhaps suggesting that he had died. William's brother George E, the youngest in the family, headed it up now as a conductor in a railroad.

p. 68 *Pamela Billings:* TAIB, #48601, 1876. She was born Pamela Allen in 1822 in East Windsor, Connecticut, daughter of Gauis and Agnes (FS). She is in the 1850 census in Enfield, Connecticut, at which point the family was living with in-laws Abraham and William Allen, Agnes, and Bradley Billings. In 1860 they are in Keokuk, Iowa, living in the family of Oscar Thorton a merchant; Jabez is 35, Pamela 32, no occupations are listed (USC, 1860). Jabez is found three more times. In the 1870 census in Keokuk he is a dry goods merchant with $3,000 in personal property and Catherine who must be his new wife has $6,000 in personal property (USC, 1870). In the 1880 census he is still there, but is a boarder, still with Catherine, a retired merchant, but has a "general debility" (USC, 1880). In 1900 he is in the census in Denver, Colorado, still with his wife Catherine to whom he has now been married for thirty years. She was from Massachusetts and either she or he is listed as housekeeper.

p. 69 *Stuart Robinson:* TAIB, #74659, 1885.

p. 69 *Charles Feeney:* TAIB, #87157, 1890.

p. 69 *Peter Burns:* TAIB, #102148, 1895.

p. 70 *During the War:* Mintz & Kellogg, *Domestic Revolutions,* p. 76.

p. 70 *Riley Carr:* TAIB #25225, 1865.

p. 70 *Daniel Rooker:* TAIB #25794, 1865.

p. 70 *Nelson Williams:* IBAMPHM #45989, 1875.

p. 70 *Rachel Hodges:* TAIB #34298, 1870.

p. 71 *John Andrew:* TAIB #41115, 1873.

p. 71 *At the end of the Civil War:* See Leslie Fishel on the African American Experience, Chapter 7, in Calhoun, *The Gilded Age.*

p. 71 *Thernstrom's detailed portrait:* See for example Table 8.4 (p. 185). In 1880, Northern-born blacks were 9% white collar, while Southern-born were 7%; 19% of the Northern-born were skilled workers, while only 9% of the Southern-born were; and 73% of Northern-born African Americans were "low manual workers," but even more—84%—of the Southern-born were.

p. 71 *John Andrew (above) died:* MVS, NEGHS, 1875.

p. 71 *Nelson Williams:* IBAMPHM #45989, 1875.

p. 71 *William L Baronett:* TAIB #34123, 1870.

p. 72 *Frances Day:* TAIB #59128, 1880.

p. 72 *Baronett was born:* Birth, marriage, and death information from FS.

p. 72 *Frances Day and her husband Edward:* USC, 1860 (Boston, Ma), 1870 (Easton, Ma). Death, MVS, NEGHS, 1880.

CHAPTER 4 *Falling Down: Yet a Surprising Resilience*

p. 73 *William Fowler:* TAIB #59158, 1880.

p. 73 *James Dooley:* TAIB #43439, 1874.

p. 73 *over $13,000 in 1860:* USC, 1860 (Lynn, Ma.), Fowler was listed as having $8,250 in real estate and $5,000 in personal property. Comparisons of living standards between the 19th century and today are quite tricky, but one measure is the average weekly salary in this period was in the $40s while a house might cost under $5,000.

p. 74 *As Alan Dawley notes:* Dawley, *Class and Community,* p. 169.

p. 74 *a "competence":* ibid., p. 152–3. The development of this term by the Massachusetts Commission of Labor is discussed in Bedford, *Their Lives and Numbers,* p. 76.

p. 74 *Table 4.1:* The census in the years 1850, 1860, and 1870 collected data on real estate and personal property. The census eliminated this question until 1930 when real estate value was returned to the questions.

p. 74 *the use of $500 by Alan Dawley:* See pp. 151–6 of *Class and Community.*

p. 74 *average yearly wages:* There are many methodological questions about the statistics gathered in Massachusetts, as they were pioneers in labor statistics. The 1875 study led by Carroll Wright gave a $462 average wage for workers, while in 1880 it declined to $401 (see Bedford, *Their Lives and Numbers,* p. 65).

p. 76 *Hayford was listed:* This is another problem with the enumeration sheets, the inability to make definite determinations of living partners. Usually in these three censuses, the hired help were referred to as domestic servants, whereas housekeeping implied unpaid domestic duties, but this case is hard to be certain of.

p. 77. *although usually the male head of household:* Despite the generally chauvinistic property laws, wives' separate property was certainly recognized, and many of the cases studied which involved separation and (more rarely) divorce did see property divided between couples.

p. 77 *sharing in the value:* There are some clear examples of communal property such as among the Shakers, with whom a number of our sample lived. The problem is discerning from census enumeration sheets whether the property placed under the first name belongs only to he (usually) and then whether the others are farm laborers or other workers or have some other status.

p. 77 *"boarding out:"* As we shall discuss in Chapter 7, millions of poor children were boarded out and sometimes apprenticed to other people. They usually had no property rights. However, since there was no legal process of adoption, those cases in which a young person was made a family member are hard to separate from those who were boarded.

p. 77 *Fundin et al:* Fundin, TAIB #87073, 1890; Joseph Thompson, TAIB #40271, 1873; Henry L. Joy, TAIB #40337, 1873; Henry Morris, TAIB #101123, 1895; Thomas Graham, TAIB #43162, 1874; Solomon Pollack, TAIB #95306, 1893; Frank L. Wyman, TAIB #95924, 1893; Edward Monroe, TAIB #74393, 1885; John O'Flaherty, TAIB #25152, 1865; William Johnson, TAIB #60679, 1880; Robert Fraser, TAIB #95398, 1893; John Perkins, TAIB #95965, 1893; Joseph Farrell, TAIB #59814, 1880; Hugh Donahoe, TAIB #59814, 1880; Mary Burke, TAIB #45419, 1875; Frederick L. Taylor, TAIB #43602, 1874; James W. Ross, TAIB #86919, 1890.

p. 77 *William Fowler:* TAIB #59158, see also NEGHS for burial plots of Fowler and Ingalls' family, USC, 1850 (Lynn, Ma.), 1860 (Lynn, Ma.), and 1870 (Wenham, Ma.). For Charles, USC, 1880 (Washington, D.C.); for William H, USC, 1880 (Hyde Park, Ma.), 1900 (Boston, Ma), and 1910 (Melrose, Ma.).

p. 78 *Ruth May:* TAIB #59798, 1880. Birth, Marriage, Husband death FS. USC, 1850 (Windham, Ct), 1860 (Woodstock, Ct), and 1880 (Northampton, Ma). Son William, USC, 1870 (Dedham, Ma) and 1880 (West Roxbury, Ma), and sister and brother-in-law USC, 1870, 1880 (Northampton, Ma).

p. 78 *Charles Hatfield:* TAIB #102138, 1895. USC, 1870 (Medford, Ma). Charles Edward, 1900 (Newton, Ma) and 1910 (Newton, Ma). Wife's death, MVS, NEHGS. Son's birth on MVS, NEHGS, Charles's death, MVS, NEGHS.

p. 79 *Charles Hand:* TAIB #34156, 1870. His death, FS. For family, USC, 1850 (Madison, Ct) and 1860 (Madison, Ct).

p. 79 *Delia Stafford:* TAIB #59019, 1880. Her birth, FS. USC, 1850 (Cambridge, Ma), 1870 (Waltham, Ma), 1880 (Saugus, Ma), and 1910 (Saugus, Ma). Brother, USC, 1880 (Cambridge, Ma) and 1910 (Worcester, Ma). Death of brother, FS.

p. 80 *Augustus Flint:* TAIB #87244, 1890. USC, 1860 (New Sharon, Me) and 1870 (Lewiston, Me). Marriage, MVS, NEGHS. Death of Josiah and Frances, FS. Death of George and Augustus, FS.

p. 80 *George Ball:* TAIB #38233, 1872. USC, 1850 (Boston, Ma), 1860 (Boston, Ma), and 1870 (San Francisco, Ca). Nahum Ball birth, FS; death, MVS, NEGHS.

p. 81 *Observers of the Gilded Age:* Trachtenberg, *Incorporation of America,* p. 90.

p. 81 *even official observers noted:* Carroll Wright, the pioneering Commissioner of the Bureau of Labor Statistics, noted in 1875 that most workers earned less than two-thirds of the necessary wages to support their families when employed; a small amount of earnings were contributed by wives, but their wages were generally speaking so small that families had to rely on children for between one-third and one-quarter of the entire family's earnings. Bedford, ed., *Their Lives and Numbers.* Ithaca, NY: Cornell University Press, 1995, p. 55.

p. 81 *Mary Loftis:* IBAMPHM #45278–80, 1875.

p. 81 *Thomas* Gallagher: TAIB #46550, 1875

p. 81 *John Ellis and Albert Ellis:* TAIB #102453–4, 1895.

p. 82 *Rob Rawson:* TAIB #102348, 1895.

p. 82 *Ellen Aldrich:* TAIB #25666–67, 1865. Husband birth, FS. Marriage, MVS, NEGHS; death of husband, MVS, NEGHS. USC, 1860 (Ashland, Ma), 1870 (Ashland, Ma), and 1880 (Ashland, Ma). Birth of illegitimate child and death, MVS, NEGHS.

p. 82 *Matilda Connors:* TAIB #42736–7, 1874. USC, 1850 (husband in Hampstead, NH), 1870 (Haverhill, Ma), 1880 (Haverhill, Ma), and 1920 (Haverhill, Ma). 1894 Haverhill City directory accessed on Ancestry.com.

p. 83 *Mary Bennett:* TAIB #102122, 1895. Birth, FS. USC, 1860 (Sudbury, Ma), 1870 (Marlboro, Ma), and 1900 (Marlboro, Ma).

p. 83 *John F. Conlin:* TAIB #103005, 1895. USC, 1870 (Chelsea, Ma), 1880 (Chelsea, Ma), and 1910 (Bridgewater, Ma).

p. 83 *Simon Davis:* TAIB #87238, 1890. USC, 1850 (Friendship, Me), 1860 (Friendship, Me), 1870 (Cape Elizabeth, Me), and 1880 (Cape Elizabeth, Me). Death, MVS, NEGHS.

p. 83 *Henry Turfey:* TAIB #64886, 1882. USC, 1870 (Philadelphia, Pa) and 1880 (Philadelphia, Pa).

p. 83 *George A. Wells:* TAIB #74333, 1885. USC, 1850 (Boston, Ma). Marriage, MVS, NEGHS.

p. 83 *James H. Arnold:* TAIB #74353, 1885. USC, 1870 (Brooklyn, NY), 1880 (New York, NY), and 1910 (New York, NY).

p. 83 *Hubert Brooks.* IBAMPHM #74328, 1885. Found family of origin USC, 1880 (Holyoke, Ma). Found Hubert Brooks back in London 1901 census, Ancestry.com

p. 83 *William Meek.:* TAIB #74598, 1885. USC 1870 (Philadelphia, Pa) and 1900 (Los Angeles, Ca).

p. 83 *Thomas Shea:* TAIB #79411, 1887. USC, 1870 (Lawrence, Ma), 1880 (Weymouth, Ma), and 1900 (Lawrence, Ma). He was listed through most of this time period in Lawrence, Massachusetts, City Directory.

p. 84 *Approximately one in six of the inmates:* I arrived at this number simply by calculating the number in the sample of 361 who died at Tewksbury, but I suspect it is higher. The difficulty is the *Inmate Biographies* themselves are highly uneven in recording death. They seem to have done so religiously when the inmate died within a short time period, but less so in the longer term. Also, because some inmates had multiple admissions, the count becomes complex. For example, I found some people who died many years after their sampled admission at the Tewksbury facility, but I did not count these as it would appear to me that their later admission, say six years later, would have little to do with why they were there the first time.

p. 84 *such as possibly Ellen Aldrich:* Not only is there no centralized list of people dying in poorhouses, but because of the poor quality of records we can only speculate. Aldrich died in Ashland's poorhouse, but in the case of Connors, Bennett, and Conlin all we have is the last census they appeared in listing them as residents of an almshouse. None are listed in the databases with a death date.

p. 84 *probably subject to a certain amount of changing:* I know of no study of this, but in addition to the complexity of women changing their names with marriage, and sometimes back again (or not) with separation, the *Inmate Biographies* themselves list frequent aliases, indicating that many poor people went by different names, and may have represented their names differently (I have had this experience in my work and research with poor people today). Add to this the Yankee clerks' tendency to mishear or Anglicize foreign names and researchers have a great deal of trouble!

p. 84 *difficult conceptual issue:* It seems to me that the only way to adequately compare people over time would be to have statistical data by age available for each year, but even then we would need this broken down by factors such as gender, ethnicity, and class.

p. 85 *Realizing this, I struggled:* I struggled with many types of samples of my data and with different methods. I was able to achieve reliable results (with about half downwardly mobile and the rest stable or upward) but whether these subjective measures are valid I can't say. My bias in determining mobility was to place those who "ended up" in the almshouse in the downwardly mobile category because of my historical reading of what the institution meant. I also categorized people as downward if they or their parents had been property owners but were no longer so at the last census. Conversely, those who had achieved property or occupational gain either through their own achievement or through family members were categorized as moving upward.

p. 86 *occupational attainments, family occupational attainments (usually husbands or grown children) and/or in terms of property ownership:* Any and all of these measures can be, and have been, challenged.

p. 86 *Bernard Roesing:* USC, 1880 (Chicago, IL).

p. 86 *James Waddington:* USC, 1900 (Boston, Ma).

p. 86 *John Batchelder:* USC, 1920 (Allentown, NH).

p. 86 *Frank Briggs:* USC, 1930 (Burlington, Wa).

p. 86 *Frederick Briggs:* Along with his brothers, TAIB #102213–16, 1895. Frederick's life span October 24, 1881, to August 1964, FS. See USC, 1900 (Lowell, Ma), 1910 (Holyoke, Ma), 1920 (Tewksbury, Ma), and 1930 (Tewksbury, Ma). Draft card, 1917, Ancestry.com has him living in Holyoke, Massachusetts, married to Ellen. He moved to Tewksbury some time between his return from the war and the 1920 census.

p. 86 *Such transitions, however, are not entirely unusual:* I make this comment based on a long history of poorhouses, asylums, hospitals, and other institutions using inmates and former inmates to do work. Though some are scandalized by this, there are many interesting examples of compassion in this situation. Two that come to mind are my documentation of some former poorhouse inmates at the Carroll County, New Hampshire, poor farm who came to work or volunteer there (*The Poorhouse,* pp. 128–9) and the inspiring whistle-blowing actions of Joey Almeida, a former patient at the Fernald State School (for the retarded) in Massachusetts, who years after he was judged "feeble minded" got a job there and helped find documents that revealed how the facility used the patients for radioactivity tests during the Cold War. See Michael D'Antonio, *The State Boys Rebellion.* New York: Simon and Schuster, 2004.

p. 89 *Werner Rusing and Clemens Rusing:* IBAMPHM #45882–83, 1875.

p. 89 *James Waddington:* TAIB #58970, 1880. His marriage on December 22, 1880, MVS, NEGHS, USC, 1900 (Boston, Ma.) and 1910 (Cambridge, Ma.); also James in USC, 1880 as a Tewksbury inmate, and his wife Helen was in the Boston Consumptives Hospital as a patient in 1920. She was a widow, so James had died between 1910 and 1920 (USC, 1920, Boston, Ma).

p. 89 *Irwin children:* TAIB #59470–3, 1880. All the children were listed at Monson in 1880 (USC, 1880). Ida and William Irwin, USC, 1900 (Boston, Ma), 1920 (Boston, Ma), and 1930 (Boston, Ma). Robert Irwin, USC, 1930 (Idaho).

p. 90 *Charles Tarby:* TAIB #59532, 1880. USC, 1900 (Lynn, Ma), 1910 (Everett, Ma), 1920 (Everett, Ma), and 1930 (Everett, Ma).

p. 90 *Jennie Grafton:* TAIB #48278, 1876. Her birth and marriage, FS. USC, 1870 (New Bedford, Ma) and 1900 (Montville, Me). Her and her husband's death, FS.

p. 90 *Eliza Ruffley:* TAIB #74685, 1885. USC, 1900 (Boston, Ma), 1920 (Bow, NH), and 1930 (Concord, NH). Her son is listed as Robert Upton and she is listed as a widow, indicating she married at some point.

p. 91 *Augusta Lee:* TAIB #64511, 1882. Marriage, MVS, NEGHS. FS entry as Augusta Andersson, born in Herrestad, Bohusland, Sweden. USC, 1880 (Longmeadow, Ma), 1900 (Springfield, Ma), 1910 (Springfield, Ma), and 1920 (Springfield, Ma).

p. 91 *David Glass:* TAIB #51289, 1877.

p. 91 *Patrick Good:* TAIB #51274, 1877.

p. 91 *Alfred Williams:* TAIB #51351, 1877.

p. 92 *When David Glass is next found:* Marriage, December 10, 1896, MVS, NEGHS. USC, 1900, Glass is actually in the Soldiers Home in Chelsea, Massachusetts, but listed as a slate and tin roofer.

p. 92 *Patrick Good is in the 1880:* Good is in 1860 (Boston, Ma), 1870 (Boston, Ma), and 1880 (Boston, Ma) censuses, and in the Boston directory in 1890 as a boilermaker at 750 E. Broadway (Ancestry.com). He did, however, commit suicide in 1890 (MVS, NEGHS).

p. 92 *Alfred Williams:* USC, 1860 (Lynn, Ma), 1880 (Boston, Ma), and 1900 (Boston, Ma). Marriage in 1878 to Adeline and birth of child Ruby in 1879, MVS, NEGHS.

p. 92 *William Garvey:* TAIB #102359, 1895. Garvey married Martha Keogh in Fall River, on April 21, 1887, FS. USC, 1900 (Providence, RI), 1920 (Altoona, Pa), and 1930 (Altoona, Pa).

p. 92 *Joseph Leadbetter* : TAIB #103070, 1895. His draft card (Ancestry.com) indicates he was born on March 23, 1875. He was at this time a farmer who worked for himself and had registered for the draft in Gardiner, Massachusetts. USC, 1910, 1920, 1930 (all Princeton, Ma).

p. 92 *William Mullen:* TAIB #102971, 1895.USC, 1870 (Wayland, Ma), 1880 (Wayland, Ma), and 1900 (Boston, Ma).

p. 93 *many others in Table 4.2:* Of course we don't want to overgeneralize from the small numbers, but it is noticeable how many more western and central European immigrants came with resources and succeeded when compared with, say, Irish immigrants.

p. 93 *mobility is a complex family enterprise:* This is certainly not a new point, particularly for economic historians and others who study mobility. The family, whether nuclear or extended, is in a unique position to assist its members in achieving economic resources or in some cases denying them.

p. 93 *Alan Dawley perhaps puts this the best:* Dawley, *Class and Community*, pp. 170–1.

Part II The "Crisis" in the Family

p. 97 *For at least 150 years:* Gordon, *Heroes*, p. 3.

p. 97 *But overall, conventional observers:* In my book *The New Temperance: America's Obsession with Sin and Vice.* Boulder, Co: Westview Press, 1997, I draw an analogy between the 1980s and 1990s and movements such as the Temperance, Social Purity and Vice and Vigilance Societies of the Victorian times. While the movements of the 1960s and 1970s seemed to lead America to sexual abandon, by the 1980s these movements had changed from a more libertarian position to various social control positions, after the New Right had succeeded along with media portrayals in pathologizing what they saw as a culture of "sex, drugs, and rock 'n roll." Democrats and even many liberals responded with campaigns such as those against teen pregnancy, "deadbeat dads," pornography, and even "welfare dependency."

p. 97 *The bourgeois nuclear family:* Much feminist history and sociology since the early 1970s has focused on both redefining "family" and tracing the roots of the so-called "traditional" family. See, for example, the work of Stephanie Coontz, *The Way We Never Were* (New York: Basic Books, 2000) and *The Social Origins of Private Life* (London: Verso Press, 1988).

p. 98 Ten Broek, *Family Law,* p. 148.

p. 98 *supposed sexual repressiveness of the Victorians:* Michel Foucault, *History of Sexuality,* Volume 1. New York: Vintage, 1990. Many other writers have commented on the contradiction of supposed Victorian sexual reticence with the continued Victorian tendency to discuss and dissect sexuality constantly.

CHAPTER 5 *"Criminal Intimacies": Out-of-Wedlock Births*

p. 101 *"She was seduced by ... and after that was":* This phrase and the following one come from about eight to ten of the inmate biographies.

p. 102 *Michael Grossberg: Governing the Hearth: Law and Family in Nineteenth Century America.* Chapel Hill: University of North Carolina Press, 1985, pp. 46–47.

p. 102 *As Sherri Broder:* Broder, *Tramps, Unfit Mothers, and Neglected Children,* p. 3.

p. 103 *"She says she complained":* The lines are from the biographies of Nellie Haskins, TAIB #36570, 1871; Margaret Walsh TAIB #41586, 1873; Winnie Hessian, TAIB #38175, 1872, and Joanna Connors, TAIB #42086, 1873.

p. 103 *In the case below of Ida Hackett:* TAIB #41220, 1873.

p. 104 *In fact prostitution often paid far more than the most common women's job:* This point was frequently made by the Massachusetts Bureau of Labor itself; see Bedford, *Their Lives and Numbers,* pp. 122–126.

p. 104 *D'Emilio and Freedman argue in their history of sexuality:* John D'Emilio & Estelle Freedman, *Intimate Matters: A History of Sexuality in America.* New York: Harper and Row, 1988, p. 57.

p. 104 *Flora Nickerson:* TAIB #28385, 1867.

p. 105 *Alice Scott:* IBAMPHM #48515, 1876.

p. 105 *Josephine Barney:* TAIB #41161, 1873.

p. 105 *Ida McGeorge:* TAIB #95356, 1893.

p. 106 *Margaret Feeley:* TAIB #87117, 1890.

p. 106 *Salia Cunningham.* TAIB #61521, 1880.

p. 106 *Ellen Morin:* TAIB #23348, 1865.

p. 107 *The word "common" in the statute:* William Novak, *The People's Welfare: Law and Regulation in Nineteenth Century America.* Chapel Hill: University of North Carolina Press, 1996.

p. 107 *Men in bastardy and other legal proceedings:* Grossberg, *Governing the Hearth,* Chapters 1–4.

p. 107 *or slightly under a tenth were sentenced to Bridgewater:* The sentences varied from six months to eighteen months dependent on prior convictions; however, inmates were routinely "pardoned" from their full sentences, so that less than a six-month term seemed typical for drunkenness or prostitution.

p. 109 *Some historians have debated how positive such changes:* see, for example, Barbara Hobson, *Uneasy Virtue.* New York: Basic Books, 1987; Regina Kunzel, *Fallen Women, Problem Girls: Unmarried Mothers and Professionalization of Social Work, 1890–1945.* New Haven: Yale University Press, 1995; and Ruth Rosen, *The Lost Sisterhood: Prostitution in America, 1900–1918.* Baltimore: Johns Hopkins University Press, 1982.

p. 109 *Ellen Jones:* TAIB #27909, 1867.

p. 109 *Two women named Mary Welch:* TAIB #s 28328 and 28450, 1867.

p. 110 *discharged to the State Board of Charities:* From the context of the notes, these cases that ended with such a notation appear to have been problematic either because of settlement (in the post-1885 years some inmates who had arrived in the United States without resources were deported and this involved federal matters) or because their disposition generally was problematic, in which case they would go to another institution, state, or auspices.

p. 110 *Etta Brown:* TAIB #48961, 1876.

p. 110 *Elizabeth Heaney:* TAIB #48290, 1876.

p. 110 *and would be exceptional from what we know of the history of this time:* Some have made the argument that poorhouses arose from "utopian ideals" in the Jacksonian period (see Rothman). However, workhouses were more rarely viewed this way, and always had prison and punishment functions.

p. 111 *Ellen Morin:* TAIB #23348, 1865.

p. 112 *George Kingston:* Ann Kingston, TAIB #40239, 1873.

p. 112 *James Moore:* Mary Moore, TAIB #41189–90, 1873.

p. 112 *John Florence:* Mary Glassed, TAIB #22903–4, 1865–66.

p. 112 *Frank Brigel:* Eliza Killips, TAIB #42993, 1874.

p. 112 *William Grey:* Mary Logan, TAIB #46180–81, 1875.

p. 112 *Most Kettough:* Catherine Burns, TAIB #102944, 1895.

p. 116 *Margaret Walsh:* TAIB #41586, 1873.

p. 116 *Amelia Millios:* TAIB #95441, 1893.

p. 116 *Robert Silverman: Law and Urban Growth: Civil Litigation in the Boston Trial Courts 1880–1900.* Princeton, NJ: Princeton University Press, 1981, pp. 128–9.

p. 116 *1914 Study:* Cited in Grossberg, *Governing the Hearth,* p. 228.

p. 117 *in many other states "common law" marriages were more recognized:* According to Grossberg, *Governing the Hearth,* Chapter 3, many states had begun by mid-century to recognize common law marriages, with New England and the "upper South" being notable exceptions (p. 73). However, by the 1870s reformers were targeting the vagueness of marital law and social purity and temperance reformers and others soon began to restrict marriage by age (age-of-consent laws), health (venereal disease, feeblemindedness), and race (miscegenation laws).

p. 117 *Mary Moore:* TAIB #41189–90, 1873.

p. 117 *Anna Barker:* TAIB #46006, 1875.

p. 117 *Anna Donnelly:* IBAMPHM #48571, 1876.

p. 118 *Mary Freeman:* IBAMPHM #51148, 1877.

p. 118 *Mary Roach:* TAIB #64515, 1882.

p. 118 *Ann Marshall:* TAIB #42897, 1874.

p. 118 *Mary Hickerman:* TAIB #87050, 1890.

p. 118 *Minnie Payne:* TAIB #60983, 1880.

p. 119 *Rosa Silva:* TAIB #51223, 1877.

p. 119 *Hannah McQuaid:* TAIB #41318–19, 1873.

p. 119 *Mary Carter:* TAIB #28213, 1867.

p. 119 *Citing post–Civil War sources:* A. Calhoun, *Social History,* p. 80.

p. 119 *1875 book by Azel Ames:* Cited in *ibid.,* p. 90.

p. 120 *James Burn worried that:* ibid., p. 150.

p. 120 *Mary Ganey:* IBAMPHM #48518, 1876.

p. 120 *Anna Perkins:* TAIB #48641, 1876.

p. 120 *Mary Owens:* TAIB #41254, 1873.

p. 120 *Clarissa Wheeler:* TAIB #40614–5, 1873.

p. 120 *Kate Mulligan:* TAIB #38258.

p. 121 *when women reached menarche much later than today:* see Daniel Smith & Michael Hindus, "Premarital Pregnancy in America 1640–1971: An Overview and Interpretation." *Journal of Interdisciplinary History,* 4 (Spring 1975), pp. 537–570 and Tamara Harevan & Maris Vinovskis, eds., *Family and Population in Nineteenth Century America.* Princeton, NJ: Princeton University Press, 1978.

p. 121 *The vast majority of unwed mothers:* Although domestic service was the most frequent female job in the last third of the nineteenth century, the percentage of service workers (I included cooks and laundresses with domestics) was far above the expected levels (75% as opposed to the 50–60% expected from the censuses). Of the 241 women who were pregnant out of wedlock, 180 had occupations listed and 135, or three-quarters, were service workers, only 28 were factory workers (15.6%), and the remaining 17 were listed with other occupations. It is not possible to generalize due to the nature of the sample. It may be that servants' social networks supported using Tewksbury as a lying-in hospital more than, for example, factory workers' networks.

p. 121 *woman named Anna Pooler:* TAIB #38207, 1872.

p. 121 *The account of a Mary A. Coran in 1874:* TAIB #43449, 1874.

p. 122 *Mary Flynn:* TAIB #34286, 1870.

p. 122 *Mary Leary:* TAIB #38308, 1872.

p. 122 *Ellen Ayer:* TAIB #43131, 1874.

p. 122 *Eva Bowen:* TAIB #46448, 1875.

p. 122 *Emma Jones:* TAIB #48324, 1876.

p. 122 *Rather the Post–Civil War period through the end of the 1870s:* Certainly there were many interpretations of contemporaries that support a sexual revolution, see for example, Calhoun, *Social History of the Family,* 1919. See also Smith and Hindus for some evidence of a statistical rise in premarital pregnancy in the latter part of the nineteenth century.

D'Emilio and Freeman are certainly correct in noting the different class and ethnic counternorms which produced very different subcultures around sexuality. But what I am suggesting here is, unlike some activity, for example gay subcultures, these norms were not particularly hidden at this time, nor were they restricted to an ethnic or geographic area. Young women in the almshouse in the 1860s and 1870s often simply stated their encounters and they were from very different ethnic groups and geographic areas.

p. 123 *Social Purity:* This movement gained ground in the 1880s and 1890s and focused on raising the age of consent for marriage, on promoting chastity pledges, promoting prosecution of men, and supporting censorship of literature and the temperance movement. See David Pivar, *Purity Crusade: Sexual Morality and Social Control 1868–1900.* Westport, Ct: Greenwood Press, 1973.

p. 124 *Ruth Bateman:* TAIB #102490, 1895. USC, 1900 (Everett, Ma), she was married to Louis a carpenter, USC, 1910 (Boston, Ma) as well. USC, 1920 (Boston, Ma) listed her as divorced. She was a label stitcher in a shoe factory.

p. 124 *Selma Bostrum:* TAIB #86958, 1890. USC, 1900 (Springfield, Ma), as Selma Holden. USC, 1920 (Northampton, Ma), Northampton State Hospital as a patient.

p. 125 *Lizzie Garfield:* TAIB #38222, 1872. MVS, marriage in 1890 at 40 to L. Bradford Howard, a photographer. She was described in a special line as "legally divorced."

CHAPTER 6 *Family Conflict and Desertion*

p. 127 Calhoun, *Social History of the Family,* p. 215. The phrase is apparently quoted from the *Nation,* Volume 10, 1870 (no page given).

p. 127 Schwartzberg, "Lots of Them Did That," p. 577.

p. 128 *from their origin:* See Wagner, *The Poorhouse.*

p. 128 *Ellen Hylie and family:* TAIB #25926–29, 1865.

p. 128 *Frances Forest and Frank:* TAIB #41209–10, 1873.

p. 128 *Ellen Burns:* IBAMPHM, #74261, 1885.

p. 129 *Michael Cook:* TAIB #46713, 1875.

p. 129 *Helen Sanborn:* TAIB #38267, 1872.

p. 129 *Many explanations have been offered for this;* For the Irish dominance in institutions and prisons, see, for example, Diner, *Erin's Daughters in America,* Chapter 5, and Cole, *Immigrant City: Lawrence, Massachusetts, 1845–1921.* Chapel Hill: University of North Carolina Press, 1963, p. 59. However, Gordon makes the interesting point that while the Italians were deeply poor, they never made up more than a small percentage of almshouse inmates (*Heroes,* p. 10). Clearly ethnicity and nationality have an independent role to play.

p. 129 *Augustus Halloran:* TAIB #45824, 1875.

p. 130 *Margaret Flynn:* TAIB #41162l, 1873.

p. 130 *Only in the 1870s when the famous case of "Mary Ellen":* See, for example, Elizabeth Pleck, *Domestic Tyranny.* New York: Oxford University Press, 1987, and Barbara Nelson, *Making an Issue of Child Abuse.* Chicago: University of Chicago Press, 1984.

p. 130 *In the Gilded Age, immigrant families who sent their children:* See Broder, in particular, for a fine discussion of behavior that was seen as neglectful by the upper classes and officials.

p. 130 *Silas Kimball:* TAIB #51340, 1877.

p. 131 *Josephine Randolph:* TAIB #59113, 1880.

p. 131 *Martha Dimond:* TAIB #46375–77, 1875.

p. 131 *Mary J. Kelly:* TAIB #103147, 1895.

p. 131 *Henrietta Smith:* TAIB #87232, 1890.

p. 132 *Catherine Cran and Catherine Jr:* TAIB #48023–24, 1875.

p. 132 *observer making statements:* Duvergier De Hauranne in Calhoun, *Social History of the Family,* p. 163.

p. 132 *For Charles Eliot Norton:* Cited in *ibid.,* p. 164.

p. 132 *And A. Maurice Low opined:* ibid.

p. 132 *French observer De Hauranne:* ibid., p. 217.

p. 132 *The National Divorce Reform League cited:* Calhoun, *Social History of the Family,* pp. 217–18.

p. 132 *a sociologist estimated:* C.A. Elwood, cited in *ibid.,* p. 265.

p. 133 *Beverly Schwartzberg noted that:* Schwartzberg, "Lots of Them Did That."

p. 133 *Linda Gordon's study:* Linda Gordon, *Heroes of Their Own Lives.*

p. 133 *The high degree of deserted women:* Gordon, "Single Mothers and Child Neglect, 1880–1920," *American Quarterly* 37 (1985), p. 176.

p. 134 *this does not include eighteen nonoverlapping cases:* 14 cases of bigamy and 38 of adultery were arrived at independently of the separations. Not surprisingly there were overlaps, but eighteen of the fifty-two had not formally said they were separated, deserted, or divorced.

p. 134 vast majority ... Roman Catholic: I have not seen this point made either in the contemporary expressions of outrage of the time nor by more contemporary observers of the period.

p. 135 *William Fahey:* TAIB #74517, 1885.

p. 135 *Annie Long Lawton:* TAIB #102387, 1895.

p. 135 *Charles Manning:* TAIB #46539, 1875.

p. 135 *Mary Feeley:* TAIB #43187, 1874.

p. 135 *Catherine Lynch:* TAIB #27899, 1867.

p. 136 *Philomena DeAugustine:* TAIB #102973, 1895.

p. 136 *Delia Kilcoyne:* TAIB #79358, 1887.

p. 136 *Hannah Hutchinson:* TAIB #59628, 1880.

p. 136 *Mary Maginnis:* TAIB #38275, 1872.

p. 136 *Anna Florinda:* TAIB #25516, 1866.

p. 137 *Jeremiah Sheehan:* case of Agnes, TAIB #102572–3, 1895.

p. 137 *Mary Matthews:* TAIB #59834, 1880.

p. 137 *Elbridge Gerry Hardy:* IBAMPHM #51243, 1877.

p. 137 *Jabez Bradbury:* TAIB #43575, 1874.

p. 137 *Patrick Murphy:* TAIB #45575, 1875.

p. 137 *Bridget Cahill:* IBAMPHM #45329, 1875.

p. 137 *neither set of reasons:* Only eighteen of the 171 cases of separation cited infidelity and seventeen cited intemperance.

p. 137–38 *unfortunately although it appears:* Despite the frequent intrusiveness of the interviewers, no attempt was made to take a sexual history or a history of prior childbirth, so that we cannot assume one way or the other whether a young woman's child was her first.

p. 138 *a not insubstantial number:* It is important to note that, unlike with out-of-wedlock births, the almshouse officials did not seem to inquire as to the father of the child with a married woman, perhaps such inquiry being deemed too personal in Victorian times. The nine cases are likely a minimum number.

p. 138 *in many instances:* Unfortunately the notes are highly uneven over time, and that, combined with human forgetfulness and the self-interests of both officials and inmates, makes developing a clear chronology of a family drama difficult. Whether adultery preceded a pregnancy or not, or whether the man knew the wife was pregnant, to take some examples, is not clear from many notes.

p. 138 *Mary Feeley:* TAIB #43187, 1874

p. 139 *Isabelle Cataldo:* TAIB #102643–44, 1895.

p. 139 *It does seem to reflect the point:* Arthur Calhoun, *Social History of the Family, Volume III,* p. 160.

p. 139 *Gordon:* Linda Gordon, *Heroes of Their Own Lives,* p. 91.

p. 139 *Diner adds that for the Irish:* Diner, *Erin's Daughters,* pp. 53–55.

p. 144 *Mary Erickson:* IBAMPHM #74124–25, 1885. USC, 1900 (Holden, Ma) and 1910 (Chicago). Mary is a widow living alone in USC, 1930 (Worcester, Ma).

p. 144 *Sadie Polinsky:* TAIB #102392, 1895. Sadie herself, USC, 1910 (Waltham, Ma) in the family of Alice J. Mears. Parents Hyman and Mary in USC, 1910 (New York), they were married sixteen years. In USC, 1930, they are in Bronx, New York, married twenty-five years.

p. 145 *such as Linda Gordon's:* The most important difference between many studies on the poor at this time through social welfare records and my own study is that of "outdoor relief" or aid at home and the almshouse as an institution. Recipients could more easily access charity, and in the absence of a husband, even if brief, secure treatment as "deserving poor" from charities. The almshouse was a course of last resort for most people, and distress that would cause someone to enter an almshouse as a general rule might be far harsher than receiving outdoor relief. Also, since Tewksbury was located in a small town, inmates gave up, at least for a time, their home and home lives (this is not to say they were all homeless; some retained family who owned homes or who continued to rent).

p. 145 *Michael Dennison:* TAIB #48397, 1876. They are found together in the English census of 1861 in Yorkshire; he was a cooper, 11 years older than Bridget. USC, 1880 (Cambridge, Ma), he is 60 and a cooper; he is listed as having rheumatism; he was unemployed for ten months that year; they evidently had no children. It looks like from NEGHS that they both died at different points in 1891. NEGHS has Bridget as will administrator, which seems to confirm Michael's death and then a Bridget Dennison of Cambridge died that year.

p. 146 *Ellen and Benjamin Mortimer:* TAIB #48965, 1876. USC, 1880 (Somerville, Ma) still, Benjamin was a 39-year-old laborer born in England and she was 50, keeping house and born in England. Ellen actually died at Tewksbury almshouse in 1892 at age 62 while Benjamin too appears to end up at Tewksbury, as he is in the 1900 census there as a 58-year-old widower born in England. He arrived in 1873, was naturalized in 1875, and had been a day laborer (USC, 1900, Tewksbury, Ma).

p. 146 *Raphael or Isabelle Cataldo:* TAIB #102643–44, 1895. USC, 1900 (Boston, Ma), Angelo was 55, Isabelle 39. They had been married eleven years and he was a day laborer. Their daughters were Elizabeth, Mary A., Catherine, and Josephine. USC, 1920 (Chelsea, Ma), he was 65, she was 59 as in the write-up. It was an Irish-Italian marriage; both had no occupation, but all children present, Mary, 24; Catherine, 22; Elmira, 21; and Joseph, 19, were working at a candy factory.

p. 146 *Margaret Mushet:* TAIB #48633. FS reports death of Margaret Mushet, 1884, aged 45 in Greater Manchester, England. William is in the USC, 1880 (Philadelphia, Pa), as a widower with three of his children, working as a shoe finisher.

p. 146 *Elinora Wallis:* TAIB #47661–62, 1875. Elinora's maiden name was Halry, she married (MVS) Samuel on July 15, 1874. He was 41 and she was 25. He was listed as a farmer, parents William and Nancy. He was born in Scotland. Her parents were William and Catherine Halry. It was her first marriage and his second. USC, 1880, she is in the Worcester Lunatic Hospital. Samuel is listed in USC, 1880, in Newburyport, Massachusetts, as a boarder. A Samuel M. Wallace died in 1899 in Worcester, Massachusetts.

p. 147 *Albert J. Fischer:* TAIB #40436, 1873. USC, 1880 (Webster, Ma), Albert was single and a painter. Albert was in USC, 1860 and 1870 (Falmouth, Ma) with parents, Betheiel from Maine and in 1860 had $100 in real estate and $30 in personal property. In 1870 Betheiel was listed as a mariner, as was Albert, and real estate value of $300 for Betheiel. Albert had a previous marriage just one year before in 1871 to Phebe R. Blakely of Melrose (MVS); she was 6 years his senior, from Melrose, and he was listed as a farmer from Falmouth, but the correct parents are listed. Sara Grover was in USC, 1870, census in Melrose, Massachusetts. Her father, George W., was a laborer born in Massachusetts with no ownership. Her mother, Mary A., was also from Massachusetts. Sara was born in 1852 and listed with no occupation. Albert and Sara were married in 1872 (MVS), listed as Albert's second marriage. He was 26, she 20; he was now listed as a laborer.

p. 147 *They found it demoralized:* Broder, *Tramps, Unfit Mothers, and Neglected Children,* p. 16

p. 147 *Stephanie Coontz argued:* Coontz, *The Social Origins of Private Life.* London: Verso Press, 1988, p. 287

p. 147 *Mintz and Kellogg: Domestic Revolutions,* p. 84.

Chapter 7 *Being "Put Out": Children in and out of the Almshouse*

p. 153 *There is a great superiority:* J.C. Ferris, "Child Helping in Tennessee." *Proceedings of the National Conference of Charities and Corrections,* 1883, p. 339 (in Arno Press, 1974).

p. 153 *The advocates of this system:* Lyman C. Alden, "The Shady Side of the 'Placing-Out System.'" *Proceedings of National Conference of Charities and Corrections,* 1885, p. 201 (in *ibid.*).

p. 153 *Many of the reform movements:* See the brief review of the "child savers" and "child rescue" movements in Lela Costin, "The Historical Context of Child Welfare," in Joan Laird & Ann Hartman, eds., *A Handbook of Child Welfare.* New York: The Free Press, 1985, pp. 34–60.

p. 154–55 *In the 1865 Annual Report of Tewksbury:* Massachusetts State Public Document, October 1865.

p. 155 *C. D. Randall, a Michigan social welfare official:* C.D. Randall, "Michigan: The Child; The State." *Proceedings of the National Conference of Charities and Corrections,* 1888, p. 263 (in Arno Press).

p. 155 *Well-known social welfare:* Homer Folks, "The Removal of Children from Almshouses." *Proceedings of the National Conference of Charities and Corrections,* 1894, pp. 122, 123, *ibid.*

p. 155 *William Letchworth, another famous social welfare reformer:* Cited in Michael Katz, *In the Shadow of the Poorhouse,* p. 111.

p. 155 *in his work on the history:* Homer Folks, *The Care of Destitute, Neglected, and Delinquent Children,* p. 15.

p. 156 *the theory and practice of officials:* Katz's *In the Shadow of the Poorhouse* still presents the best treatment of how superintendents and other local officials nearer to public scrutiny had different interests than social reformers. See also Wagner, *The Poorhouse.*

p. 157 *Thomas Donahoe:* TAIB #29954, 1867.

p. 157 *Philip Snow:* TAIB #38239, 1872.

p. 158 *Mary Ferrin:* TAIB #59990, 1880.

p. 158 *Albert and John Ellis:* TAIB #102453–4, 1895.

p. 158 *Martha McVey:* TAIB #47578, 1875.

p. 158 *Lucy A. Moore and Sarah E. Moore:* TAIB #64451–2, 1882.

p. 158 *Daniel L. Darwood:* TAIB #103263–4, 1895.

p. 159 *Llewellyn Westcott:* TAIB #34207, 1870.

p. 159 *John Kirby:* TAIB #48407, 1876.

p. 159 *Michael Boland:* IBAMPHM #74263, 1885.

p. 159 *Margaret (see Arthur Froitingham):* IBAMPHN #51208, 1877.

p. 159 *Biagio Frezza:* TAIB #102409, 1895.

p. 160 *From the very origins of the Anglo American poor relief system:* See, for example, Trattner, *From Poor Law to Welfare State: A History of Social Welfare in America*; Schneider, *The History of Public Welfare in New York*; and Bruce Jansson, *The Reluctant Welfare State.* Belmont, Ca: Brooks-Cole, 4th Edition, 2000.

p. 160 *Like the indentured servants who made up a fairly large number of Colonial immigrants:* For more on indenture generally see John Van Der Zee, *Bound Over: Indentured Servitude and the American Conscience.* New York: Simon and Schuster, 1985.

p. 160 *"acquittal of anyone who committed homicide":* Cited in Holt, *The Orphan Trains,* p. 33.

p. 160 *Homer Folks stated in his history:* Homer Folks, *The Care of the Destitute,* p. 29.

p. 160 *Charles Loring Brace's:* For a contemporary critique of Brace, see Hastings H. Hart, "Placing out Children in the West." *Proceedings of the National Conference of Charities and Corrections,* 1884 (in Arno Press).

p. 161 *as noted social welfare figure Grace Abbott argued:* Abbot was referring to apprenticeship, but certainly could be speaking of any of the placing out processes. Cited in Ten Broek, *Family Law and the Poor,* p. 132.

p. 161 *The 1864 annual report:* See State of Massachusetts Public Document 19, 1864, pp. 266–69. The situation was serious enough that a report was ordered by the Governor.

p. 161 *A special report was commissioned after the Civil War:* Report of the Visiting Agent of the State Almshouse, Tewksbury. Boston: Wright & Potter, 1869.

p. 161 *Children are charged to families: ibid.,* p. 4.

p. 161 *Elliot did find some "excellent families:* See examples, *ibid.,* pp. 12–15.

p. 161 *"no uncommon occurrence": ibid.,* p. 7.

p. 162 *The president of Girard College:* Cited in Lyman C. Alden, "The Shady Side ... ," p. 203.

p. 162 *Lyman Alden sounded like a critic: ibid.,* p. 207.

p. 162 *Robert W. Hebberd:* "Placing Out Children: Dangers of Careless Methods."

Proceedings of the National Conference of Charities and Corrections, 1899, p. 172 (in Arno Press).

p. 162 *Josephine Shaw Lowell:* "Report of the Institutions for the Care of Destitute Children of the City of New York." Reprinted from the New York State Board of Charities Annual Report for the Year 1885, Arno Press.

p. 162 *Homer Folks remained militant:* "The Child and the Family." *Proceedings of the National Conference of Charities and Corrections,* 1892, p. 420 (in Arno Press).

p. 162 *Homer Folks in fact was ahead: ibid.,* p. 423.

p. 164 *Margaret Lovett:* TAIB #43495, 1874.

p. 164 *William Livingston:* TAIB #61552, 1880.

p. 164 *Ellen Rice:* TAIB #102248, 1895.

p. 165 *Mary Burke:* TAIB #45419, 1876.

p. 165 *Harold Wilson:* TAIB #102713, 1895.

p. 165 *Lizzie Fleming:* TAIB #40334, 1873. Marriage, MVS, NEGHS, 1874 (Clinton, Ma). Her husband, William Augustus Hunting, was from Lancaster, 24, a farmer; she was 19.

p. 166 *Ann Ilsley:* TAIB #43463, 1874.

p. 166 *Minnie A. Payne:* TAIB #60983, 1880.

p. 166 *Kate Jackson:* TAIB #48426, 1876.

p. 166 *Isabella Gillespie:* TAIB #24115–16 (with daughter Ann), 1865.

p. 166 *Mary L. Ryder:* TAIB #102112, 1895.

p. 167 *John Mann:* IBAMPHM, #45418, 1875.

p. 167 *Alice Chase:* TAIB #48273, 1876.

p. 167 *Agnes Goddard:* TAIB #45857, 1876.

p. 167 *John Bridge:* TAIB #48395, 1876.

p. 168 *Ellen McCarty:* TAIB #27912, 1867.

p. 168 *John Higgs:* TAIB #36467, 1871.

p. 168 *Jane Richardson:* TAIB #64862, 1882.

p. 171 *We can tell that generally those bound out did not differ:* I compared 146 cases of children admitted to Tewksbury with the 59 bound-out cases (most of the latter are contained in the former figure, but not all, as some reported being put out who were now adults). Generally, both groups were more U.S.-born than the average inmate, partly reflecting their later births than adult almshouse residents. Both groups had a far higher number of nonwhites than the overall inmate population (16.4% of the children and 10% of the bound-out children were "colored"). Both groups contained large numbers of orphans and half-orphans. Of the bound-out children 10.2% were noted to be illegitimate, but only 7.5% of the overall children were. Disabilities including blindness, epilepsy, "simple"-mindedness, and others and accounted for 14.1% of the children, and 16.9% of the placed out. The last sets of figures are not statistically significant.

CHAPTER 8 *"We Can Do Nothing for Him": The Fate of the Elderly*

p. 173 *Cornelius McCuddy:* TAIB #25494, 1865.

p. 173 *James Fitzpatrick:* TAIB #48977, 1876.

p. 173 *By the late nineteenth century:* See Stewart, *The Cost of American Alms-*

houses; Carole Haber & Brian Gratton, *Old Age and the Search for Security*. Bloomington: Indiana University Press, 1994, see Chapter 4; and Carole Haber, "'And the Fear of the Poorhouse:' Perceptions of Old Age Impoverishment in Early Twentieth-Century America." *Generations* 17(2) (Spring/Summer 1993), pp. 46–51.

  p. 173 *Will Carleton's 1870s:* There are many printed versions. The first verse is from *Farm Ballads* (New York: Harper and Brothers, 1882*)*. The later verses are quoted from Ethel McClure, *More than a Roof: The Development of Minnesota Poor Farms and Homes for the Aged*. St. Paul: Minnesota Historical Society, 1968, pp. 30–31.

  p. 174 *Early work on the history:* See, for example, Donald Cowgill & Lowell D. Holmes, eds., *Aging and Modernization*. New York: Appleton-Century-Crofts, 1972, and Ernest W. Burgess, *Aging in Western Society*. Chicago: University of Chicago Press, 1970. David Hackett Fisher's well known work, *Growing Old in America* (New York: Oxford University Press, 1977) challenged elements of modernization theory which saw a natural connection between the decline in the power and status of the elderly and industrialization, but still agreed on the diminution of the elderly's status and power.

  p. 174 *More recent work has questioned this:* Haber and Gratton, *Old Age and Security*.

  p. 175 *it is important to acknowledge that relatively few:* ibid. and Carole Haber, "'And the Fear of the Poorhouse.'"

  p. 175 *"a reverence for God, the hope of heaven, and the fear of the poorhouse":* Quoted in Stewart, *The Cost of American Almshouses*, p. iii.

  p. 176 *Annie Sullivan who was an inmate:* Quoted in Nella Braddy, *Anne Sullivan Macy: The Story Behind Helen Keller*. Garden City, NY: Doubleday and Company, 1933, pp. 19–25.

  p. 178 *James McIntire:* TAIB #36538, 1871

  p. 178 *Mary A. Kearns:* TAIB #43105, 1874.

  p. 178 *Evart A. Van Gogh:* TAIB #65007, 1882.

  p. 178 *Paul Gruzot:* TAIB #74562, 1885.

  p. 179 *It is also likely that clerks writing these notes:* Under the Poor Laws, close relatives (and in some jurisdictions even distant relatives) were held accountable for care of their elders and might not have been aided. On the one hand, some inmates and families may then have had motivation to stress the family disengagement or, on the other hand, it may be that inmates who found themselves at Tewksbury, as compared with the local town relief, already were rejected by town's aid.

  p. 179 *Frederick Merritt:* TAIB #24892, 1866.

  p. 179 *John Lyons:* IBAMPHM, #45954, 1875.

  p. 180 *Dennis Brooks:* TAIB #48342, 1876.

  p. 180 *Fanny Austin:* TAIB #26171, 1866.

  p. 180 *Felix Neptune :* TAIB #34189, 1870.

  p. 180 *John Gale:* TAIB #34245, 1870.

  p. 180 *Lucy Mason:* TAIB #79367, 1887.

  p. 181 *Dennis O'Neil:* TAIB #25986, 1866.

  p. 181 *Thomas Fallon:* TAIB #25997, 1866.

  p. 181 *Philip B. Cook:* TAIB #86887, 1890.

  p. 181 *Willett G. Brown:* TAIB #38185, 1872.

  p. 181 *Honora Murphy:* TAIB #41289, 1873.

  p. 182 *Timothy Kenney:* TAIB #41639, 1873.

p. 182 *Catherine Quinn:* TAIB #25970, 1866.

p. 182 *James Farrell:* TAIB #28579, 1867.

p. 182 *Morris O'Connell:* IBAMPHM #48573, 1876.

p. 182 *Thomas Pratt:* IBAMPHM #48519, 1876.

p. 183 *young children and women:* The wages in Massachusetts were so low, on average families had to rely on children for between 25% and 33% of their income; see Bedford, ed., *Their Lives and Numbers,* p. 55. One of the major differences between immigrants and upper class reformers was the cultural divide over child labor; see, for example, Broder, *Tramps, Unfit Mothers, and Neglected Children.*

p. 183 *James Mellen:* TAIB #34144, 1870.

p. 184 *Mary Wilkenson:* TAIB #41306, 1873.

p. 184 *Amelia Mellett:* TAIB #46317, 1875.

p. 184 *John Coffin:* TAIB #51461, 1877.

p. 184 *Hugh Lohan:* TAIB #34304, 1870.

p. 184 *Hannah Granger:* TAIB #41153, 1873.

p. 185 *James Kalugher: TAIB* #102172, 1895.

p. 185 *David Hackett Fisher called the "gerontophobia:"* Fisher, *Growing Old in America.*

p. 185 *Alexander Keyssar cites:* "Social Change in Massachusetts in the Gilded Age," in Tager & Ifkovic, p. 140.

p. 186 *James Stevenson:* TAIB #41654, 1873.

p. 186 *Thomas Gallagher:* TAIB #46550, 1875.

p. 186 *William Curtis:* TAIB #48236, 1876.

p. 186 *James Mount:* TAIB #51138, 1877.

p. 187 *Henry L. Joy:* TAIB #40337, 1873.

p. 187 *Charles B. Allen:* IBAMPHM #45389, 1875.

p. 187 *Patrick Conley:* TAIB #52682, 1877.

CHAPTER 9 *From History's Shadows: Partial Views of the Poor*

p. 190 *Ruth Bateman:* TAIB #102490, 1895; FS, born in 1878 in New Brunswick. Marriage, MVS, 1898 (Boston) to Duchene. In Canadian census, 1881, Shediac, New Brunswick, Ancestry.com. USC, 1900 (Everett), 1910 (Boston), and 1920 (Boston).

p. 190 *Frank Edward Cole:* TAIB #42031, 1873. USC, 1860 (Dover, Me), 1870 (Dover, Maine), 1900 (Cambridge, Ma), and 1910 (Bourne).

p. 191 *Patrick Jennings:* TAIB #1880. USC, 1870 (Gloucester, Ma), 1900 (Boston), 1910 (Boston), 1920 (Boston), and 1930 (Boston).

p. 191 *Ellen Quilty:* TAIB #59178, 1880. MVS, 1868 (Boston), marriage to Joseph. USC, 1900 (Lawrence, Ma), 1910 (Lawrence, Ma), and 1920 (Lawrence, Ma). The spelling in 1910 and 1920 changed to "Juilty."

p. 192 *Joseph Rice:* TAIB #103214, 1895. USC, 1900 (Shenandoah, Pa), 1910 (Schuykill, Pa), and 1930 (Schuykill County, Pa).

p. 192 *Elizabeth Sandford:* TAIB #43066, 1874. MVS, marriage 1/16/1838, Holliston, Ma. USC, 1850, Giles (Holliston, Ma), 1860 (Milford, Ma), and 1870 (Milford, Ma). Elizabeth, USC, 1850 (Holliston, Ma), 1860 (Bellingham, Ma), 1870 (Hopkinton, Ma). Death, MVS, NEGHS, 1874, Tewksbury.

p. 194 *It is important to note that most people compare themselves to their own reference group:* See, for example, psychological theory in Argyle, *The Psychology of Social Class.* London: Routledge, 1994, pp. 223–27.

p. 198 *Catherine Cunningham:* TAIB #34109, 1870.

p. 198 *William Fallowfield:* TAIB #38184, 1872.

p. 198 *Delia Turner:* TAIB #48275, 1876.

p. 198 *Jennie Baker Canad:* IBAMPHM #51221–22, 1877.

p. 199 *For example, child labor laws were put on the books in New England states:* Legislation moved slowly but steadily around child labor and protective legislation for women. Other ideas like unemployment insurance and mothers' pensions would take two decades to move further. For information on Massachusetts legislation and political reform, see Hart, *Commonwealth History of Massachusetts,* and essays in Tager & Ifkovic, *Massachusetts in the Gilded Age.*

Bibliography

Abbot, G., *The Child and the State*. Chicago: University of Chicago Press, 1938.

Alden, L.C., "The Shady Side of the 'Placing-Out' System." *Proceedings of National Conference of Charities and Corrections,* 1885, p. 201 (Arno Press).

American Social History Project, *Who Built America? Working People and the Nation's Economy, Politics, Culture and Society: Volume 2, From the Gilded Age to the Present*. New York: Pantheon Books, 1992.

Argyle, M., *The Psychology of Social Class*. London: Routledge, 1994.

Barron, H., *Those who Stayed Behind: Rural Society in Nineteenth-Century New England*. Cambridge, UK: Cambridge University Press, 1984.

Beard, R., ed., *On Being Homeless: Historical Perspectives*. New York: Museum of the City of New York, 1987.

Bedford, H., ed., *Their Lives and Numbers*. Ithaca, NY: Cornell University Press, 1995.

Bodnar, J., *The Transplanted: A History of Immigrants in Urban America*. Bloomfield: Indiana University Press, 1985.

Braddy, N., *Anne Sullivan Macy: The Story Behind Helen Keller*. Garden City, NY: Doubleday and Company, 1933.

Brecher, J. *Strike!* Boston: South End Press, 1972.

Breckinridge, S., *The Family and the State*. University of Chicago Press: Chicago, 1934

Broder, S., *Tramps, Unfit Mothers, and Neglected Children: Negotiating the Family in Nineteenth Century Philadelphia*. Philadelphia: University of Pennsylvania Press, 2002.

Brumberg, J., "'Ruined' Girls: Changing Community Responses to Illegitimacy in Upstate New York 1890–1920." *Journal of Social History* 18(2) (1984), pp. 247–272.

Calhoun, A., *A Social History of the American Family from Colonial Times to the Present*. New York: Barnes and Noble, 1945 (original 1919).

Calhoun, C., ed., *The Gilded Age: Essays on the Origins of Modern America*. Wilmington, De: Scholarly Resources, 1996.

Campbell, B., *The Human Tradition in the Gilded Age and Progressive Era*. Wilmington, De: Scholarly Resources Inc., 2000.

Cole, D., *Immigrant City: Lawrence, Massachusetts, 1845–1921*. Chapel Hill: University of North Carolina Press, 1963.

Coontz, S., *The Social Origins of Private Life*. London: Verso Press, 1988.

———. *The Way We Never Were*. New York: Basic Books, 2000.

Costin, L. "The Historical Context of Child Welfare," in Laird, J., & Hartman, A. (eds), *A Handbook of Child Welfare*. New York: The Free Press, 1985.

Cott, N. ed., *Root of Bitterness: Documents on the Social History of American Women*. Boston: Northeastern University Press, 1986.

Cresswell, T., *The Tramp in America*. London: Reaktion Books, 2001.

D'Antonio, M., *The State Boys Rebellion*. New York: Simon and Schuster, 2004.

Dawley, A., *Class and Community in Lynn*. Cambridge, Ma: Harvard University Press, 1976.

D'Emilio, J., & Freedman, E., *Intimate Matters: A History of Sexuality in America*. New York: Harper and Row, 1988.

Deutsch, A., *The Mentally Ill in America*. New York: Columbia University Press, 1949.

Diner, H., *Erin's Daughters in America*. Baltimore: Johns Hopkins University Press, 1983.

Dodd, D., *Historical Statistics of the United States*. Westport, Ct: Greenwood, 1993.

Dubofsky, M., *Industrialization and the American Worker 1865–1920*. Arlington Heights, Ill.: AHM Publishing, 1975.

Eno, A.L., ed., *Cotton Was King: A History of Lowell, Massachusetts*. Lowell: Lowell Historical Society, 1976.

Erickson, C., *Invisible Immigrants: The Adaptation of English and Scottish Immigrants in Nineteenth-Century America*. Coral Gables, FL: University of Miami Press, 1972.

Ferris, J.C., "Child Helping in Tennessee." *Proceedings of the National Conference of Charities and Corrections*, 1883, p. 339 (in Arno Press, 1974).

Fink, L., *Major Problems in the Gilded Age and the Progressive Era*, Second Edition. Boston: Houghton Mifflin Company, 2001.

Fischer, D.H., *Growing Old in America*. New York: Oxford University Press, 1977.

Folks, H., *The Care of Destitute, Neglected, and Delinquent Children*. New York: Arno Press, 1971 [original 1900].

————. The Child and the Family." Proceedings *of the National Conference of Charities and Corrections*, 1892 , p. 420 (in Arno Press).

————. "The Removal of Children from Almshouses." *Proceedings of the National Conference of Charities and Corrections*, 1894, pp. 122, 123.

Foucault, M., *History of Sexuality*. Volume 1. New York: Vintage, 1990.

Frisch, M., "Poverty and Progress: A Paradoxical Legacy." *Social Science History* 10:1 (Spring 1986), pp. 5–32.

Gordon, L., *Heroes of Their Own Lives: The Politics and History of Domestic Violence*. New York: Penguin Books, 1988.

————. "Single Mothers and Child Neglect, 1880–1920." *American Quarterly* 37 (1985), pp. 173–192.

Grossberg, M., *Governing the Hearth: Law and Family in Nineteenth Century America*. Chapel Hill: University of North Carolina Press, 1985.

Grusky, D., & Fukumoto, I., "Social History Update: A Sociological Approach to Historical Social Mobility." *Journal of Social History* 23:1 (Fall 1989), pp. 221–232.

Gutman, H., & Kealey, G., eds., *Many Pasts: Readings in American Social History 1865–The Present*. Englewood Cliffs, NJ: Prentice–Hall, 1973.

Haber, C., & Gratton, B., *Old Age and the Search for Security*. Bloomington: Indiana University Press, 1994.

Handlin, O., *Boston's Immigrants 1790–1880*. New York: Atheneum, 1977.

————. *The Uprooted*. Boston: Little, Brown and Company, 1952.

Harevan, T., ed., *Transitions: The Family and the Life Course in Historical Perspective*. New York: Academic Press, 1978.

Hart, A.B., ed., *Commonwealth History of Massachusetts,* Volume IV. New York: The States History Company, 1930.

Hart, Hastings H., "Placing Out Children in the West." *Proceedings of the National Conference of Charities and Corrections,* 1884 (in Arno Press).

Hebberd, R., "Placing Out Children: Dangers of Careless Methods." *Proceedings of the National Conference of Charities and Corrections,* 1899, p. 172 (in Arno Press).

Henderson, D., *Quiet Presence: Franco-Americans in New England*. Portland, Me: Guy Gannett Publishing Company, 1980.

Hill, R.N., *Yankee Kingdom: Vermont and New Hampshire*. New York: Harper Brothers, 1960.

Hobson, B., *Uneasy Virtue*. New York: Basic Books, 1987.

Holt, M., *The Orphan Trains: Placing Out in America*. Lincoln: University of Nebraska, 1992.

Ingham, J., "Comment and Debate: Thernstrom's Poverty and Progress: A Retrospective after Twenty Years." *Social Science History* 10:1 (Spring 1986), pp. 1–44.

Jansson, B., *The Reluctant Welfare State*. 4th edition. Belmont, Ca: Brooks–Cole, 2000.

Jasper, J., *Restless Nation: Starting Over in America*. Chicago: University of Chicago Press, 2000.

Jensen, J., "The Death of Rosa: Sexuality in Rural America." *Agricultural History* 67:4 (Fall 1993), pp. 1–12.

Jewett, S.O., *Betsey's Flight: The Country of Pointed Firs and Other Stories*. Garden City, NY: Doubleday, 1956.

Jones, H.M., & Jones, B.Z., eds., *The Many Voices of Boston*. Boston: Little, Brown and Company, 1975.

Judd, R., Churchill, E., & Eastman, J., *Maine: The Pine Tree State from Prehistory to the Present*. Orono: University of Maine Press, 1995.

Katz, M., *In the Shadow of the Poorhouse: A Social History of Welfare in America*. New York: Basic Books, original, 1986, second edition, 1996.

————. *Poverty and Policy in American History*. New York: Academic Press, 1983.

Keller, H., *Teacher: Anne Sullivan Macy*. Garden City, NY: Doubleday and Company, 1955.

Kelso, R., *Public Poor Relief in Massachusetts 1620–1920*. Boston: Houghton-Mifflin, 1922.

Keyssar, A., *Out of Work: The First Century of Unemployment in Massachusetts*. Cambridge, Ma: Cambridge University Press, 1986.

Kirkland, E.C., *Men, Cities, and Transportation: A Study of New England 1820–1900,* Cambridge, Ma: Harvard University Press, 1948.

Knights, P., *Yankee Destinies: The Lives of Ordinary Nineteenth-Century Bostonians*. Chapel Hill: University of North Carolina Press, 1991.

Kunzel, R., *Fallen Women, Problem Girls: Unmarried Mothers and Professionalization of Social Work, 1890–1945*. New Haven: Yale University Press, 1995.

Kusmer, K., *Down and Out, On the Road: Homelessness in American History*. New York: Oxford University Press, 2002.

Levitan, S., *Programs in Aid of the Poor.* 6th Edition. Baltimore: Johns Hopkins Press, 1990.

Lowell, J.S., "Report of the Institutions for the Care of Destitute Children of the City of New York." Reprinted from The New York State Board of Charities Annual Report for the Year 1885, Arno Press.

Massachusetts, Commonwealth of. *The Census of the Commonwealth of Massachusetts: 1895.* Boston: Wright & Potter Printing Company, 1896–7.

Massachusetts Public Document, No. 19, 1864, Board of State Charities.

McClure, E., *More than a Roof: The Development of Minnesota Poor Farms and Homes for the Aged.* St. Paul: Minnesota Historical Society, 1968.

Mintz, S., & Kellogg, S., *Domestic Revolutions: A Social History of Family Life.* New York: Simon and Shuster, 1989.

Mitchell, B., *The Paddy Camps: The Irish of Lowell 1821–61.* Urbana: University of Illinois Press, 1988.

Monkkonen, E., ed., *Walking to Work: Tramps in America 1790–1935.* Lincoln: University of Nebraska Press, 1984,

Montgomery, D., *Citizen Worker: The Experience of Workers in the United States with Democracy and the Free Market during the Nineteenth-Century.* New York: Cambridge University Press, 1993.

Moran, W., *The Belles of New England: The Women of the Textile Mills.* New York: Thomas Dunne Books, 2002.

Nelson, B., *Making an Issue of Child Abuse.* New York: Oxford University Press, 1984.

Novak, W., *The People's Welfare: Law and Regulation in Nineteenth Century America.* Chapel Hill: University of North Carolina Press, 1996.

Nugent, W., *Crossings: The Great Transatlantic Migrations 1870–1914.* Bloomington: Indiana University Press, 1992.

O'Connor, T., *The Boston Irish: A Political History.* Boston: Little, Brown and Company, 1995.

O'Leary, E., *At Beck and Call: The Representations of Domestic Servants in Nineteenth-Century American Painting.* Washington, D.C.: Smithsonian Institution Press, 1996.

Pessen, E., ed., *Three Centuries of Social Mobility in America.* Lexington, MA: DC Heath, 1974.

Pivar, D., *Purity Crusade: Sexual Morality and Social Control 1868–1900.* Westport, Ct: Greenwood Press, 1973.

Piven, F.F., & Cloward, R., *Regulating the Poor: The Functions of Public Welfare.* New York: Vintage, 1993 (original 1971).

———. *Why Americans Do Not Vote.* New York: Pantheon, 1989.

Pleck, E., *Domestic Tyranny.* New York: Oxford University Press, 1987.

Randall, C.D., "Michigan: The Child; The State," *Proceedings of the National Conference of Charities and Corrections,* 1888, p. 263 (in Arno Press).

Report of the Visiting Agent of the State Almshouse, Tewksbury. Boston: Wright & Potter, 1869.

Rischin, M., "A Significant Part of History Deals with Mankind in Motion." *Journal of American Ethnic History* 15(3) (Spring 1996), pp. 44–52.

Rosen, R., *The Lost Sisterhood: Prostitution in America, 1900–1918.* Baltimore: Johns Hopkins University Press, 1982.

Rothman, D., *The Discovery of the Asylum*. Boston: Little, Brown and Company, 1971.

Sappol, M., *A Traffic of Dead Bodies: Anatomy and Embodied Social Identity in Nineteenth-Century America*. Princeton, NJ: Princeton University Press, 2002.

Schlereth, T., *Victorian America: Transformations in Everyday Life*. New York: Harper Perennial, 1991.

Schneider, D., *The History of Public Welfare in New York*. New York: New York State, 1939.

Schlup, L., & Ryan, J., *Historical Dictionary of the Gilded Age*. Armonk, NY: M.E. Sharpe, 2003.

Schwartzberg, B., "'Lots of Them Did That': Desertion, Bigamy, and Marital Fluidity in Late-Nineteenth-Century America." *Journal of Social History* 2004 (4), pp. 573–600.

Silverman, R., *Law and Urban Growth: Civil Litigation in the Boston Trial Courts 1880–1900*, Princeton, NJ: Princeton University Press, 1981.

Smith, D.S., & Hindus, M., "Premarital Pregnancy in America 1640–1971: An Overview and Interpretation." *Journal of Interdisciplinary History* 4 (Spring 1975), pp. 537–570.

Stanley, A.D., "Beggars Can't be Choosers: Compulsion and Contract in Postbellum America." *Journal of American History* 78 (March 1992), pp. 1265–93.

Stewart, E., *The Cost of American Almshouses*. Washington, D.C.: Government Printing Office, 1925.

Tager, J., & Ifkovic, J., eds., *Massachusetts in the Gilded Age*. Amherst: University of Massachusetts Press, 1985.

Temin, P., ed., *Engines of Enterprise: An Economic History of New England*. Cambridge, Ma: Harvard University Press, 2000.

Ten Broek, J., *Family Law and the Poor*. Westport, Ct: Greenwood Publishers, 1971.

Thernstrom, S., *The Other Bostonians: Poverty and Progress in the American Metropolis 1880–1970*. Cambridge, Ma: Harvard University Press, 1973.

———. *Poverty and Progress: Social Mobility in a Nineteenth Century City*. Cambridge, Ma: Harvard University Press, 1964.

Trachtenberg, A., *The Incorporation of America: Culture and Society in the Gilded Age*. New York: Hill and Wang, 1982.

Trattner, W., *From Poor Law to Welfare State: A History of Social Welfare in America*. 4th Edition. New York: The Free Press, 1989.

Ueda, R., "Immigration and the Moral Criticism of American History: The Vision of Oscar Handlin." *Canadian Review of American Studies* 21(2) (Fall 1990), pp. 183–202.

United States Census, *Paupers in Almshouses* 1903. Washington, D.C.

Van Der Zee, J., *Bound Over: Indentured Servitude and the American Conscience*. New York: Simon and Schuster, 1985.

Vecoli, R. The Resurgence of American Immigration History." *American Studies International* 12 (Winter 1979), pp. 46–71.

Wagner, D., *The Poorhouse: America's Forgotten Institution*. Lanham, Md: Rowman & Littlefield, 2005.

Wilson, H.F., *The Hill Country of Northern New England: Its Social and Economic History 1790–1930*. New York: AMS Press, 1936.

Wright, C., *The Census of Massachusetts 1875.* Boston: Albert J. Wright, 1876.
Yans-McLaughlin, V., ed., *Immigration Reconsidered: History, Sociology, and Politics.*
    New York: Oxford University Press, 1990.

Index

About the Author

David **Wagner** is a professor of social work and sociology, as well as the coordinator of the masters program in social work, at the University of Southern Maine. Prior to entering academia, he worked as a social worker and labor organizer in Massachusetts and New York. He holds degrees from Columbia University (B.A., History, Masters in Social Work), University of Massachusetts (Masters in Labor Studies), and City University of New York (Ph. D. in Sociology). He is the author of five previous books including *Checkerboard Square: Culture and Resistance in a Homeless Community,* which won the C. Wright Mills award; *The New Temperance: America's Obsession with Sin and Vice,* which won the Northeast Popular Culture Book Award; and most recently, *The Poorhouse: America's Forgotten Institution.*